FROM HERE TO MATERNITY

CONNIE MARSHALL R.N., M.S.N.

Congratulations! By reviewing this book, you are taking an important step toward a healthy pregnancy.

By visiting your physician early and often and following the important advice in this book, you can help give your baby the best chance for a healthy start in life.

By offering you *From Here To Maternity,* your company is also helping the March of Dimes and its Campaign for Healthier Babies. Up to 5 percent of proceeds from the sale of this book goes to help the March of Dimes carry out its mission of improving the health of babies by preventing birth defects and infant mortality.

We at the March of Dimes wish you a happy and healthy pregnancy.

Dr. Jennifer L. Howse
President
March of Dimes Birth Defects Foundation

Composition by Col D'var Graphics
Production by Carol Dondrea, Bookman Productions
Copyediting by Eva Marie Strock
Interior design by Renee Deprey
Cover design by The Dunlavey Studio
Cover illustration by Mary Engelbreit / © 1992 Mary Engelbreit

Prima Publishing
Rocklin, CA

In agreement with:
Conmar Publishing, Inc.
P.O. Box 641
Citrus Heights, CA 95611
(916) 332-9872

Library of Congress Cataloging-in-Publication Data

Marshall, Connie C. (Connie Clydene)
    From here to maternity : a pregnant couple's guide for the nine-month journey toward parenthood / by Connie Marshall.
        p.   cm.
    Originally published: Rev. ed. Sacramento, Calif. : C. Marshall Pub., c1984.
    Includes bibliographical references and index.
    ISBN 1-55958-077-1
    1..Pregnancy.   2. Childbirth.   I. Title.
[RG525.M333   1991]   90-49113
618.2′4—dc20   CIP

92 93 94 95 MAL 10 9 8 7 6 5 4 3

Printed in the United States of America

Table of Contents

PART III
The Experience

Acknowledgments

To my husband, Byrne, the father of this "baby," who provides inspiration, coaching, support, and encouragement through the delivery of each edition of this book.

To Kathi, my sister, friend, and business partner, whose loyalty, integrity, commitment, and persistence has enabled us to grow and prosper.

To Cheryl, the third member of our team, whose indispensable organizational talents and expertise keep us on track, and whose faith has never wavered.

Sincere appreciation goes to the professional friends and associates who made valuable contributions to this book: Judy LaPray R.N., M.S.N., for the comprehensive information on breast-feeding; Larry Bertolucci, R.P.T., for his contribution to the Common Complaints chapter; Ciri Sriyan, reflexologist, for his expertise on acupressure techniques; Rae Kuhn, R.N., B.S.N., for her helpful information on baby care in the Postpartum chapter; Lynn Fraser, B.S., international pregnancy fitness expert, for her important contribution to the exercise section in the Pregnancy Fitness chapter; and Joyce Higley, R.D., for her help with the nutrition section.

A special thanks to all the childbirth educators who use this book as their teaching guide and who continue to be a valuable resource.

Publisher's Note:

The information, procedures, and suggestions included in this book are not to be used as a substitute for your chosen health care provider. Medically supervised care is a necessity during your pregnancy.

Foreword

Thomas J. Garite, M.D.

Professor and Chairman of Obstetrics and Gynecology
University of California, Irvine

Even when a pregnancy is planned and truly desired, normal fears and conflicting emotions sometimes infringe on the joy of knowing your new baby is indeed growing inside you: Is everything going to be all right with my baby? Are we really ready to be parents? What are pregnancy and childbirth going to be like? As the introduction to this not-to-be-missed manual for expectant parents, *From Here To Maternity*, by Connie Marshall, R.N., so clearly points out: *Reality lies somewhere in between.*

In the last 10 to 20 years, no other area of medicine has changed more drastically than obstetrics. New information and technology have changed the important relationship between you, the expectant mom, and your doctor or midwife. Today the expectant couple has a lot more to learn, which creates its own questions regarding decisions that must be made.

Because every pregnancy is unique, turning to parents or friends for answers based on their experiences may not provide you with the most accurate information, however well intended it is. When you don't have all the necessary information, anxiety can be created or aggravated. The best solution for new parents-to-be is to obtain as much quality information as possible without inundating yourselves to the point where you become overwhelmed.

When I visit bookstores, I check out the books on pregnancy and childbirth. I search for the best ones to recommend to my patients. My practice is limited to "high-risk" pregnancies, and my patients' anxieties are amplified by the complications and the technologies imposed. I feel it is critical to find reading material that will both inform them and relieve their fears.

I highly and enthusiastically recommend *From Here To Maternity* to expectant parents. This book meets all my criteria. It is complete, thorough, accurate, up-to-date, and written in clear and understandable language. **Virtually every question commonly asked by my patients is addressed, and I agree with virtually every answer. I only wish I could explain things as clearly to my patients at all times as this book does.**

Finally, no book can answer all your questions or relieve all your fears. If you need more information, write down your questions and discuss them with your caregiver/doctor. Expect clear information or, when they don't know the answer, an admission to that effect.

Since only God can give guarantees, we in the medical community can only promise to do our best. Your assistance, understanding, and participation are critical. May you be ultimately blessed with a healthy, happy baby.

Introduction

Pregnancy is a nine-month journey to the state of motherhood. The experiences along the way vary greatly from woman to woman, but some are common to all pregnant women. It is comforting to know that others have made the journey before you and that those currently doing so are experiencing many of the same things. You are not alone.

The information in this book provides an overview of the varied emotions and experiences you and your husband can expect during your pregnancy. While there are many common experiences, every pregnancy is unique, and you will find yourself at times bouncing between the two extremes below.

Reality

Lies

Somewhere

in

Between

The information presented in this book is based, in part, on *Standards for Obstetric-Gynecologic Services and Guidelines for Perinatal Care*, published by the American College of Obstetricians and Gynecologists (ACOG) and the American Pediatric Association (APA), respectively. The information contained herein is current and accurate. There is a review of the literature listed in the bibliography as it relates to the various chapters, if you feel the need to read the medical literature.

The Recommended Resources section of books and tapes is purposely limited; those included were chosen for their quality, credibility, and objectivity. I am sure there are others that have equal merit, but a long list would be like going to the bookstore—too overwhelming with all the choices.

You will notice in the text the baby is alternately referred to as he and she. Equal time is nice, but I didn't keep a strict count. I'm not that compulsive. It's the thought that counts.

The man in your life is referred to as your husband. It has a nicer ring than "significant other" or "partner." The majority of prenatal books neglect this very important person in your pregnancy. He may be mentioned briefly, if at all. While it wasn't practical to present every aspect of pregnancy from his perspective, I did address the more important aspects as they relate to him. If he would like a prenatal book, we recommend *The Expectant Father*, a pregnancy guide devoted specifically to his needs.

For simplicity, your health care provider is referred to as doctor. As with the baby, the doctor is alternately referred to as he and she. Since most babies are delivered by doctors, the majority rules. It's too awkward to keep repeating "doctor or midwife." If the balance tips the other way someday...doctor is out, midwife is in.

Humor is used throughout the book for good reason: it helps to put any situation into proper perspective. Humor is a great anxiety reliever, healer, and equalizer. It is meant to add a little extra smile or two on your trip through pregnancy. Many of the current books dwell on the sacred mystical aspects of childbirth, making it sound like strictly serious business. It's a wonderfully satisfying, creative time in your life, but it does have a lighter side. A sense of humor helps, no matter where you are.

Have a great time on your way to parenthood. This is my gift to you. I hope you like it.

PART I

The
Adjustments

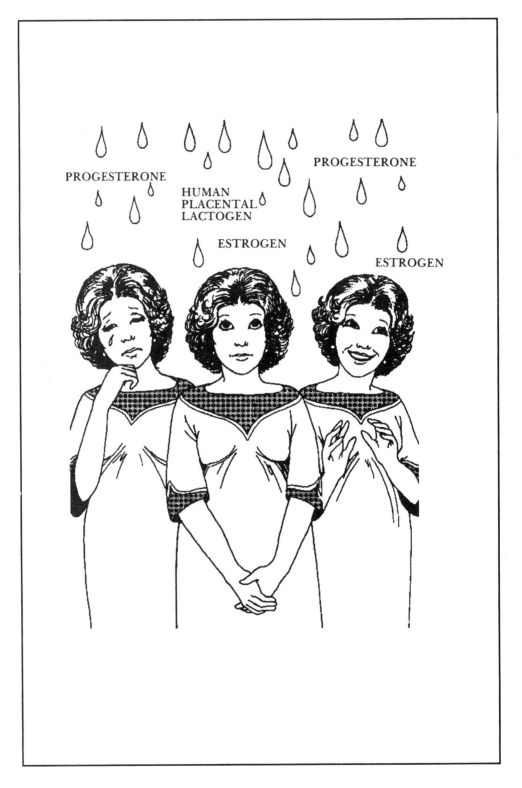

1

Emotions of Pregnancy

CHANGES IN ATTITUDE AND LATITUDE

Your pregnancy will cause obvious physical changes. It will also cause gradual and dramatic emotional changes. At times, these changes may show up as drastic mood swings; at other times they may be so subtle that they elude even the most intimate observer. The hormones of pregnancy are largely responsible for the emotional changes. The physical changes produce a shift in latitude, the emotional ones a change in attitude.

Psychologists have isolated three distinct phases a woman goes through during pregnancy. These phases are referred to as developmental tasks. In the beginning, she has to accept the fact of her pregnancy; then she accepts and feels the baby as part of her body. Finally, she perceives the baby as a separate being and is ready to release the baby from her body through childbirth. The husband shares these phases to some degree as he accepts his new or expanded role as the father-to-be. You can both be assured that these changes are real and no cause for alarm. Pregnancy does change your lives, so be prepared for some adjustments.

First Trimester

In the first 3 months when you realize pregnancy will indeed change your life, you may feel ambivalent and have mixed emotions no matter how you planned or hoped for a baby. You may feel nauseated and tired, which is enough to make anyone "snarky" and out-of-sorts. You may find your sex drive on hold for fear that intercourse may harm the baby or cause you to miscarry. It won't, but the feelings are normal. You begin to wonder if pregnancy is all that it's cracked up to be. Most women spend some time mulling over their mixed emotions during this time and bouncing back and forth emotionally like a boomerang.

In addition to their regular job of ensuring a successful pregnancy, the hormones of pregnancy seem to intensify your moods and feelings; at times you can feel as if you're riding an emotional roller coaster. One minute you're deliriously happy about your pregnancy and everything else. You and Mary Poppins are soul sisters. The next minute you find yourself in tears over nothing in particular. Take heart! You aren't going crazy. You have the entire first trimester of your pregnancy to resolve your feelings and settle in to the fact that you really are pregnant.

Second Trimester

Everything usually evens out in the second 3 months. Your nausea and mind-numbing fatigue subside, and you can take great delight in your belly button sticking out. So, there really is a baby in there! You've mastered the second developmental task and incorporated your baby as part of your own body. You experience the meaning of real togetherness as you become accustomed to the kicks and flutters you're now feeling.

The good news is that your bustline has undoubtedly increased; the bad news: so has your waistline. You may find as many women have, that it's a relief not to have to hold in your stomach. For the next 6 months, your stomach is on vacation!

Emotionally, you'll probably find that you're more dependent on your husband. You have a strong desire to have him share in your pregnancy, feel the baby move, and talk about your impending parenthood. The topic dominates your thoughts and your conversation. You may also find it hard

4

to make even simple decisions like what to have for dinner or what to wear. If you have always been a very decisive person, this may be disconcerting, but this too shall pass.

Third Trimester

The last 3 months of pregnancy are often call the trimester of anticipation. You can be quite content to sit back and let other people make decisions and take care of you. Your thoughts focus inwardly, and you dream of things to come—labor and delivery and, of course, babies. You try to settle on names, and you wander reflectively through the baby department picking out the "right" clothes, the perfect crib.

This is a very reflective time. Serene and passive are the key emotional adjectives. You're earth mother, and your nesting instinct becomes irresistible as you clean the nursery several times a day, scrub floors, rearrange furniture. You're getting ready to finish that last phase: tying up the loose ends of your psychological growth spurt. You're preparing yourself psychologically to release your baby from your body through birth. You are now able to picture the baby "inside" as being "outside," a separate being from you. You're really ready to be a mother.

THE FATHER-TO-BE

As an expectant father, you also have some emotional adjusting to do. You may find yourself going through the same feelings of ambivalence about the pregnancy as your wife. You may find initially that you crave some emotional and physical distance from her and the reality of the pregnancy until you can sort out your feelings. This doesn't mean that you don't love your wife or that you aren't happy about the baby; you just need some time to let the dust settle in your brain. Many men take this time to pursue a new hobby, go back to school, or just go fishin'.

If you're already a father, you aren't immune to the ambivalence and introspection. You will also need some emotional room to reevaluate your fathering role.

Even though in recent years our culture has come to accept tender, nurturing qualities in men, you're not sure just how that applies to you personally. Some men become frightened or confused by the intensity of their feelings toward the pregnancy. You may feel the urge to engage in some extra male bonding to counteract the strange emotions you are feeling. At the other end of the behavior spectrum, you might experience "couvade," the feeling that "we" are both pregnant. When this happens, your feelings about your own feminine creativity are intense. You so strongly desire to share in the creation and growth of your child that you find yourself experiencing decreased appetite, nausea, and other gastrointestinal upsets. You might even put on a few pounds around your middle.

Becoming a family man with all its added responsibilities can weigh heavily on you, especially if you haven't had a strong role model to guide

you. You spend some time thinking about your relationship with your own father and trying to decide how you want your relationship with your new baby to be. If you find that you're having problems adjusting to the idea of being a father, get some help to resolve your difficult feelings. You want your relationship with your new family to be healthy, just like your new baby.

Once you've resolved your feelings and feel back on track, you'll take a more active interest in your wife's pregnancy. "Taking hold" of the fathering role occurs somewhere between the twelfth and thirty-sixth week of pregnancy. You now want to spend time with friends who have children. You feel more enthusiasm for the coming birth and think about fixing up the baby's room, shopping for a crib with your wife, and even taking prepared childbirth classes. You're ready to expand emotionally your one-to-one relationship with your wife to the new family that will occupy your attention. You, your wife, and your marriage are changing and growing.

2

Sexuality

FEAST OR FAMINE

Pregnancy, especially a long-awaited one, usually brings great joy to a marriage; however, even the most stable marriage experiences some stress and strain along with the joy. Naturally, changes occur in your sexual relationship. Your roles evolve as you begin to see yourselves as parents of this baby as well as the companions, friends, and lovers you were before. Your marriage undergoes a reorganization that can cause a few temporary crises until you adjust to the changes.

First Trimester

Generally, in the first trimester your sexual appetite will be relatively unchanged. However, your nausea, vomiting, fatigue, and tender breasts can put a damper on your usual healthy libido.

Second Trimester

During the second trimester, famine turns into feast. Your energy levels are back. In spite of an enlarging abdomen, it's common to experience a heightened eroticism through sexual fantasies and dreams. The gleam is back in your eye, and you may find yourself eagerly planning sexual encounters with your husband. Your sexual and pelvic organs are filled with extra blood during pregnancy, which gives your libido a jump start. Many women experience their first orgasms during the second trimester. This can be a fun time for both of you. Remember it for later.

Third Trimester

By the third trimester, the lustful fire of desire that crackled between you in the previous months has now become flickering embers of faded ecstasy. Emotionally, you may find yourself becoming quite introspective as you concentrate on the coming labor and delivery. Sex may not be high on your list. You and your husband can be assured that the situation is temporary and normal.

"We shall overcome" is your new theme song as you struggle to find positions that work and are comfortable as your uterus grows ever larger. At the very end of pregnancy, when the "missionary" position is a memory, the only realistic position left may be with you on your side facing away from your husband. In this position, you can rest your abdomen on a pillow, and the penis won't penetrate the vagina as deeply as in other positions. Several excellent books that deal with sexuality during pregnancy can be helpful. See the Recommended Resources section in the appendix.

It is not uncommon, especially in the last weeks of pregnancy, for you to feel some cramping or mild contractions after intercourse, for several reasons. The seminal fluid (semen) contains substances called prostaglandins, which can cause the uterus to contract for a short time. The contractile effect doesn't usually cause any problems except some discomfort. If you're concerned because you're cramping frequently after intercourse, try having your husband wear a condom or ejaculate outside your vagina (coitus interruptus). Discuss your concerns with your doctor for other suggestions.

Cramping after intercourse may also come from stimulation of your nipples. Nipple stimulation can cause the release of a hormone, oxytocin, which makes your uterus contract. The degree of cramping varies from woman to woman. The amount of intermittent nipple stimulation during lovemaking is rarely enough to trigger labor.

HUSBANDLY CONCERNS

You also are influenced by the psychological and physical changes taking place in your wife's body and have your own adjustments to pregnancy to make. Your satisfying sexual relationship can change very quickly when your wife is tired, irritable, and moody and has morning sickness. Even if you were her favorite movie star, she wouldn't be interested. Don't take it personally; your libido would take a nose dive too if you thought you had to run for the bathroom any minute. She may be spending more time hugging the toilet bowl than you.

As pregnancy advances, you may find that you're embarrassed or hesitant to approach an increasingly unfamiliar body. By the third trimester, your wife may feel more like a lumbering bear headed for hibernation than the prepregnant girl of your dreams. This woman who used to start forest fires in your southern region just doesn't look the same. She looks . . . motherly. You might find those long forgotten little boy "feelings" you used to have for your own mother resurfacing to confuse you. Don't worry; you're normal. It's also common to feel anxious, even guilty, because you fear injuring your wife and/or the baby, but you won't.

Even though there will be times when your wife may not be interested in the physical act of love, she strongly desires closeness, affection, and comfort from you. If you're conditioned to the idea that physical affection always proceeds to sex, both of you may be very disappointed. If ever there was a time to be very sensitive of each other's needs, this is it. Talk to each other! Tell her how you feel and what you need—her heart will melt faster than an ice cream cone on the fourth of July. Listen when she shares her feelings with you. Cultivate your sense of humor because it'll help you cope and keep your perspective. You are in this together.

A FEW GENERAL RULES

As a rule, sex during pregnancy is safe, and there is no reason to alter your routine. If you perceive a potential problem regarding intercourse during pregnancy or if you have any fears, discuss them freely with your doctor. Try not to be shy and embarrassed; your doctor has heard it all.

Only rarely will intercourse be prohibited. For example, if you have a history of preterm labor or if your membranes rupture prematurely (your water bag breaks too soon), your doctor will prescribe celibacy until you deliver. When penetration isn't allowed, many couples rely on more oral-genital activities as a way of maintaining intimate physical closeness.

A few sexual practices must be restricted during pregnancy. Air blown into the vagina can be very dangerous because the air can enter your bloodstream and result in death for both you and your baby. It's unwise to insert plastic vibrators into the vagina because the plastic is very rigid and could damage your cervix or, in rare cases, cause your water bag to break.

A big question for most couples is when to stop having intercourse. Very few, if any, doctors still recommend abstaining from sex for 6 weeks before you deliver. Usually, you can continue until your water breaks. If your pregnancy remains normal, there's no reason why you can't make the decision yourselves. You'll find that your physical changes will be a prime factor in whether or when you decide to give up sex for the duration. For example, the extra engorgement that caused such delight in your second trimester can cause great discomfort in your third trimester. It can prove too much of a good thing. Many positions are very uncomfortable, and even if you manage to find one that allows you to complete the act, orgasm doesn't relieve your fullness, so it may seem more trouble than it's worth to you (at times you may consider it a mercy mission). A simple rule to follow is: If it still feels good, carry on.

△△△

3

Your Body and Baby's Growth

CALCULATING YOUR DUE DATE

Pregnancy usually lasts 265 days from conception, or 280 days from the first day of the last menstrual period, assuming a 28-day cycle. The rule for calculating your due date is to subtract 3 months from your last period and add 7 days. For example, if the first day of your last menstrual period was September 7, your due date would be June 14. Deciding how far along you are can be confusing because pregnancy duration is calculated in lunar months of 28 days as opposed to calendar months of 31 days. Consequently, pregnancy lasts 10 lunar months (40 weeks) or 9 calendar months.

About 50 percent of all pregnant women will deliver 1 week before the due date and 1 in 10 will go 2 weeks beyond the due date. As you can see, your due date is merely a ballpark figure; you can't use it as an absolute.

1 TO 2 LUNAR MONTHS

The baby is still an embryo during the first 8 weeks and is about 1-1/2 inches (4 centimeters) long. The heart is the most developed organ at this point. The arms and legs are still buds, and the umbilical cord is beginning to form.

3 TO 4 LUNAR MONTHS

Between 12 and 16 weeks, the baby is about 3 inches in size and weighs only 1/4 of a pound (110 grams). Arm and leg buds have blossomed, and nails are developing. Hair begins to appear on the body, and sexual development is apparent. The baby's skin is very transparent. The heartbeat can now be heard.

Now you can feel your uterus just above your pelvic bone, and probably you're spending a lot of time in the bathroom urinating because of the pressure on your bladder.

5 LUNAR MONTHS

You're halfway through your 10 lunar months or 40 weeks of pregnancy. The uterus has reached your navel. You're becoming accustomed to the baby's kicks and movements you're feeling. There really is a baby in there, and you're thrilled every time you feel even a little flutter. You can also feel the Braxton-Hick's (false) contractions by now, and you're definitely looking pregnant.

Your baby now weighs a little under a pound (300 grams) and has fine silky hair (lanugo) all over the body. Hair on the head is beginning to sprout.

16

6 LUNAR MONTHS

At 6 lunar months, the average weight of a baby is 1-1/2 pounds (630 grams). Her skin is wrinkled, but fat deposits are forming and in time will smooth out the wrinkles. The head is noticeably larger than the body. Eyebrows and lashes are present. Babies born at this time may be able to breathe briefly, but their immature lungs and other body systems give them a very slim chance of survival.

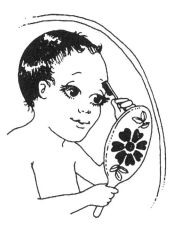

Your body is definitely looking pregnant. Your navel may be sticking out, and the round ligaments holding up your uterus may be stretched enough to make you feel at times as if your bottom is falling out.

7 LUNAR MONTHS

Your little sweetheart now weighs a little over 2 pounds and is 16 inches long. The skin is red and covered with nature's "cold cream," called vernix caseosa. With expert care in a sophisticated neonatal intensive care unit, most babies born at this point survive. You may experience pregnancy aches and pains, but at least you're over the nausea, and you aren't spending half your life in the bathroom urinating.

8 LUNAR MONTHS

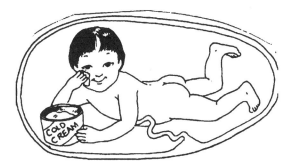

At 8 lunar months, you may have problems with your round ligaments again and soreness of your pubic bones, not to mention those funny shooting pains in your vagina. In spite of the aches and pains, you can relax. Babies born at this time have an excellent survival rate. Their average weight is around 4 pounds (1800 grams).

9 LUNAR MONTHS

A baby at this state is 16 to 18 inches long and about 5-1/2 pounds. The wrinkles are almost gone and your little superman may be keeping you awake at night. You wearily watch your abdomen rock and roll as you swear he's doing the tango about 2 A.M.

Your uterus is now near your rib cage, and you may find yourself short of breath because your diaphragm is being crowded. The thrill of being pregnant usually wears thin at this point. You yearn for the day when you'll have your body all to yourself again.

10 LUNAR MONTHS

This is it! The end is in sight, and boy, are you ready. You're sick of maternity clothes, swollen ankles, and all the other aches and pains. The latest pinup

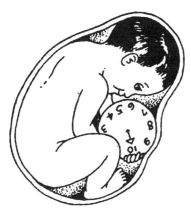

in PLAYGIRL could interest you less. Again, you're spending more time in the bathroom relieving your bladder, which seems to be full all the time. Your Braxton-Hick's contractions keep you guessing if it's the real thing. Your baby is fully developed and raring to meet the world. It's getting very crowded in there.

△∧△

4

Pregnancy Fitness

WEIGHT GAIN

The ideal woman of the 1800s was built for comfort, not speed. She was a stout, hearty Brunhild. Since pregnancy was a "delicate" condition, she remained in "confinement" like a fragile flower and probably ate herself into oblivion out of boredom. The turn-of-the-century Gibson girl "porked up" because she was eating for two.

In the 50s and 60s, the tide turned; fat was unfit. Gaining more than 10 pounds during pregnancy supposedly gave you toxemia, and eating salt was a sin. The tide turned again by the 70s and 80s. Since today's nonpregnant ideal is the slim, trim health food jogger, what's considered ideal for the pregnant woman these days?

To eat or not to eat is no longer the question. According to the Committee on Nutritional Status During Pregnancy, a weight gain of 25 to 35 pounds produces the healthiest babies. Pregnancy is no time to lose weight. If you've spent the better part of your adult life fighting flab, you may have to adjust your mind-set.

For some, the expectation to gain weight is akin to dying and going to hog heaven. These are the women who lose control and gain 60 pounds before they regain their senses. For others who fought the hard fight and were winning the battle of the bulge, the prospect of calling even a temporary truce can be disheartening.

It may help your adjustment to understand why you need to gain those extra pounds. There's a direct correlation between adequate maternal weight gain and healthy babies. Newborns who weigh between 6-1/2 to 8 pounds are healthier and just do better. Low birth weight babies, those under 6 pounds, generally have a higher rate of stillbirth, neonatal death, poor infant development, cerebral palsy, mental retardation, and lowered intelligence. In contrast, those women who choose hog heaven run the risk of having much larger babies which may complicate labor. The lesson is to avoid feast or famine. There's a happy medium.

PRODUCTS OF PREGNANCY
Average Weight

Component	Pounds
Baby	7.5
Placenta	1.0
Amniotic fluid	2.0
Uterus, weight increase	2.5
Breast tissue, weight increase	3.0
Blood volume increase	4.0
Maternal fat stores	4.0 to 8.0
Total	24.0 to 28.0

The rate at which you gain is just as important as how much you gain. Slow, steady weight gain during the whole pregnancy is ideal. A gain of more than 6-1/2 pounds in a month is too much; less than 1/2 pound in 1 month after the first trimester is too little. The formula is simple to follow. You'll probably gain about 2 to 4 pounds by the end of the twelfth week, depending on how nauseated you are. After that, the usual weight gain is 1 pound a week for the last 28 weeks. If you're overweight, you should still gain 15 to 25 pounds. Overweight women who gain less than 15 pounds have infant mortality rates twice those of overweight women with adequate weight gains. Consult your doctor for more specific recommendations based on your individual weight. The chart on page 20 shows where the additional weight goes.

During the second trimester, the weight you gain is added to your own fat stores. These are the new, more lush contours you notice on your abdomen, breasts, hips, and thighs. This is important because during the third trimester, when the baby is gaining weight rapidly, your metabolism changes. The weight stored during the second trimester nourishes your body, while the calories you consume go to your growing baby. Mother Nature also stores those extra pounds in preparation for breast-feeding.

NUTRITIONAL KNOW-HOW

Even with our all-consuming preoccupation with food, few people, pregnant or not, really understand what constitutes a healthy diet. There's no mystical, magical, miracle diet for pregnancy; it's fairly simple.

CALORIES

The old adage of eating for two isn't quite accurate. One and a half is the current standard. The single most important factor nutritionally for your baby is adequate calorie intake by you. You need dietary extras in the form of calories, proteins, carbohydrates, fats, vitamins, and minerals, which you get from a sensible balanced diet.

You need approximately 300 extra calories a day while pregnant and breast-feeding. Figure 17 to 18 calories per pound of your normal or ideal body weight. For most women this amount will be 2200 to 2400 calories. Again, consult your doctor if you have questions or special needs.

PROTEINS, CARBOHYDRATES, AND FATS

The types of calories you eat each day are as important as how many. Nutritional experts agree that your daily diet should be divided into three components. Proteins should constitute 20 percent of your diet, fats 30 percent or less, and carbohydrates 50 percent. Few people meet these requirements. The typical American diet is high in fats and proteins, low in carbohydrates. To find out where you fit in between the typical and ideal diet, do a 48-hour diet recall. Write down everything you eat, and see where you need to reform—this is a real shocker for most people.

Proteins

Proteins are important tissue builders for both you and your baby, but you don't need as much as you think. Most American diets provide more than enough protein. While your body can use protein as an energy source, its prime function is to rebuild tissues and cells. It's not the most efficient energy source for your body. Too much protein can make you feel sluggish and put a strain on your kidneys. During pregnancy you need 70 grams of protein per day.

Carbohydrates

Carbohydrates are appropriately called "protein sparers." They fuel your body so protein can be used for tissue building instead of energy. Next to fats, "carbo's" are the most misunderstood and maligned component in our diet. It's important to understand their function in order to use them efficiently.

Carbohydrates are divided into two groups: starches and sugars. The starches provide the complex carbohydrates that maintain a steady source of fuel being released into your system. They satisfy your hunger for longer periods of time in contrast to the simple sugars found in processed junk food. Potatoes, pastas, and breads are excellent complex carbohydrates and they aren't fattening. Anything can be fattening if you plaster butter all over it, so try using plain, low-fat yogurt on your baked potato instead of sour cream and extra butter (the plain yogurt tastes very similar to sour cream).

While fresh fruits contain sugar, they also provide high fiber, which keeps blood sugar on an even keel. The fiber content also keeps your colon working efficiently. Remember, complex carbohydrates from fresh vegetables, grains, and fresh fruits should constitute at least 50 percent of your daily diet. The following foods are good sources of carbohydrates for your diet, especially during pregnancy:

Starches	Sugars
Potatoes	Fresh fruits
Pasta	Fresh vegetables
Rice	Fruit juices
Breads	

Fats

Fats are another important energy source; just don't overdo them. Your body stores fat as an emergency supply for those times when you use up your carbohydrate fuel. Stored fat is the body's insurance policy. Fats such as butter, margarine, and salad oils make your diet more appealing to eat, and are a necessary part of your diet. Just keep the amount of fat in your diet to 30 percent or a little less.

Your basic food intake each day should contain 4 servings of milk or milk products for your calcium requirement; 3 servings of meat or meat substitutes such as eggs, beans, dried peas, peanut butter, and nuts; 4 servings of vegetables, fruits, bread, and cereals. See on page 24 the sample menu of a well-balanced, nutritious diet for 1 day; it contains adequate calories and components, including calcium.

NUTRITIONAL HINTS

Cereals

All cereals are not created equal. The most nutritious cereals are those without added sugar, salt, or fat and have a high content of carbohydrates and fiber. For example, granola has a high fat content and a higher caloric value than many other cereals. Shredded wheat is ideal because it doesn't contain salt, sugar, or fat—you add the only sugar—and its fiber and carbohydrate content are slightly higher than that in other leading brands. Read the labels on the boxes to help you make informed choices.

SAMPLE MENU

Food group		Calories	Carb. (gm)	Prot. (gm)	Fat (gm)	Calcium (mg)
	Breakfast					
1 cereal	3/4 cup Wheat Chex	100	23	3	0	12
	2 tsp. sugar	32	8	0	0	0
1 dairy	1 cup low fat milk	120	12	8	5	300
1 fruit	1 small orange	60	15	1	0	50
	Snack					
2 fruit	1 banana	105	23	2	0	0
	Lunch					
2 bread	2 slices whole wheat	120	22	6	2	60
1 fat	2 tsp. mayonnaise	67	0	0	7	0
1 meat	1 oz. turkey breast	60	0	7	3	3
1 veg	1 oz. romaine lettuce	9	2	1		20
2 fruit	1 cup V-8 juice	50	10	2	0	30
1 bread	8 Wheat Thins	70	9	1	3	0
	Snack					
1 milk	cottage cheese 1/2 cup	100	4	16	3	78
1 fruit	raisins 1/3 cup	150	40	1	0	25

SAMPLE MENU *(continued)*					
Food group		**Calories**	**Carb. (gm)**	**Prot. (gm)**	**Fat (gm)**	**Calcium (mg)**

Food group		Calories	Carb. (gm)	Prot. (gm)	Fat (gm)	Calcium (mg)
	Dinner					
3 meat	3 oz. baked chicken	165	0	21	9	0
1 veg	Baked potato	145	39	8	0	8
2 fat	1 tsp. butter/ margarine	36	0	0	4	1
	1 oz. low-fat plain yogurt	18	2	1	0	51
2 veg	1/2 cup peas	67	12	4	0	22
1 veg	Salad with ro-maine lettuce and 1/2 cup tomatoes	33	6	2	0	28
4 fats	salad drsg					
	4 tbs (oil/ vinegar)	290	0	0	32	0
1 dairy	1 cup low-fat milk	120	12	18	5	300
	Snack					
1 bread	1 slice French bread	80	13	3	1	22
1 fat	1 tsp. peanut butter	95	3	5	8	5
1 milk	8 oz. low-fat milk	120	12	8	5	300
	Total	2212	262	108	87	1322
			57%	24%	20%	

The Battle of the Sweeteners

A word about sugar versus substitutes. Sugar has been unjustly maligned for a long time. Advertisers have programmed us to believe that sugar is the "killer white" to be avoided at all costs. Let's look at the cost of a 5-pound bag of pure cane sugar at approximately $1.21 versus $7.61 for 7 ounces of Nutrasweet (aspartame), which gives you 400 teaspoons of sweetener. Economically, there's no contest. In the battle of the calories, it's hardly worth the effort since sugar has only 16 calories per teaspoon. So what's the big deal? Honey sounds better, but it has slightly more calories than sugar, and your body doesn't know the difference. Sugar is sugar to your metabolism. As with most things in life, moderation is the key. It's no different with sugar. You can have a few teaspoons a day for your coffee and cereal and not feel guilty. If you still feel aspartame is your sweetener of choice, then go ahead—experts conclude that it's safe to use during pregnancy.

Fresh Fruits versus Juices

Here's the difference between fresh fruits and fruit juices. The whole fruit has the fiber that keeps your colon happy and stabilizes your blood sugar. Orange juice is healthy, but it gives you an instant sugar high without the fiber. Be aware of the difference between juices and fruit cocktail drinks: The fruit cocktail may contain as little as 10 percent fruit juice, the rest is water and sugar. Fruit cocktail drink isn't a good buy money-wise or nutritionally.

Salt

Normal amounts of salt should remain in your diet. *Salt does not cause toxemia.* Unless you're eating huge amounts of very salty food, salt doesn't cause you to retain water. Continue to use salt moderately unless your doctor directs otherwise.

Great Greens

Lettuce and other green leafy vegetables can be good sources of vitamins and fiber. If you aren't wild about the exotic greens like mustard or kale, become more creative with salads. Experiment with something other than iceberg lettuce, which has very little food value or fiber. Try mixing romaine and leafy, salad bowl lettuce with raw, chopped Swiss chard. Shred some cabbage and toss it in. The combinations are endless. Keep in mind that salads are very nutritious and low in calories, but salad dressings aren't.

26

Oil and vinegar-based dressings have fewer calories than mayonnaise-based dressings. You need some fats in your diet, but this is where many people get carried away.

Vitamins and Supplements

Have you ever forgotten to add the baking powder to your cake recipe? Even if you added all the other ingredients, without the baking powder as the catalyst, your cake was probably a flop. Eating sufficient calories without adequate vitamins and minerals as a catalyst is a similar experience: Your body isn't able to absorb its necessary quota of nutrients.

For example, without enough B complex vitamins (B, B6, and B12), your body can't utilize the fats, carbohydrates, and proteins you put into it. Vitamin C is another example—besides rebuilding tissues, vitamin C enhances your body's ability to absorb iron.

Vitamin pills are not a substitute for a good balanced diet. Experts agree that a healthy diet provides all the vitamins and minerals you need during pregnancy, except iron and folic acid. In spite of that belief, most doctors prescribe supplements during pregnancy. If you feel that you want or need vitamin supplements during pregnancy, talk to your doctor. The key is to not use them as a substitute for a poor diet or to embark on megavitamin therapy, which is dangerous to your developing baby.

Calcium

Calcium is lacking in most diets. Pregnant women need far more calcium than the average person—1200 milligrams per day. Your growing baby needs calcium to build strong teeth and bones. The old wives' tale is true: The baby will drain the calcium from your bones' stores if you don't supply enough of it through proper diet and, if necessary, pill supplementation. Depleting your bones' calcium stores can result in osteoporosis (softening of the bones) in later life. Adequate calcium intake

now is good insurance so you won't be caught short in later life. If you have any questions about your calcium intake, ask your doctor for advice.

Calcium comes from many sources, including green leafy vegetables, but the most readily available sources are dairy products, the best being milk. People are rarely neutral about milk. They either love it, or hate it, or it doesn't love them. Many adults have an intolerance to the lactose in milk, which gives them uncomfortable and embarrassing intestinal eruptions. They drink milk and their colon does an imitation of Mount St. Helens.

Milk

If you love milk and it loves you, you're in luck. You can obtain all the calcium you need by drinking just four 8-ounce glasses of milk a day. If milk disagrees with you, there's still hope. Most markets now carry milk with Lactaid added, which allows for easier digestion. Some producers even add extra calcium. Yogurt is also a good source of calcium. If you'd rather kiss a toad than drink milk, your only source is lots of green leafy vegetables and pill supplements. You don't need a prescription for calcium. The most digestible and easily absorbed form of calcium is calcium carbonate—the kind in TUMS. Each TUMS contains 500 milligrams of calcium carbonate. Other calcium sources include those shown in the following table.

CALCIUM SOURCES Daily requirements second /third trimesters = 1200 mg		
Food	**Serving size (oz.)**	**Calcium (mg)**
Fortified milk	8	359
Raw turnip greens	3-1/2	246
Raw collard greens	3-1/2	203
Raw beet greens	3-1/2	119
Romaine lettuce	3-1/2	68
Boston lettuce	3-1/2	35
Iceberg lettuce	3-1/2	35

Pregnancy is a perfect time to evaluate your diet and eating habits. You have a real incentive to lead a healthier life-style. If you feel you're hopeless, or want some special attention, ask your doctor to recommend a registered dietician for a consultation. It's a wise investment for your baby and you.

EXERCISE

For those addicted to the joys of jogging or aerobic dance, the burning question is whether one has to sacrifice cardiovascular fitness, firm thighs, and a great rear end for the sake of a healthy baby. Only in the last several years has anybody tried objectively to evaluate the effects of exercise on human pregnancy. A lot of pregnant rats and sheep have been exercised into oblivion looking for some answers. So far, it doesn't look as if the old running shoes will have to be put into moth balls.

Researchers find that even though blood shunts away from the uterus during strenuous exercise—even to the point of exhaustion—the baby is able to compensate quite well and suffers no ill effects. Original fears about growth retardation and lower birth weight babies are not a concern. The increase of body temperature during exercise doesn't cause spinal defects in babies either. Olympic athletes, joggers, and even aerobic dance enthusiasts were studied to determine the effects of regular exercise during pregnancy. They were compared to pregnant non-exercising women. The outcomes for the two groups were the same. If you embark on an exercise routine in the belief it will make your labor shorter and easier, you may be disappointed. A look at the Olympic athletes showed a longer first stage of labor but a shorter second stage. The aerobics and jogging group showed no differences at all in either stage.

If you're experiencing a complicated pregnancy, exercise isn't advised. A baby that already has problems with reduced oxygen levels may not tolerate even light exercise by mom. Talk to your doctor if you have any questions.

General Guidelines

Whether you're fit or not, pregnancy brings some physical changes that alter your ability to engage in physical activity. Due to the hormones of pregnancy, joints are more unstable, and ligaments and tissues are more relaxed. Your center of gravity changes as pregnancy advances. Your balance is more precarious. Your chances of injury increase. You have to honor those temporary changes and make adjustments for them.

The safe and realistic goal of exercise during pregnancy is to maintain a reasonable level of fitness. Now is no time to try to transform yourself from couch potato to iron woman. If you're healthy, and your pregnancy is low-risk, exercise is safe. If you have an established exercise routine, there's no reason to alter it. Listen to your body and use common sense combined with moderation. If you haven't exercised before pregnancy, there are safe and effective exercise programs for you too. Begin with physical activity of very low intensity and advance activity levels very gradually.

If you're a high-performance athlete such as a marathon runner or aerobic dance instructor, you may need to reevaluate your current exercise program and make some temporary adjustments. No matter what your level of fitness, discuss your past and current exercise habits with your doctor to decide the best level and type of exercise for you.

The exercise guidelines on pages 32–33 are adapted from the recommendations of the American College of Obstetricians and Gynecologists (ACOG). These guidelines are very conservative and may not fit the needs of the conditioned athlete.

ENERGIZING EXERCISE

Aquafitness

Swimming or other water exercises are particularly safe and suited to pregnancy. You can achieve aerobic fitness, and you don't have to worry about falling. When you get tired, you can float and relax. To get the most out of your sessions, keep the major portion of your body in the water while exercising. The water should be at a comfortable temperature. Many health clubs now offer aquafitness programs for pregnant women.

Walking

Walking is another very safe exercise during pregnancy because it's gentle on the body, low impact, and easier on the joints. Resist wearing weights on your arms or legs since they add stress to already unstable joints. Wear good walking shoes to maximize stability and comfort. Drink plenty of fluids, and don't exercise when it's too hot or humid. Keep your bladder in mind lest you stray too far from potential pit stops. Take your husband for evening walks—walking is a great stress reliever.

Bike Riding

A stationary bike is the safest during pregnancy. You can't fall over, you don't have to wear a helmet, and you don't have to worry about traffic. Make sure the seat and height are comfortable. Avoid overextending knee and hip joints while pedaling. Check your pulse to avoid exceeding the 140 beats per minute limit.

Aerobic Classes

If aerobic classes were a regular part of your routine before pregnancy, you can continue during pregnancy with a few adjustments. Be sure your instructor knows you're pregnant. Don't try to keep up with your nonpregnant cohorts. Some days you just won't have the energy, so listen to your body. Be aware as your center of gravity shifts. Study the Don'ts in the ACOG guidelines and modify your moves accordingly to avoid the jerky, bouncy moves. Monitor your pulse and stay within the guidelines.

Aerobic video tapes are very popular because you can stay home in the privacy of your living room. Low-impact videos are generally the best for the pregnant woman. Make sure you have enough room to move around and good ventilation. Monitor your heart rate.

If aerobics weren't a part of your exercise routine, find a class for pregnant women. Ask if your instructor is trained to teach pregnant women. If she

EXERCISE GUIDELINES

Pregnancy and Postpartum

Do

1. Regular exercise of at least three times per week.

2. Precede vigorous exercise with a 5-minute period of muscle warm-up. Slow walking or stationary cycling with low resistance is effective.

3. Gradually decrease activity. For example, if you have been fast walking, finish with very slow walking. Conclude with gentle stationary stretching. Make your stretches slow and steady. Hold the stretch for about 20 seconds and relax into it. Avoid bouncy movements that snap your muscles like rubber bands. That's how you injure yourself.

4. Take your pulse during peak activity. Keep target heart rate within limits set by your physician. *Maternal heart rate should not exceed 140 beats per minute.* You need a watch with a second hand. If you count 23 beats in 10 seconds, you are within the limits. Athletic stores also sell devices that strap on your finger and give you a continuous recording of your pulse rate. In general, if you're able to carry on a conversation comfortably while exercising, your heart rate is probably within the recommended limits. Check to make sure.

5. Exercise on a wooden floor or a tightly carpeted surface to reduce shock and provide sure footing.

6. Rise gradually to avoid dizziness from floor-lying exercises. Periodically move your legs to keep your blood circulating.

is familiar with the ACOG guidelines and has a certificate from an organization such as "Mom's On the Move," the American College of Sports Medicine, or the Aerobics Fitness Association of America you are on the right track. The advantages of an all-pregnant class is the opportunity to meet with other pregnant women and share experiences.

EXERCISE GUIDELINES *(continued)*

7. Drink liquids before and after exercise to prevent dehydration. Replenish fluids as necessary.

8. Assure adequate caloric intake to meet both the extra energy needs of pregnancy and the exercise performed.

9. Consult your physician if any unusual symptoms occur during exercise.

Don't

1. Exercise in hot, humid weather or during any illness if you have a fever.

2. Engage in exercise that requires deep flexion or extension of joints, jumping, jarring motions, or rapid changes in direction. Don't use jerky, bouncy motions such as those used in racquet-ball, tennis, or high impact aerobics. However, If you are well conditioned and have been engaging in these sports previous to pregnancy, listen to your body. You will know when you need to modify your exercise regimien.

Pregnancy Only—Don't

3. Exercise strenuously for longer than 15 minutes.

4. Lie flat on your back after the fourth month of pregnancy has been completed.

5. Raise your core temperature more than 38 degrees centigrade (100.4 degrees Fahrenheit).

6. Use exercises that require you to hold your breath or bear down (Valsalva maneuver).

Pump You Up—Weight Training

Weight training is an effective way to strengthen and tone your muscles. It can provide the complement to your aerobic exercise. Use light to moderate weights. Avoid exercises that may stress your lower back or place pressure on your abdominal muscles. Remember to breathe while lifting weights, exhaling on exertion and inhaling on relaxation. Nautilus equipment is safer than free weights because it's more stable. Be careful to not overextend joints if you use free weights. Your warm-up stretching and cool-down exercises are especially important with weight lifting because your muscles become tight. If possible, consult with someone who's knowledgeable about weights and explain the limits of the ACOG guidelines to assure you have a safe, effective program.

Yoga

Mention yoga and most people immediately conjure the stereotypical picture of someone sitting in the lotus position with eyes closed, the mind quietly engaged in contemplating the mysteries of the universe—or their navel. Yoga is not only for the mind. Some types of yoga such as Iyenegar, focus on the body. Properly done, yoga strengthens, tones, and stretches your muscles. It's a proven stress reliever, and you don't need any special equipment. It also helps you learn concentration, persistence, and patience—ideal qualities for your upcoming labor and birth experience. The exercises in the excellent *Stretch and Relax* book in the Recommended Resources section are based on yoga poses. Check your local YWCA, YMCA, or health clubs for yoga or stretch and tone classes.

Remember, exercise will give you a sense of well-being, lift your spirits, and decrease stress. There is something for everyone. See the recommended exercises in Appendix 1.

ΛΛΛ

5

Common Complaints of Pregnancy

While you may enjoy your new pregnancy figure, the increased hormones and blood volume combine with your enlarging uterus to produce those on-again/off-again discomforts throughout pregnancy. Although some women have more discomfort than others, you'll probably have your share. You can expect more, or different, discomforts with each succeeding pregnancy. It's trite but true: "Every pregnancy is different." "Uncommon" remedies can be found in the acupressure/massage section of Chapter 16—"Labor and Delivery."

BACKACHE

It's a rare pregnant woman who can escape backaches. Your enlarged uterus throws your weight forward and puts great strain on your back and leg muscles. Normal body mechanics shift, causing muscle stress and increasing back joint compression. Pain, even all-out muscle spasm, can result.

■ HELPFUL HINTS

Prevention, as usual, is the best treatment. Observe good body mechanics:

1. Bend with your knees, not your back! Lift with your legs, hold objects close to your body, and plan ahead to avoid sudden load shifts. Lift objects only chest high. When the load is heavy, get help. Always be sure of your footing.

2. Stand with one foot up; change positions often. A small footstool will help you, especially when you're washing dishes or ironing. Walk with good posture, keeping your head level, your breastbone up, shoulders relaxed. Wear comfortable, flat shoes with heels no higher than 1 inch.

3. Move your car seat forward to keep your knees bent and higher than your hips. You might want to use a small pillow to support the low back area.

4. Sit in chairs low enough for you to place both feet on the floor with your knees higher than your hips.

5. A good night's sleep is imperative. You should have a firm mattress. Some people find a waterbed really helps; it's an individual preference. Sleep on your side with your knees bent toward your chest. A pillow between your knees helps you be more comfortable. As your uterus grows, a pillow under your stomach also helps.

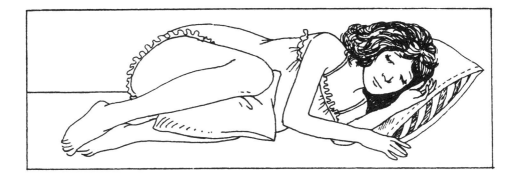

The following exercises help stretch and rest your back muscles, alleviating discomfort. If back pain persists, you may want to have your doctor recommend a physical therapist who can outline for you a more detailed

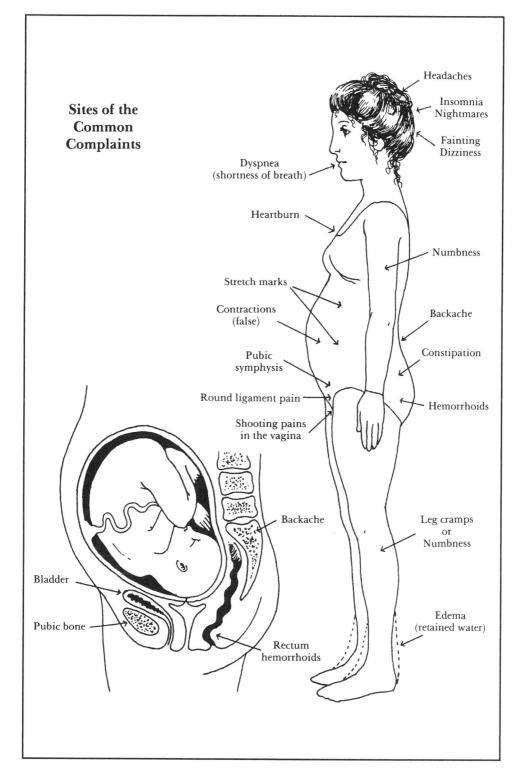

Sites of the Common Complaints

Headaches

Insomnia
Nightmares

Fainting
Dizziness

Dyspnea
(shortness of breath)

Heartburn

Numbness

Stretch marks

Contractions
(false)

Backache

Pubic
symphysis

Constipation

Round ligament pain

Hemorrhoids

Shooting pains
in the vagina

Backache

Bladder

Leg cramps
or
Numbness

Pubic bone

Rectum
hemorrhoids

Edema
(retained water)

37

regimen to strengthen your muscles. Certain types of yoga exercises, such as Iyenegar, help you strengthen, stretch, and tone your back muscles. Check the Recommended Resources section for a helpful book.

If you're at work and experiencing back strain, take a few moments every hour and give your back a break. This is especially important if you sit at a computer all day! Here are some rest positions that can relieve your back by straightening your spine and tilting your pelvis backward.

■ **HELPFUL HINTS**

1. Using the back of a chair to support and balance yourself, assume a squatting position for a 30-second interval, and then rest for 15 seconds. Repeat this exercise at least six times, six times a day.

2. At work or home, lean forward in your chair and lower your head to your knees for 30 seconds. Raise up and repeat six times, six times a day.

CONSTIPATION

The pregnancy hormones mentioned earlier slow down bowel function. Nature does that to assure maximum absorption time for nutrients and vitamins. If you tend to constipation anyway, you may begin to feel that dynamite is the only solution. Laxatives may help, but they offer only short-term relief, and with their repeated use, your colon becomes even lazier and addicted to the artificial, harsh stimulation laxatives provide.

■ **HELPFUL HINTS**

Instead of using laxatives, add 3 tablespoons of unprocessed bran to a high-fiber cereal such as Bran Flakes or Grapenuts at breakfast, or just mix the bran with milk or juice. If that hasn't worked by the next morning, add another tablespoon to the original 3. Continue adding more each morning until you get results; some people require more than others. This is the safest, most reliable method available for treating constipation, as well as the cheapest. Try adding more leafy green vegetables and fresh fruits to your diet.

CONTRACTIONS, "FALSE"

By your fourth month, you may notice your abdomen occasionally becoming tight, as if the baby had rolled into a ball. You might feel some pressure in your lower abdomen and slight discomfort, but no real pain. These are Braxton-Hick's or "false," contractions. The uterus is just warming up for the real thing. The uterine muscle exercises to keep its tone and do a good job during labor.

DYSPNEA (SHORTNESS OF BREATH)

As yet, there's no certain explanation for the shortness of breath some women experience during pregnancy. What we do know is that the increase of the hormone progesterone makes the respiratory center more sensitive. Progesterone causes you to breathe faster (hyperventilate), and some women, more sensitive to this change, feel short of breath.

EDEMA (SWOLLEN FEET AND ANKLES)

At least half of all pregnant women have swollen feet and ankles during pregnancy, which is normal and considered a sign of a healthy pregnancy. Swelling, or water retention, called edema, is most noticeable at the end of the day. It results from the extra blood volume you normally acquire during pregnancy. Your growing uterus exerts pressure on your lower extremities, where blood pools. The pressure of the trapped blood forces water into the tissues of your feet and ankles. Overindulgence in salty foods may aggravate the situation. The fluid forced into your feet and ankles isn't excess fluid; it's merely displaced and needs to be returned to your circulatory system.

PRECAUTION

Do not take diuretics (water pills). Doctors no longer recommend them for edema. Taking them during pregnancy can cause a serious chemical imbalance in your body.

■ **HELPFUL HINTS**

There is a safe, simple, relaxing solution to the problem of edema. Lie on your left side twice a day for a 1/2 hour and the problem will take care of itself. This position relieves the pressure and lets your system reabsorb the fluid. If there's any excess fluid, your kidneys will eliminate it. Now you know why you spend so much time at night running to the bathroom!

FAINTING AND DIZZINESS

These two symptoms, alone or in combination, can result from the way you're sitting or standing, from eating the wrong foods, or from not eating often enough. If you lie flat on your back, your uterus compresses major arteries and cuts off a lot of the blood supply to both you and the baby. You feel faint, nauseated, and dizzy. If left on your back, you can actually faint and undergo a dangerous drop in blood pressure. Some women are more prone than others to fainting spells, but you can avoid the possibility.

■ **HELPFUL HINTS**

After the fifth month of pregnancy, don't lie flat on your back; sleep or lie on your side or in a semipropped position. Inform your husband that if you do faint, he's to turn you on your left side so your blood pressure can recover.

Feeling dizzy while standing in one spot for a long time, as in a grocery line, is fairly common. Again, your uterus compresses major arteries, trapping blood in your legs and causing your blood pressure to drop. It can be a little embarrassing to conk out waiting in line; people get very excited.

If you start to feel dizzy, shift your weight from one leg to the other. The movement will get your circulation going again. Your mother called it "fidgeting."

The prime source of fuel for your baby is your blood sugar. For your system to supply this fuel, you too need a steady source of your own: food. If you skip meals or go too long without eating, your blood sugar drops and you start feeling dizzy, irritable, shaky, and headachy, a condition known as hypoglycemia.

Consider this analogy: What happens when you build a fire and try to keep it going using only paper as fuel? The fire burns fast, and you must keep adding more paper frequently to keep it going. It just isn't efficient. If you use wood to fuel the fire, it slowly and steadily releases its energy. This principle applies to your food intake and its relationship to your blood sugar levels.

■ **HELPFUL HINTS**

Avoid eating simple carbohydrates (sugar). Processed foods usually have large amounts of sugar added. Because your system burns them so quickly, the simple carbohydrates keep your blood sugar level on a roller coaster with unhealthy peaks and valleys. Eat food that stays with you, such as milk, cheese, fresh fruit, bread, and cereal. Complex carbohydrates keep your blood sugar even. Junk food is the paper fuel for your system; complex carbohydrates are the wood. You may find that eating four to six small meals a day helps you avoid the "sugar blues."

HEARTBURN

The enlarging uterus and the hormones of pregnancy are the culprits of this common complaint. The uterus pushes the stomach upward as it grows. Pregnancy hormones slow digestion, so the stomach doesn't empty as fast, making it possible for stomach acid to shoot up into your throat and bounce off your tonsils. It's uncomfortable and tastes terrible!

Do not use bicarbonate of soda. It is high in salt and can aggravate swollen feet and ankles by causing your body to retain more water than it needs.

■ **HELPFUL HINTS**

Avoid large or unusually spicy meals before bedtime. Antacids like TUMS and Amphojel often help. (See the discussion of antacids in Chapter 7.) Sleep in a semipropped position, with two or three pillows. The cure for heartburn comes when you have your baby.

HEADACHE

Headache is a common complaint, especially in the first trimester. No one knows the cause.

During the first trimester of pregnancy, *do not take any medication of any kind without consulting your doctor.* No one knows for sure what effects even common medications have on the baby in early pregnancy. After the first trimester, you can take Tylenol, but in the last trimester avoid aspirin because it can adversely affect both you and your baby's blood clotting mechanism. Chronic ingestion of aspirin in pregnancy can increase anemia, hemorrhage, prolonged pregnancy, fetal mortality, and low birth weight. Tylenol is safer than aspirin for minor discomforts. See the discussion of over-the-counter drugs in Chapter 7.

■ **HELPFUL HINTS**

1. Lie down with a cold, wet cloth on your forehead, and rest. You might find it helpful to use the relaxation techniques of meditation or those you learn in prepared childbirth training.

2. Don't go long periods without eating. Have an apple or a glass of milk.

3. Have your husband give you a foot massage. The big toes are the acupressure sites for the head. Firm, kneading pressure to these areas can help relieve a headache.

HEMORRHOIDS

Hemorrhoids are large veins distended with blood (varicosities), usually in the rectal area and sometimes in the vagina also. Slowed, impaired circulation caused by the growing uterus, and constipation, usually aggravate the problem during pregnancy. Delivery relieves the pressure in that area, and the hemorrhoids usually disappear.

■ HELPFUL HINTS

Avoid constipation by including adequate bran and fiber in your diet. Don't stand or sit in one place too long. You can treat pain and swelling with warm soaks and anesthetic agents sprayed on the tender areas.

INSOMNIA

In early and again in late pregnancy, you may find it hard to get to sleep. New information suggests a link between caffeine and insomnia in pregnant women. Caffeine breakdown and elimination during pregnancy are slow. Even drinking small amounts might affect your sleep. Eliminate caffeine for a few days and see if it helps.

1. Take a warm bath.

2. Practice some meditation or prepared childbirth techniques to help you relax enough to drift off to sleep.

LEG CRAMPS AND "RESTLESS" LEGS

Just when you get to sleep (and right in the middle of your Robert Redford dream), here comes an aggravating leg cramp to wake you up again. Leg cramps are possibly caused by a calcium deficiency, although drinking more milk or taking calcium pills hasn't been wildly successful in curing leg cramps. Researchers now feel that several factors may cause leg cramps. One is a diet high in phosphorus, an element commonly found in highly processed junk foods and milk. The altered posture of pregnancy plays a big role also; the forward shift of your weight strains those leg muscles, contributing to the cramping at night.

■ **HELPFUL HINTS**

Practice the preventative exercises described below. If a leg cramp should strike, have your husband push the ball of your foot toward you so your toes point toward your knees. If he exerts steady pressure for about a minute, the cramp will go away. If he isn't handy, get up and do the exercise described below.

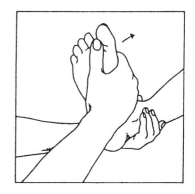

You can prevent leg cramps by following a simple routine before bedtime. Take a warm bath to loosen those tight, tired muscles. Before bed, do the exercise runners use to stretch calf muscles: Stand about 2 feet away from the wall, with your hands on the wall at about eye level. Extend one leg behind you keeping your knee straight. Keep your heels on the floor and lean forward until you feel a stretch in the back leg. Hold the stretch for 20 to 30 seconds, making it a steady stretch, not a bouncy one that snaps your muscles like rubber bands. Repeat the stretch until you no longer feel any tension in your calf muscles.

Stretching your calf muscles also alleviates "restless" legs. You try to drift off to sleep, but your legs seem to have a life of their own, moving and twitching as though possessed by little gremlins. Your calves are telling you that they need relaxing, so get up and do the wall stretch.

NAUSEA AND VOMITING (MORNING SICKNESS)

Nausea is the plague of pregnancy. There's no way to prevent it or even predict who'll get it. Usually it strikes around the sixth week of pregnancy and lasts another 6 to 12 weeks. The cause remains unknown. The pattern of nausea can vary from woman to woman—some experience nausea only in the morning, while others find nighttime the worst. The smell and taste of certain food also trigger nausea. These uncomfortable and inconvenient symptoms can come and go during the day, may disappear for a day, and then recur.

Nausea remedies have run the gamut from simple to very bizarre—from vitamin B12 to intravenous administration of honey, husband's blood, and the male hormone testosterone. None of the aforementioned have met with any success. Currently, no drugs on the market are recommended as safe for pregnancy-induced nausea. But studies show the use of transcutaneous electrical nerve stimulation (TENS) to the acupressure site for nausea located on the wrist is very effective in alleviating nausea and vomiting, and it has no side effects or risk to the baby. The Federal Drug Administration (FDA) has recently approved the **Relief-Band™***, a small battery-operated wristband, for use. The **Relief-Band™** is available by prescription. You can ask your doctor if you would like to try one.

If your nausea and vomiting aren't overwhelming, you can usually handle them with the following simple solutions.

■ **HELPFUL HINTS**

1. Before bedtime, eat a protein/carbohydrate snack such as milk or an apple to help prevent hypoglycemia and the nausea that goes with it in the morning.

---

* Maven Laboratories, 1401-21st St. #340, Sacramento, CA 95814, (916) 442-7110

2. Keep crackers by your bedside to munch on before you get up in the morning.

3. Eat small but frequent meals, and avoid foods that aggravate your discomfort.

If you still feel lousy, find it difficult to function, and start losing weight, don't be a martyr. When severe nausea and vomiting persist, your body can develop a serious metabolic disturbance that requires hospitalization with IV therapy. Consult your doctor before things get out of control.

If you're vomiting continuously without relief, remember that acupuncture has been highly successful in studies with chemotherapy patients. Acupuncture has become an accepted part of our western medicine. Many insurance companies cover the cost of acupuncture therapy. Many HMOs offer it as an optional therapy. Acupuncture is certainly cheaper than hospitalization and it seems worth trying, especially if nothing else works. Ask your doctor for a reference to a certified acupuncturist licensed by your state.

NIGHTMARES

Scary dreams of deformed babies and miscarriages plague some women during early pregnancy. In late pregnancy, nightmares may center on labor and delivery and the approaching role of motherhood. You'll naturally be anxious about your new or extended motherhood role. Even the most confident of women will have doubts from time to time.

If you aren't sure what your dreams mean and you find them disturbing, buy a dream book to help you figure them out. Discuss your dreams with your husband or a friend; just talking about them makes them less frightening. Chances are someone you know had similar dreams when pregnant.

NOSEBLEEDS

Nosebleeds are very common in pregnancy. The increased blood supply puts a strain on the delicate veins in the nose, and they sometimes rupture quite easily.

■ **HELPFUL HINTS**

1. When a nosebleed occurs, pinch your nostrils together tightly.

2. Remain sitting up. If you lie down, the blood runs into your stomach and you may become nauseated and vomit.

3. Apply tight pressure for at least 4 to 5 minutes.

4. It may help to apply a cold cloth to the back of your neck.

NUMBNESS IN LEGS OR ARMS

Not infrequently, a pregnant woman will find that one of her legs refuses to function when she stands up; it just gives way. You wake up in the morning but one of your arms feels asleep. Such symptoms can be scary, but rest assured that you don't have a brain tumor or worse. Your altered posture of pregnancy causes the problem. Your shifted weight puts pressure on sensitive nerves, causing numbness and tingling. If you bound out of bed in a hurry, one of your legs might not cooperate, and you may also feel dizzy.

■ **HELPFUL HINTS**

Learn to wake up slowly and give your body a chance to get its act together. Sit on the edge of the bed and take inventory of what seems to be working and what isn't. This gives your circulation a chance to recuperate.

PUBIC SYMPHYSIS PAIN (PELVIC PAIN WHEN WALKING)

Hormonal influences cause increased movement of the hip and groin (sacroiliac) and tail bone (coccygeal) areas. In some women, the bones actually separate a little and it hurts. Sorry to say, this is one of the aches and pains you can't do much about.

■ HELPFUL HINTS

Get off your feet and elevate them. This temporarily relieves pressure on the bones.

Severe and persistent pubic symphysis pain can be treated with the transcutaneous electrical nerve stimulation (TENS) mentioned earlier in the discussion on nausea. You wear this electrical stimulator device externally, like a beeper. Electrodes placed over acupuncture sites control pain and muscle spasms. If your pain is chronic and you are unable to function, ask your doctor to recommend a physical therapist who's familiar with TENS therapy. Check to see if your insurance will pay for it.

SORE RIBS

Around the eighth month, some women complain that their ribs are sore. Because the top of the uterus (fundus) is just below the edge of the rib cage, the upward pressing of the uterus produces the sensation of stretching or soreness.

■ HELPFUL HINTS

It helps to raise your arms over your head and do a tall stretch, although this won't alleviate the problem entirely.

ROUND LIGAMENT PAIN

Because of increased blood supply and hormonal changes, your ligaments become softened and stretch slightly. The round ligaments hold up your uterus. As the uterus grows, the added weight puts stress on those ligaments, making them ache.

48

The location of the pain varies, but it's constant and intense, and it can be on one or both sides and radiate to your lower abdomen as well. Many women graphically describe the pain as "feeling as if your bottom is falling out." The feeling of pressure can last for hours, even days. Round ligament pain happens sporadically, but it's most common in the fifth and eighth months of pregnancy.

■ HELPFUL HINTS

Get off your feet. Try the following "wheelbarrow" and pelvic tilt exercises.

To do the wheelbarrow: lie on your back semipropped and have someone grasp your ankles; then bend your knees and elevate your hips off the bed. Doing this exercise several times a day will help relieve the pressure of your ligaments and give you some relief from the pain.

SHOOTING PAINS IN THE VAGINA

This problem is usually fleeting and rarely causes too much discomfort. It's just a little startling when you first experience it. Uterine pressure on adjacent nerves causes the pain. The sensation is of shooting or needle-like pains inside the vagina.

■ HELPFUL HINTS

If you're very uncomfortable, get off your feet to relieve the pressure.

STRETCH MARKS

Avoiding stretch marks during pregnancy is strictly a matter of luck and the right genes—nothing more. Either you have the right kind of skin tissue or you don't. Contrary to popular belief, what you put on the outside of your skin doesn't prevent stretch marks, which occur from the inside, influenced by the type of skin you inherited. So don't spend hours slathering cocoa butter or any other touted prevention for stretch marks all over your body; it won't work.

If you do get stretch marks, they'll fade after you have your baby. In most women, they become silvery lines you can barely see, but they don't fade entirely. It's one of the trade-offs for being a mom.

VAGINAL DISCHARGE

Pregnancy produces increased vaginal discharge that's white, clear, and mucousy, and that has no odor. It's normal, and no treatment is needed. If your discharge turns white with a cheesy consistency and itches, you probably have a yeast infection. Disagreeable vaginal odor is also abnormal. If the aforementioned conditions occur, discuss them with your doctor. A sample of the discharge is cultured to see specifically which type of infection you have, if any. Your doctor will then prescribe the appropriate medication.

VARICOSE VEINS IN LEGS AND LABIA

Women commonly develop varicose veins in their legs, even in the labia or vulva during pregnancy. These distended veins result from the pressure from your growing uterus that traps blood in your lower extremities. The varicosities almost always disappear after delivery.

■ HELPFUL HINTS

Relieve the pressure of your uterus on those extremities. Don't sit or stand for long periods of time. Rest periodically with your feet up. Wearing support hose is often a great help. For severe problems, special support hose can be tailor-made; ask your doctor if you think you need them.

URINARY TRACT INFECTIONS

The urinary tract is a common infection site in pregnant women. Suspect an infection if you have burning on urination. You feel as if you're passing razor blades, and you're able to urinate only small amounts at a time, even though you feel as if you're floating up to your eyeballs. Untreated urinary tract infections are the most common cause of preterm labor symptoms, so see your doctor if you think you have such an infection.

△△△

6

Work and Play

The present-day ideal superwoman works all day, jogs home, and still has time and energy to clean house and make gravy. When she gets pregnant, she doesn't plan to alter her life-style. Should she? The answer seems to be "no" for the healthy, low-risk, pregnant woman.

WORK

Doctors' opinions vary as to how long a pregnant woman may continue working. As long as your pregnancy remains uncomplicated, most doctors will agree to your working until your due date. Others may suggest that you stop working 2 to 4 weeks before your due date. If you're a lumberjack, trucker, furniture mover, or a CIA agent stationed in the Middle East, you may have to transfer temporarily to less physically demanding or stressful work. Your doctor may advise you to become a homebody the last 6 to 12 weeks. You may also have to "retire" at least 12 weeks before term if you have pregnancy complications such as

twins, previous history of premature rupture of membranes, preterm labor, or high blood pressure. There are no absolute strict guidelines; your doctor will evaluate your situation and discuss your options and alternatives.

After your baby is born, plan on staying home 4 to 6 weeks if you can. You really need the time to get yourself physically and emotionally back on track. Going back to work right away can make the adjustment period more difficult, especially when you're operating on a sleep deficit. It's a fairly sure bet you'll end up singing those "Postpartum Blues." Some companies even give new fathers maternity leave. Check it out. Take all the help you can get.

There has been some concern of late regarding the hazards of computer video display terminals (VDTs), particularly for the pregnant woman. The concern is for increased risks for miscarriage. You can discount the initial concern about low-frequency magnetic fields and ultraviolet radiation because it isn't a problem. There isn't the risk for miscarriage either. You can relax if you're one of the millions who use VDTs daily in your work.

Many physicians do recommend a 15-minute break every 2 hours to improve circulation, reduce eye strain, and relax those back muscles. See the exercises in Chapter 5, "Common Complaints of Pregnancy," for helpful ways to relax those tired back muscles. The following are simple exercises to relax stressed, tired eyes.

Blinking and Breathing

1. Close your eyelids and inhale and hold for 1 to 2 seconds.

2. Exhale, open your eyes, and focus on objects that are small and far away, at least 20 feet or more.

Palming

1. Sit in a comfortable position and rest your elbows on a table.

2. Place your palms over your eyes in a crisscross fashion and then cup your eyes.

3. Close your eyelids and breathe deeply; exhale and relax.

4. Visualize an object such as a saltshaker in front of you. Concentrate on every detail. Develop your power of concentration.

Near and Far

1. Fix your gaze on an object that is far away.

2. Quickly move your gaze to a small object in front of you such as a word on a piece of paper.

3. Alternate your gaze, back and forth, between the two objects for 30 seconds.

Eye Push-ups

1. Holding a pencil 2 to 3 inches from your nose, visualize a clock in front of you at the 1 o'clock position.

2. Hold a pencil 2–3 inches from your nose at the one o'clock position.

3. From the 1 o'clock position, move the pencil slowly and touch your nose; follow its path with your eyes. Do not move your head.

4. Repeat the exercise around the entire clock from the 1 o'clock to 12 o'clock position.

Discuss your job with your doctor, especially if you feel you have a hazardous job or are being exposed to potentially harmful chemicals or pollutants. Generally, working during pregnancy is like sex—if it still feels OK, keep going.

SPAS AND HOT TUBS

There may be a relationship between hyperthermia and spinal column defects in babies. Sitting in water heated to 102 degrees causes your core body temperature to rise to 102 degrees within 10 minutes (hyperthermia). Especially in the first trimester, avoid hot tubs and saunas with 102-degree or more heat. Getting in and out every 10 minutes won't avoid the problem because it takes 45 minutes for your body temperature to return to normal. Keep water temperatures 100 degrees or below for safety. Avoid prolonged soaking sessions. Also, there's no truth to the rumor that you can catch herpes from sitting in a hot tub.

SPORTS

Some sports become hazardous during pregnancy because of the possible risks of falling. The amniotic fluid cushions the baby well, but the force of an impact may cause the placenta to separate from the uterus, causing, at the least, a decrease in oxygen, and at worst, death for the baby and possibly you from hemorrhage. Use good judgment. Pregnancy is no time to take up skydiving or mountain climbing. Hazardous sports include:

- Horseback riding, especially for the inexperienced rider.

- Snow skiing.

- When water skiing after the first trimester, wear a wet suit. When you fall, water can be forced into your vagina and uterus, which may result in a fatal embolism.

Even if you're proficient at these sports, you stand a greater than average chance of injury because the additional weight and relaxed ligaments and joints alter your balance. Your muscle memory is now dealing with an unfamiliar body. You have to decide if the risk is worth it. See the various exercises in Chapter 4, "Pregnancy Fitness," and Appendix 1 for suggestions on how to maintain your fitness.

TRAVEL

We're a very mobile society, and questions about travel during pregnancy frequently crop up. Generally, traveling "afar" in the first 6 months of your pregnancy is safe. Negotiate trips the last 3 months of pregnancy with your doctor. Give some thought to what you would do if you went into labor in a strange place. Talk to your doctor before you leave on vacation and ask him to recommend a colleague in the city you'll be visiting in case you have a medical problem. Check to see if your insurance will cover an out-of-territory delivery. (We could be talking a lot of money and emotional trauma.) It may not be worth it to jet off to Tahiti just to darken your tan. Think about it.

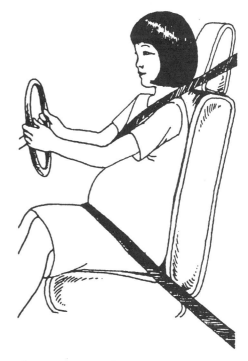

Pregnant women can be prone to blood clots in the legs from long periods of inactivity. If you travel by car, plan to stop every hour to stretch and walk around to get your circulation going. If the back seat is vacant, take a pillow and lie on your side for 20 minutes periodically during long trips, to help keep your feet and ankles from swelling.

Whenever you travel by car, use your three point seat belt restraint! Secure the lap belt low on your thighs. Half the automobile injuries to pregnant women can be avoided by use of a seat belt.

Air travel restrictions for pregnant women have changed. (Some credit goes to all those pregnant flight attendants who fought to stay on the job). Hypothetical dangers to the fetus included:

- Noise and vibrations

- Dehydration from low humidity

- Decreased oxygen from pressure changes at high altitudes

- Cosmic radiation at 30,000 feet

None of the purported dangers has proved true. Flying isn't hazardous to the fetus. Most major domestic carriers have discarded their rules prohibiting pregnant women, near term, from flying. Overseas flying is a little different. If you have plans to catch a plane for exotic places, check with the airline in question to see if they require any doctor's certificate. In your last month, they may require your doctor or "other qualified person" to accompany you on your flight through the "friendly skies."

ΔΔΔ

7

Drugs in Pregnancy

THE RIGHT STUFF

We have prescription drugs, over-the-counter (OTC) drugs, and the ever popular social/recreational drugs. There's something for everyone. Pregnancy provides the opportunity for many women to examine their particular pattern of drug use.

Everyone wants a healthy baby with all the designated parts in the proper places. Pregnant women worry about birth defects and try to do everything possible to avoid harmful substances that might harm their developing baby. There's much confusion and anxiety about what causes birth defects and the role that drugs play. When a miscarriage or abnormality in the baby occurs, the normal reaction is to look for a place to lay the blame. But it's not that simple most of the time.

Pregnancy normally carries a 2 to 4 percent risk for abnormalities, and only 2 to 3 percent have a known cause. Drugs are implicated in approximately 6 percent of birth defects.

THE POROUS PLACENTA

There's no placental barrier as previously thought. The placenta functions more like a sieve. Picture the strainer you use to drain spaghetti and you get the idea: Only the largest of particles can't drain through the porous membrane.

Whether a drug affects a developing fetus depends on the drug, the particular period of pregnancy, how much is taken, how often, and so on. Some drugs can be dangerous at any time during pregnancy, not just during the first 12 weeks. The baby's genetic susceptibility can also play a part. For lack of a better explanation, fate seems to be the only explanation as to why some babies have problems while most don't. At least right now we don't have all the answers. Avoiding all drugs during pregnancy is ideal but not always practical. Following are commonsense guidelines to drug use during pregnancy.

PRESCRIPTION DRUGS

Most people believe in the magic of medicine. We want quick cures and rely on pills, potions, and powders to cure what ails us. For every symptom there must be a pill to alleviate the misery. Suffering isn't our strong suit.

Half of all pregnant women use at least one prescription drug during pregnancy. Antibiotics are frequently prescribed during pregnancy because infections have more potential to cause harm than an antibiotic. Ampicillin and penicillin are safe to take during pregnancy; there are others.

There are two antibiotics to avoid during pregnancy. *Tetracycline* will stain the developing baby's teeth. *Sulfa* medications given near the time of delivery may cause the baby's skin to become yellowed (jaundiced) in the first days of life. Your doctor has to weigh the benefits and risks of prescribing medications for you. For example, the risk of preterm labor from a urinary tract infection is higher than taking the medication. If you have the miseries from the flu or a cold, you don't need medication; you can take to your bed and wait it out.

OVER-THE-COUNTER (OTC DRUGS)

OTC drugs are the ones you prescribe for yourself. Sixty-five percent of pregnant women medicate themselves for various ailments. A sound rule to follow is to avoid all medications for the relief of minor aches and pains in the first trimester. **Only take medications ordered by your doctor and follow the directions to the letter.** Here's a review of some common OTC drugs used during pregnancy.

Aspirin

Aspirin is the most commonly used drug in pregnancy. It's a great drug but not the best one for the pregnant woman. In excessively high doses, aspirin can cause congenital defects. Aspirin also alters the body's clotting mechanism in both mom and baby, which is why it's not recommended during pregnancy, particularly in the last trimester.

Acetaminophen

Acetaminophen is the generic name for products such as Tylenol, Datril, and Tempra, which have a safe track record in pregnancy. It has the same ability as aspirin to ease those aches and pains and to lower temperatures. In small doses, acetaminophen can be used safely during pregnancy.

Vitamins

Everyone agrees the pregnant woman needs extra iron, but what about vitamins? Physicians almost routinely prescribe vitamins during pregnancy. The experts in the field say vitamin supplementation isn't necessary; the benefits are unproven. But ask the experts if they prescribe vitamins in their practice: They do.

Vitamins aren't an acceptable substitute for a balanced diet. If you take a vitamin supplement, keep it simple. You don't need to spend a fortune on prenatal supplements. One-a-day multiple vitamins will suffice. Megavitamin therapy during pregnancy is very risky. The fat-soluble vitamins A, D, E, and K can accumulate in the body and produce toxic effects. Birth defects and other problems have been related to excessive vitamin intake. For example, vitamin C in high doses taken regularly during pregnancy can lead to scurvy in the newborn baby after birth. The baby is used to the high levels of vitamin C, and when the supply is decreased after birth, the baby gets scurvy. When it comes to vitamins in pregnancy, "A little dab will do ya."

Water Pills (Diuretics)

Swollen ankles and feet can be uncomfortable, but diuretics aren't the cure. Swelling of the feet and ankles is a sign of a healthy pregnancy. Your blood volume expands to provide nourishment for the baby. As your uterus grows larger, it compresses major vessels and traps the fluid in your lower extremities. It's not extra fluid, merely displaced fluid. If you lie on your side to relieve the pressure, the fluid shifts back to where it belongs. Diuretics can cause a serious chemical imbalance in your body so they aren't recommended for swelling.

Laxatives

There are over 700 OTC laxative products . . . you don't need. Many laxatives tend to be harsh and habit-forming if used regularly. Your bowel won't work unless it gets a daily fix. Refer to the "Constipation" section in Chapter 5, "Common Complaints of Pregnancy." Your colon needs encouragement, not dynamite.

Cold Remedies

Millions of dollars are spent every year for cough and cold remedies. Many do neither harm nor good; the benefits go strictly to the manufacturers, who make all the money. Many of the preparations are combinations of various drugs, such as aspirin, caffeine, antihistamines, and potassium iodide, which interferes with thyroid activity.

If you have a stuffy nose, take a steamy shower. Nasal sprays provide very short-term relief, and you end up with a stuffy nose again that's worse than before. You experience rebound swelling. It's not worth the trouble or expense. As one doctor tells his patients, "If you don't take anything for your cold, you'll get better in a week. If you take something, you'll feel better in 7 days." In other words, your cold will get better on its own.

Cough Remedies

There's no sound evidence that cough remedies work, contrary to what's claimed in the high-powered advertising. The alcohol content of various cough syrups is 5 to 20 percent, not the best remedy for a pregnant woman. If you have a typical cough from a cold, inhale hot or cold steam. Don't add a Vick's-type preparation to your vaporizer because it won't help. But sucking on hard candy does help, and it's cheaper than cough drops. Drinking something hot can help too; honey and lemon juice mixed in hot water is very soothing to your throat. If your cough isn't better in a week, call your doctor.

Antacids

Heartburn can be a problem during pregnancy. Avoid drugs with high sodium content such as Bromo Seltzer, Alka Seltzer, or Fizrin. Two of these products also contain aspirin and caffeine. Baking soda isn't a good idea either because it's just more salt in your system. There are two acceptable remedies: TUMS and Amphojel. TUMS contain 500 grams calcium carbonate per tablet. You can alleviate your heartburn and supply some of your daily calcium requirements. Some doctors recommend TUMS instead of calcium pills if you don't drink milk. Don't overdo the calcium, or you may become constipated; three tablets per day is sufficient. Amphojel gives effective relief from heartburn but causes even more constipation than TUMS. Use both these drugs moderately. A word of forewarning: Antacids can be like nasal sprays. When they wear off, the heartburn can be even worse than before. Avoid all other antacids on the market while pregnant.

For an eye-opening guide to medications, read *The Medicine Show* by Consumer Reports, which gives the real scoop about the effectiveness, dangers, and expense of all those drugs you learn about in the media. It's an education that could save you a lot of money.

RISKY RAYS

X-rays aren't drugs, but many pregnant women are exposed to them during pregnancy, often inadvertently when x-rays are taken before the mother-to-be even knows she's pregnant. Current medical opinion feels that there's no increased risk of abnormalities in these cases. Diagnostic x-ray studies (upper and lower intestinal series, kidney studies) generally should be avoided during pregnancy, but if they're done, there's no great reason to worry about the baby being abnormal.

SOCIAL DRUGS

Demon Rum

Alcohol doesn't discriminate between mother and baby. It's an equal opportunity drug that easily crosses through the placenta to the baby. If you become tipsy, your baby won't pass a sobriety test. You wouldn't dream of giving your newborn a martini, so don't give your unborn baby one either.

The detrimental effects of alcohol on the developing fetus have been known for centuries. Carthage and Sparta passed laws to prevent newlyweds from drinking so they wouldn't produce defective children. Thus, it's not hot news that alcohol can cause problems for babies.

The exact amount of alcohol it takes to produce adverse effects on babies is unknown, but consuming 3 ounces or more per day puts your baby in the high-risk category for Fetal Alcohol Syndrome (FAS) and Intrauterine Growth Retardation (IUGR). Low birth weight and stillbirths increase when pregnant women consume more than 1.6 ounces of absolute alcohol per day. The highest risk for problems is associated with beer, rather than wine or liquor, despite beer's lower absolute alcohol content. The reason is unknown. The risks are lower, but not zero, if you consume 1 ounce or less of alcohol per day, which is the equivalent to either 24 ounces of beer, 8 ounces of table wine, or 2 mixed drinks. No safe levels of alcohol consumption have been established for pregnancy. It's a little like playing Russian roulette—you've no way of knowing you're in trouble until it's too late. **The only safe course is to abstain during pregnancy.**

No-No Nicotine

The dangers of smoking are well known. Because 20 to 30 percent of women of childbearing age smoke, let's concentrate on the effects of smoking on your baby. Smoking causes your blood vessels to constrict, decreasing the blood flow carrying nutrients and oxygen to the baby, who won't get full rations throughout pregnancy. Smoking inhibits your ability to metabolize certain important vitamins and minerals. If you aren't absorbing those nutrients, neither is the baby.

Here's a fact that may appeal to your womanly vanity. Vitamin C builds and maintains vital tissue and cells. Smoking prevents proper absorption for both you and your baby. The result to you is . . . *wrinkles!* The lack of vitamin C robs the skin of elasticity. Show me a woman who looks younger than her age, and I'll show you a nonsmoker. The reverse is also true.

Calcium is an important requirement in pregnancy. The baby needs lots of it, and so do you. Smoking prevents calcium absorption. Calcium is drained from your bones to supply the baby, leaving you with softening of the bones—osteoporosis in later life. It's no coincidence that women under 65 who develop osteoporosis are overwhelmingly smokers.

Back to the baby. Smoking mothers produce a higher incidence of preterm births, miscarriages, stillbirths, congenital defects, and low birth weight babies. Smoking contributes to 20 to 40 percent of low birth weight infants. If you smoke 20 cigarettes or more a day, your baby will weigh approximately 1/2 pound less. Fifteen to forty-five percent of unfavorable pregnancy outcomes are attributed to smoking. And the effects don't end at birth: Children of smoking parents continue to show a decrease in their lung function as they grow older.

As with any other drug, the effects are dose-related: more smoking, more problems. Give the kid a break! If you can at least cut down during the last trimester, your baby will be healthier. He can gain more weight, and all those growing brain cells he'll need to become the next Einstein will get some extra nourishment. Should you decide to quit, the most effective way is cold turkey. Just stop. Your body is addicted to the nicotine, and trying to cut down just prolongs the agony of withdrawl. There are a number of self-help groups in the community dedicated to helping you quit—try one.

Popular Pot

Marijuana originated in central Asia about 5000 years ago. The Chinese used it as a remedy for various ills, but it never caught on with the party crowd there. In England during the 1800s, marijuana was considered a wonder drug that cured all. The Muslims used it for intoxication and to cure everything from asthma to dandruff and piles. George Washington grew pot on his farm . . . but don't look for an exposé in the *National Enquirer.* George wasn't a closet playboy. He didn't smoke the stuff; he made ropes out of it.

There's the potential to become complacent about marijuana since cocaine seems so much more dangerous. Pot continues to be a very popular "recreational" drug; some say its use is epidemic. The effects of marijuana on pregnancy are still not clear. Some studies have associated marijuana use with smaller babies and a fivefold increase to deliver a baby with FAS features. Animal studies show a greater incidence of miscarriages, decrease in birth weight, stillbirth, neonatal deaths, and IUGR. More information on humans is needed. Meanwhile, it's safer to get high on meditation or exercise, especially while you're pregnant.

Coke Catastrophe

Maternal use of cocaine during pregnancy is rising at an alarming rate. The consequences are serious for both mother and baby. Placental abruption (premature separation of the placenta from the uterine wall) can occur because of the dramatic constriction of blood vessels with cocaine use. The mother can hemorrhage, endangering her life and her unborn baby's. Cocaine increases the risk of preterm delivery and delivery of a baby small for gestational age. There's also increasing concern about neurologic problems resulting from intrauterine exposure to cocaine that may have lifelong implications. These babies have emotional and physical disabilities they may never be able to overcome. If that isn't enough, babies born to mothers who use cocaine undergo painful withdrawal from the drug in the first days of life, which isn't exactly a loving welcome to the world.

If you use cocaine, you need help. Contact any one of the several organizations available to help with cocaine problems and take advantage of their service. Do it before you become pregnant. Do it for you and your baby.

Stimulants (Coffee, Tea, Cola)

Caffeine, the socially acceptable "upper" for most of us, stimulates the central nervous system. Many people need one cup of coffee in the morning to get their heart started, and one to wake up.

Drinking caffeine during pregnancy is generally safe, but drinking more than five or six cups of coffee per day (600 milligrams of caffeine) is associated with low birth weight babies and stillbirths. Caffeine is found in a variety of medications as well as tea and cola. The following chart shows the amount of caffeine in selected foods and drugs.

Beverages	Serving Size	Caffeine (mg)
Coffee, drip	5 oz	110–150
Coffee, perk	5 oz	60–125
Coffee, instant	5 oz	40–105
Coffee, decaffeinated	5 oz	2–5
Tea, 5-min steep	5 oz	40–100
Tea, 3-min steep	5 oz	20–50
Hot cocoa	5 oz	2–10
Coca Cola	12 oz	45

Foods	Serving Size	Caffeine
Milk chocolate	1 oz	1–15
Bittersweet chocolate	1 oz	5–35
Chocolate cake	1 slice	20–30

Over-the-Counter Drugs	Dose	Caffeine
Anacin, Empirin	2	64
Excedrin	2	130

Be on the safe side and limit your caffeine intake to less than 400 milligrams per day. Caffeine is excreted less efficiently during pregnancy, and insomnia can result with even small amounts. If you have trouble sleeping, eliminate caffeine and see if it helps.

A FINAL WORD

In truth, not enough information about drugs and their exact effects on pregnancy is available . . . a lot of unknowns out there. Don't devote a major amount of time worrying about what you took during the first trimester when you didn't know you were pregnant. If you took an aspirin or had a glass of wine, don't spend the rest of your pregnancy walking on eggshells and worrying because you could make yourself crazy thinking about all the possibilities. The fact is, the vast majority of babies are healthy.

△△△

8

Food for Thought: Breast or Bottle and Baby's Doctor

One of the many decisions facing you as expectant parents is whether to breast- or bottle-feed your baby. Medical and public opinion favor breast-feeding, claiming emotional, psychological, and physiological benefits. No one argues the health benefits, but claims about emotional benefits raise more than a few hackles on those who choose to bottle-feed, and rightly so. Let's be realistic. The act of breast-feeding doesn't automatically make you a better mother. Playing the martyr and doing it begrudgingly, or feeling guilty because you don't do it, is counterproductive. So, relax. "Man does not live by bread alone," and neither do babies . . . make that milk. The emotional benefits of breast-feeding come from holding and cuddling, something mom and dad can offer the bottle-fed baby too.

BOTTLE-FEEDING

Babies under one year of age need formula, not cow's milk, which has too much of what a baby doesn't need: protein and sodium. Protein in excess can alter the baby's body chemistry and cause listlessness. Too much sodium can make the baby's kidneys work overtime, increasing water loss and making baby thirsty.

Formula is similar in composition to human milk; it has slightly more protein, calcium, and lactose, but less fat. The protein in formula is less digestible than that in human milk, and the sodium content varies. Otherwise, it's nutritionally balanced.

The bottle-fed baby's stool is more formed than that from a breast-fed baby. Bottle-fed babies are more prone to constipation and gastrointestinal upsets (colic) than breast-fed babies.

The major disadvantage of bottle-feeding is overfeeding. Formula babies double their birthweight in 14 to 16 weeks. If your baby doesn't finish the bottle, don't force the issue. A baby who cries an hour or so after a feeding may just be thirsty or tired. Offer water instead of another bottle. As with the breast-fed baby, 6 to 8 wet diapers per day indicate enough food. A great advantage to bottle-feeding is that dad can help, which keeps him from feeling left out and gives you some help with those wee-hour feedings that can kill you off.

BREAST-FEEDING

Breast milk has nutritional advantages: It's easily digested and contains all the necessary vitamins and minerals your baby needs. Breast milk promotes the growth of the protective bacteria lactobacilli in your baby's gastrointestinal tract. Consequently, breast-fed babies have fewer problems with diarrhea and intestinal infections. The early milk (colostrum) is rich in immunity factors, which are passed on to your baby as long as you breast-feed. Breast-fed babies have less allergies, colic, constipation and respiratory problems. Breast milk also offers an edge in the "fit or fat" battle because breast-fed babies tend to be leaner than their formula-fed counterparts. Breast-fed babies don't double their birth weight until they're 5 months old, in contrast to formula babies, who double their weight by 12 to 14 weeks. Convenience is a factor since you don't have to stumble around in the middle of the night warming bottles or preparing formula. The economy of breast-feeding can't be beat—it's one of the few free things in life.

The disadvantages are that you're the only one who can feed the baby unless you pump your breasts and save the milk, and you can't stray too far for too long from your baby because your breasts get full and very uncomfortable. To help you decide about breast-feeding, read Chapter 18, "Breast-feeding," and see the chart "Feeding Methods at a Glance" at the end of the chapter for a summary of the advantages and disadvantages.

CHOOSING A BABY DOCTOR

After the seventh month of pregnancy is a good time to start thinking about who'll be your baby's doctor. The same criteria you used to pick your doctor apply here also.

Let Your Fingers Do the Talking

Streamline the interview process by calling and asking one of the office staff the following questions:

- What's the procedure for after-hour's coverage? Is there a call group? Do you go to the emergency room?

- How evenly is the doctor's schedule divided between illness and wellness? Are there separate hours for wellness checks so your baby won't be exposed to illness?

- Are developmental, safety, nutritional, and educational materials provided? Are there staff persons qualified to provide phone advice?

Consider how helpful and courteous the person you're speaking to is. If your questions are answered patiently and you like what you hear, make an appointment to see the doctor; it shouldn't take you more than 5 to 10 minutes to decide if your personalities and philosophies mesh. Talk to the doctor's nurse or assistant who works with her; she and the front office staff will usually be your initial contacts when you're trying to reach the doctor. You need to decide if they'll be a help or a hindrance in getting you the information and help you need. Be considerate; this isn't the time to discuss potty training and where your child should go to college.

Ideally, the doctor's practice should offer both illness and wellness care, and should provide 24-hour coverage. Educational material should be available. The office staff should be friendly and supportive. You're going to spend many years depending on your baby's doctor and the staff, so it's important that you trust and like each other.

FEEDING METHODS AT A GLANCE

Method	Advantages	Disadvantages

Breast-feeding	**Cost:** It's free.
	
	Convenience: Milk comes ready to use; conveniently and attractively packaged. Breast-feeding aids in maternal weight loss.
	
	Infant health: Breast-feeding produces generally healthier babies. Colostrum (first milk) is especially rich in immunity factors. Babies have a decreased incidence of these problems:
	  Allergies
	  Gastrointestinal ailments (gas, colic)
	  Constipation and diarrhea
	  Respiratory problems, asthma, bronchitis and croup
	  Colds and other contagious diseases
	
	Infant nutrition: Babies digest breast milk easily and utilize all its components. The milk contains all necessary vitamins and
		Inconvenience: The mother has slightly less mobility. She will have to pump her breasts when away from the baby. The alternative is to rent a breast pump—very handy if she has to work. Her breasts may leak milk.
		
		Decreased vaginal secretions may make intercourse painful, although lubricant relieves dryness.
		
		Fatigue: Mothers who breast-feed on a demand schedule may be tired due to the more frequent feedings.
		
		Breast infection (mastitis): The infection is uncomfortable and inconvenient but can be treated with an antibiotic.

minerals. **Babies will double their birth weight in 5 months and are less prone to obesity. No other food required until 6 months of age.**

Formula feeding by bottle

Convenience: Mother has greater mobility. Dad or others can help feed the baby.

Infant nutrition: Formula contains almost all essential nutrients.

Cost: Formula is expensive.

Inconvenience: Formula requires preparation.

Infant health: Formula contains no immunity factors. Babies have more of these problems:

   Allergies
   Colic
   Constipation and diarrhea
   Colds and contagious diseases

Infant nutrition: Birthweight doubled in 14–16 weeks. Over-feeding a major problem.

PART II

The Process and Precautions

9

Prepared Childbirth

EVOLUTION

Throughout history, men have had battlefields on which to prove their bravery. Traditionally, women have viewed the labor bed as their battleground, where their strength, endurance, and courage were tested. Women still love to tell "war" stories about labor and delivery. The "warriors" engage in fierce competition as they compare tales of who had the longest labor, the most stitches, and the biggest baby. This is female macho at its worst. The story-telling doesn't change, but the battleground gets redecorated every decade or so.

Childbirth has come a long way from the 1950s and 1960s, when having babies was a very serious business. Doctors considered the process too complicated for the womenfolk to worry about and too gruesome for the men to participate in. The expectant father's place was in the waiting room while the mother of his child labored in a drug-induced twilight zone, alone and stoned.

During the 1970s, "natural" childbirth was in vogue. Childbirth without medication was an initiation rite, a way for women to attain a sort of "superwarrior" status among their peers. Any method other than cold turkey was deemed a failure by those in the know. Returning to Lamaze or Bradley class as a dropout was a fate worse than death. Yet, if you asked 10 people to define natural childbirth, you got 10 different answers. For some, it meant a home birth and no medication; for others it meant medication but a home-style delivery in the hospital. The combinations were endless.

By the 1980s, "prepared childbirth" replaced natural as the buzzword in obstetrics. Consumers wanted a more individualized approach to labor and delivery, to allow the option of doing whatever best suited their needs. This was a healthier approach than the restrictive, judgmental, pass-fail, do-or-die mentality that surrounded natural childbirth. With the resurgence of epidural anesthesia in the 90s, "Be awake, alert, and don't hurt" is replacing the old 80s mantra "No pain, no gain."

THEORY

The basic theory behind prepared childbirth, whether it be Lamaze, Bradley, Fitzhugh, or Dick-Read, is the same:

- Self-awareness

- Self-control through programmed exercises

- Reduction of pain through education and knowledge of the labor and delivery process

Remember the word "reduction." Many women and their husbands falsely expect the childbirth exercises to eliminate pain completely. Only a completely effective epidural, which numbs you from the waist down, will produce that kind of pain relief. The exercises you learn in class and practice during your pregnancy help you develop your powers of concentration, which enhance your ability to alter your pain perception and keep your self-control during labor. The exercises are helpful but not a panacea.

CHILDBIRTH CLASSES

In olden days, most childbirth educators adhered to the party line preached by Lamaze or Bradley. Strict lines were drawn. In these more modern times, many childbirth educators mix and match philosophies, exercises and attitudes. Remember, there is no right or wrong method. It's simply a matter of your choice and what best suits your needs. Find a teacher who suits your style. You can't go wrong with someone who is flexibile, practical, and has a sense of humor.

Beware of anyone who preaches a totally painless labor and birth through exercise and fanatically insists that you refuse all medication during labor. In general, beware of anyone who has an inflexible approach to your labor and birth experience. Do not set yourself up for a guilt trip if you are unable to follow the rigid guidelines set for you. Use the exercises to meet *your* needs. Keep your options open, and remember that the most important concepts of prepared childbirth are to maintain your self-control and share your arduous but happy experience with your husband. The togetherness and a happy outcome are what really count.

There are a number of good reasons for taking prepared childbirth classes. You need to learn the physical processes of pregnancy and childbirth and the types of birthing options open to you in your community. Without this knowledge, it is difficult to prepare a realistic birth plan, and you hinder your role in the decision-making process drastically.

Classes are available through community programs, doctors' offices, private instructors, and school districts. The fee for classes vary, so ask. Groups of 5 to 7 couples are considered ideal because the instructor can give more individualized attention, and smaller groups are less threatening and more amenable to learning and socializing. Classes provide a ready-made support group and the chance to meet other expectant couples. Take advantage of the opportunity to enrich your pregnancy experience by sharing it. More than a few lifelong friendships have been made in childbirth classes.

ΛΛΛ

10

Childbirth Options

In the 1950s and 1960s the childbirth landscape was a dust bowl—barren, cold and sterile. Rigid hospital policies rendered any change infertile. Childbirth was just another sterile, surgical event; consumers had no alternatives or options. Birthin' babies was a serious business.

WINTER OF DISCONTENT

By the 1970s and 1980s, consumers grew discontented with the status quo in obstetrics. Ferdinand Lamaze's philosophy of "natural" childbirth brought seeds of change on a soft breeze of new consciousness that soon became a raging hurricane of controversy. Exciting alternatives germinated in the newly fertile obstetrical field. Birth options began sprouting everywhere, amid great concern from health care providers, who viewed the changes as unnecessary and threatening.

The long winter for the consumer was over. The spring of childbirth had "sprung." Consumers saw beautiful flowers; the medical establishment saw weeds. Consumers and health care providers were at odds. Those having babies wanted to view the process as natural and normal, an event to be shared and celebrated by the whole family. Those delivering babies saw it as an intrusion into the comfortable, sterile, sanctity of their domain. Shrill hysteria emanated from many of the newly self-appointed "childbirth advocates," whose credentials and objectivities in many cases were nonexistent.

Doctors were unaccustomed to being viewed as the enemy. It was a tough time and the doctors' collective psyches took a beating. It was the best of times; it was the worst of times.

It took much of the 80s for the hysteria to die down and both sides to look more objectively at the real issues and come to a meeting of the minds. Health care providers moved from antagonism and ambivalence to acceptance of most of their patients' demands. Consumers in general decided that an adversarial role with their doctors was counterproductive. Inflexibility on both sides matured into a more accepting, adaptable relationship. It was a more fruitful climate since trust is an important component of the relationship with those caring for you at such an important time in your life.

RULES AND REGULATIONS

Health care providers, including hospitals, are now more open to and accepting of their clients' wishes. Attaining your "dream" birth is more possible now than at any previous time. Rigid rules and routines have softened. For instance, most doctors don't routinely insist on enemas. Continuous fetal monitoring and IVs are reserved for the complicated pregnancy. Fetal monitoring for the low-risk pregnancy is limited to a baseline strip of 20 minutes on admission and may then be repeated for only 10 minutes every hour or so. Some places may still limit the number of "support" persons present during labor but other hospitals just say, "Y'all come." Midwives deservedly have won privileges to practice in hospitals and birth centers and are carving a more collegial niche for themselves by joining doctors in their practice. It's a nice combination of personnel that benefits all concerned.

FAMILY CENTERED CARE

Hospitals are waging battles of survival in this era of intense competition for the consumer dollar. Young, growing families are a major target for most hospitals.

Maternity care is often the entry port for many families into a specific health facility; they have their baby there, and they return for other aspects of care. Hospitals want their business.

A popular marketing strategy for hospitals now is Family Centered Care (FCC). Unfortunately, the term means different things to different hospitals and individual consumers. FCC is a concept wherein the total family's needs are considered and addressed from the first encounter with the hospital to discharge. An important component of FCC is keeping the family together during the hospital stay, including extended family if desired. For instance, if a cesarean birth is necessary, the father and a support person could attend the birth. There are very liberal guidelines regarding visitation and the numbers of family and extended family permitted. Siblings are welcomed. Newborns spend as much time with the family as they wish. For those who elect the short stay plan, discharge within 24 hours, follow-up care is offered.

If FCC is an important component of your birth plan, check your local hospitals well in advance. Call and/or take a tour of the hospitals you may utilize. Many hospitals provide slick brochures with appealing pictures of mom, dad and baby, but if you ask pertinent questions about visitation policies, sibling participation, support people, anesthesia and cesarean birth options, you may not like what you hear. Do your homework.

SHORT STAY PROGRAMS

In 1982, the average hospital stay for a new mother was 3 days, but now most women go home in 24 hours. Not too long ago, discharge in 24 hours was considered a short stay, but now it's the norm. Some hospitals offer a short stay of 12 hours or less. There are the usual advantages and disadvantages. The primary advantages of short stay are money saving and getting to sleep in your own bed. Realistically, you'll sleep better and get more rest at home, especially if you have help. The disadvantages are the loss of educational and teaching support from the nursing staff. Teaching time for baby care and breast-feeding is curtailed. If you want to stay longer than 24 hours, check your insurance to see what they allow. If you have to go home within 24 hours, be sure you have some help at home. Find out who you can use as a resource support person in your doctor's office when you have questions in those early weeks. Buy a good baby book to help answer any simple questions that might arise. The postpartum chapter in this book will give you a head start on the first six weeks.

FROM HOMESTYLE TO SINGLE-ROOM MATERNITY CARE

The '70s homestyle room with the dying fern and rocking chair is now dated. Many obstetrical units are adopting the newer and more practical concept of single-room maternity care. This concept is the wave of the 90s in obstetrics as more women choose this option. With single-room maternity care, Mom stays in an LDRP (labor/delivery/recovery/postpartum) room, eliminating the inconvenience and discomfort of moving from a labor bed to the delivery room and then moving again to the recovery room and still again to the postpartum floor. The ideal room design usually accommodates 8 people. The labor bed converts into a birthing bed. The delivery equipment, such as oxygen and resuscitation is efficiently and conveniently located behind pictures and in drawers so as to not detract from the homelike setting. Some hospitals offer romantic, candlelight, gourmet dinners for the new parents.

Although the single-room maternity concept is ideal, many older hospitals are unable to provide this service in its purest form. What you may find is a compromise such as the labor and birthing room, combined with recovery and postpartum provided on the postpartum maternity floor. It's still a great improvement over the traditional method of a separate room for each aspect of the birthing process. The days of having to move to a gurney when you're fully dilated while the nurses frantically tell you not to push are mercifully becoming obsolete.

Hospitals are more flexible in offering the option of keeping the baby and mother together. Mom can keep baby in her room or send her to the nursery if she desires some time off. In some hospitals, one nurse cares for both mom and baby until discharge, assuring a nice continuity of care. If you find this concept appealing, call your local hospitals and ask if they offer this option.

FREESTANDING BIRTH CENTERS (FSBCs)

Freestanding birth centers are facilities independent of a hospital setting, staffed by certified nurse midwives, with obstetrician backup.

- Midwives manage labor and attend the birth.

- These birth centers accept the low-risk clientele who desire a less intrusive birth experience.

- Technology is kept to a minimum if it is used at all.

- More babies are delivered without episiotomies.

- Women aren't confined to bed and use a variety of positions to alleviate labor pain.

- Less medication is used during labor.

Approximately 13 percent of women laboring in FSBCs require transfer to a hospital because of complications. Outcomes for neonates delivered in an FSBC and a hospital setting are the same. The option of delivering in an FSBC isn't widely available, so you may have to look around.

HOME BIRTH

Home birth continues to account for only 1 percent of the obstetrical population in this country. The highest numbers of home births are concentrated in upper New England, Texas, and the Pacific Coast. Midwives are licensed in 11 states and in Arizona doctors do their share of home deliveries. Most deliveries (90 percent) are uneventful, while 2 percent involve serious, unanticipated threats to mother and baby. Previous screening helps identify some but not all problems in advance. In 1975, the stillbirth rate in California for home deliveries was twice as high as for in-hospital births. Based on this information, there is little doubt hospital births are safer. The decision for a home birth usually transcends economic and safety considerations. There is often a deep emotional commitment to a home birth experience, and a previous negative experience in the hospital can reinforce the commitment. If you are one of those people who have such a commitment, you need to plan carefully. Have your prenatal workup performed by an obstetrician, and determine if you have any medical or health problems, your pelvis is more than adequate, and your blood work is normal. A very important consideration is the time it would take you to get the hospital in case of an emergency. Ask your doctor what is considered a reasonable time limit and if he/she would agree to provide back-up if you have to go to the hospital because of complications.

If you pass the first step, you can start shopping for a birth attendant. If your area allows certified nurse midwives or doctors to do home deliveries, you are in luck. If not, you have to interview lay midwives very carefully. Some lay midwives have no experience beyond having their own babies at home; they have decided that delivering babies would be an interesting hobby. You wouldn't dream of trusting your next door neighbor to repair your expensive stereo as a hobby. Don't let her deliver your baby either! If your area has no licensing and standards, be an informed consumer. Screen your prospective birth attendant well. What training has she had? How many babies has she delivered? (Fifty is an appropriate number.) Does she have resuscitation skills? Is there a plan for complications such as bleeding, breech, or prolapsed cord? Be sure she has a well-defined disaster plan. If she is willing to care for you even if you develop a high-risk complication such as preeclampsia, look for another birth attendant.

SIBLING PARTICIPATION

The attendance of siblings at birth is slowly increasing but still not universally accepted. The more disdainful see it as an effective method of population control: They predict that little boys will grow up impotent and little girls will avoid pregnancy like the plague. No one has confirmed that such dire consequences have occurred. In fact, some parents have reported a wonderful experience and less sibling rivalry which they attribute to participation in the birth experience. The prospect doesn't appeal to everyone; you have to decide what suits your family and if the perceived benefits outweigh the potential disadvantages. Discuss the possibilities with your husband and your children.

Incorporating your kids into the birth experience requires common sense, preparation, flexibility, and a willingness to have them see you au naturel. Children need some preparation: They need to know where babies come from, how they get here and an introduction to the panting, blowing, and funny faces you may be making so they won't be frightened. Give them a preview of the hard work you will be doing, so the real experience won't scare them. Read the excellent book *Birth—Through Children's Eyes* listed in the Recommended Resource section for more comprehensive ideas. Many hospitals offer sibling preparation classes—sign the kids up. Your children also need a designated support person of their own in case they find the experience too intense or boring. Give each child something to do such as taking pictures, bringing ice chips, or stimulating acupressure points on your feet to send you energy so they will feel needed.

If you find you're spending more time worrying about your children and their reactions during labor, give yourself permission to alter your plan and have them leave for a while. Some women prefer to labor without the children and have them come in immediately after the baby is born for the family togetherness.

EPIDURAL ANESTHESIA—PAINLESS PURSUITS

The trend in obstetrics is toward more painless childbirth. While there are those women who still wish to labor without medication, many are opting to experience as little pain as possible. Epidural anesthesia is gaining in popularity after a decade or so of the cold turkey method.

Epidural anesthesia, given during the active phase of labor, numbs you from the waist down. You can use your breathing exercises until epidural time and then relax until it is time to push. See Chapter 16, "Labor and

Delivery" for more details. Hospitals are vying for the consumer dollars by offering this anesthesia option. If "No pain, no gain" isn't your cup of tea, ask your doctor if this option is available to you. Now you can really have it all ways. This is a nice time to have a baby!

△△△

Prenatal Care

CHOOSING A DOCTOR

Good Vibrations

Choosing a doctor or birth attendant without careful thought has all the pitfalls of an arranged marriage: You don't know what you've committed to until it's too late. Save yourself and the doctor wasted time and emotional trauma by doing your homework now.

Think about what kinds of personality traits make you the most comfortable. If your doctor is the autocratic type and you want to share in the decision-making process, you'll be at each other's throats in no time. If you don't like to worry about details, a take-charge type may be just your style. Decide what *is* your style and find someone who'll "wear well" over the months of your pregnancy. Breaking up after you're several months into the relationship can be inconvenient, if not painful, for both of you.

If you have insurance with maternity benefits, your first step is to know exactly what is and is not covered. It's a waste of valuable time to investigate hospitals and doctors if they don't accept your particular insurance plan. Many plans now contract with certain hospitals and doctors to provide services for their subscribers. You need to know what, if any, limitations apply. You may want to ask your insurance representative the following questions.

QUESTIONS FOR THE INSURANCE COMPANY

- Which hospitals in my area accept my insurance?

- Do you have a list of physician providers from which to choose?

- What's the total reimbursement you provide for my doctor?

- What's the total reimbursement allowance for hospital costs?

- How many hospital days do you allow for a vaginal birth and a cesarean birth?

- What type of hospital room does my plan provide for? Private? Semiprivate or ward?

- How is payment handled for services? Direct payment to physician? Reimbursement to me after delivery?

- What obstetrical costs do you cover? Ultrasound? Blood tests? Amniocentesis? Fetal well-being tests (stress and nonstress testing)? Medications?

- Is there coverage for neonatal or pediatric care?

- What coverage is there should complications occur?

Before you plunge ahead to find your doctor, give some thought to your birth preferences. If you have some very specific plans for your birth, such as epidural or single-room maternity care, keep in mind that most doctors limit their practice to one or two hospitals. If you find that your chosen doctor doesn't practice at the hospital which offers these options, you'll have to decide between your doctor and your preferences and what your insurance allows.

Call the hospitals in your area and ask to speak to a nurse in the labor and delivery department. Explain that you're pregnant and interested in what the hospital has to offer for birth options. Here are some sample questions:

QUESTIONS FOR THE HOSPITAL

- What types of birthing rooms do you offer? Traditional? Single room, labor/delivery/recovery/postpartum (LDRP), or a combination?

- Who do you allow for support persons? How many? Do you let children attend births? If you do, are sibling preparation classes offered at the hospital?

- Do you allow video cameras during delivery?

- If a cesarean has to be done, do you allow support persons in the operating room?

- Do you offer vaginal birth after cesarean?

- What types of anesthesia for delivery do you provide? Is epidural anesthesia available?

- Do you have 24-hour coverage for anesthesia in the hospital, or do you use on-call people after hours?

- After delivery, how soon can I nurse my baby?

- Does the baby have to stay in the nursery, or can I have unlimited access to him?

- How soon after delivery do you usually discharge patients?

You can add or delete questions to the list depending on what's important to you. Don't ask nurses about hospital fees; they usually don't know about those things. Labor nurses are also great resources for matching you with a suitable doctor based on your preferences. Give the nurse a sample of your high-priority preferences. For instance, if you don't want an enema or perineal shave and you want to stay out of bed as long as possible, who would go along with your wishes? If you want someone who is flexible or fatherly, ask for the names of doctors who fit your bill. Ask your friends and family for some recommendations. Call a few childbirth educators and get their input. Many resources of information are out there.

Now that you've checked around and gotten the names of several doctor candidates, call their offices and ask some more questions. Keep in mind that your prospective doctor comes with an office staff that is much like an extended family; you'll develop a relationship with each member of the staff. They'll come to know you and share in your pregnancy. Make note of how friendly and helpful you feel they are as you collect your information. The receptionist or office nurse can answer your preliminary questions. Here are more examples.

QUESTIONS FOR THE DOCTOR'S OFFICE

- At which hospital does the doctor primarily practice? Does she have practice privileges at other hospitals? Which ones?

- Is the doctor always on call for his own patients? Is the doctor in a call group? How large is the call group? What are the names of the doctors?

- Does the doctor provide care for complications in pregnancy, or does the doctor refer them elsewhere?

- If you've had a previous cesarean, does the doctor provide vaginal birth after cesarean?

- Does the doctor perform ultrasound, amniocentesis, and nonstress tests in the office?

- Does the office provide prepared childbirth or other educational classes? What kind?

Now ask to speak to the office manager or billing person for more questions.

- What's the fee for a vaginal birth? Cesarean birth?

- What's the preferred method of payment (full in advance, payment not due until delivery, and so on)?

- What insurance plans do you accept?

By now you should be able to sort out your preferences according to which hospitals and doctors can provide them for you. Now you're ready to make an appointment and talk to the doctor. If you still haven't made a decision and you just want to interview the doctor, make that clear to the appointment clerk. The doctor may or may not do interviews. She may do them but charge a fee. Find out.

When you sit down with your prospective doctor, ask diplomatic questions; no one likes to be interrogated. It's counterproductive and usually futile to ask such questions as the doctor's personal cesarean birthrate because most doctors don't keep track. Hospitals have that information but are unlikely to share it with you. In reality, cesarean birth statistics don't always give valid insight into the quality of obstetrics being practiced because too many variables enter into the decision to perform a cesarean. Read the "Cesarean Birth" section in Chapter 15 for more insight.

Be friendly and relaxed. You aren't negotiating a Middle East crisis, you're just looking for a doctor. If you ask open-ended questions you're more likely to get the candid answers you need to make your decision. Keep in mind that your mission isn't to make judgments, you just want to find a doctor whose philosophy and personality are compatible with yours. Here are some sample questions.

QUESTIONS FOR THE DOCTOR

- What do you like best about the hospital where you primarily practice?

- Do the doctors in your call group share your birthing philosophy? How do they differ?

- What is your policy regarding ultrasound exams during pregnancy? How many do you routinely do? If you do an ultrasound, can my husband and children be present?

- If I develop a complication, will you still care for me, or transfer my care elsewhere? If you'd transfer me, where would I go?

- What birth options are you comfortable providing?

- What procedures do you routinely require during labor?

- What is your policy regarding preps, enemas, fetal monitoring, and IVs?

- How do you feel about support persons? Do you limit the number of people?

- What is your approach to episiotomy and positions during delivery?

- What are your preferences regarding medications and anesthesia for labor and delivery?

- How do you feel about vaginal birth after cesarean? Do you offer that option?

Once you've made your choice, communicate your desires and preferences clearly to your doctor; mind reading wasn't a part of his medical training program. Effective communication is the key to establishing the important trust and rapport vital to any successful relationship, and it's no different with your doctor.

PRENATAL WORKUP

Getting To Know You

Your official relationship with your doctor begins with the three-part prenatal workup. First, a medical history reveals any past or current health problems for you or in your immediate family that may affect your pregnancy. The questions are very standard, so don't get excited when you're asked if you mainline heroin or have syphilis. If you have any unusual (or what the "moral majority" might consider) unspeakable diseases or habits, don't be embarrassed or withhold information. With few exceptions, health care providers are nonjudgmental or at least desensitized. The goal is to give you the best care possible and work with whatever problems exist, no matter what they are.

Next is a physical exam. Besides the usual poking, prodding, and stick out your tongue routine, your pelvis is evaluated for its potential as a gateway for your baby's journey into the new world. *Adequate* and *borderline* are two terms commonly used. "Adequate" means that the baby should slip through without problems; "borderline" means wait and see: It might be a tight squeeze. If your doctor describes your pelvis as big as the Grand Canyon, consider it a compliment. But don't get ugly and hateful if your doctor says "She has a pelvis I could deliver through" and you end up with a cesarean birth. It happens. Nothing is 100 percent guaranteed.

92

During the pelvic exam, your uterus is palpated (felt) to determine if the date of your last menstrual period (LMP) is consistent with the size of your uterus. The exam provides reference points to be sure that things are proceeding normally during the pregnancy and the baby is growing on schedule. If you're unsure of your LMP, or have risk factors, an ultrasound may be done at or before 20 weeks' gestation to more accurately pinpoint your due date. The distance from your pubic bone to the tip of the uterus (fundus) is measured in centimeters. The number of weeks you're pregnant will approximate the size of your uterus; 20 weeks will equal 20 centimeters, give or take a centimeter. This is another way to follow your baby's growth.

The last part of the workup includes lab tests done for the following various reasons.

ROUTINE TESTS

Blood Count (Hemoglobin and Hematocrit)

This test detects anemia. It is repeated around 28 weeks to monitor if blood volume has expanded adequately. Your hematocrit normally decreases during the second trimester from increased plasma volume and the slower increase in red cell production. The normal decrease is not synonymous with anemia. Since the decrease is a healthy sign, some practitioners argue against routinely giving iron supplements.

Urinalysis and Culture

This test screens for infection and other kidney disease since symptoms may not be present.

Blood Type and Rh Factor

This test establishes if there's a risk for potential incompatibility and Rh disease. See the "Blood Incompatibilities" section in Chapter 13.

Antibody Screen

Your body produces substances (antibodies) in response to exposure to other substances that are foreign to your body (antigens). Blood screening detects antibodies that may be harmful to your baby.

Rubella (Measles) Antibody Titer

This test determines if you're immune to measles. Nonimmune rates in women are about 10 percent. Measles produce serious congenital deformities if the mother is infected during pregnancy. Immunization for nonimmune women is done *after* delivery.

Serology (VDRL)

This is the test for syphilis. The positive rate is very low, but testing is required by state law.

Blood Sugar

This test screens for potential gestational diabetes (pregnancy-induced glucose intolerance). Pregnancy is the perfect time to screen *all* women for diabetic tendency. The hormones of pregnancy inhibit insulin production, and a temporary diabetic condition can result. A meal high in carbohydrates or 50-gram glucose drink is taken and the blood sugar level tested in 1 or 2 hours. See the "Gestational Diabetes" section in Chapter 13.

SUBSEQUENT VISITS

Office visits are monthly until 32 weeks, every 2 weeks until 36 weeks, and usually weekly during the last month. Your visits may be fairly brief, but they're very important. Besides answering your questions, your doctor will evaluate and record several things, including:

1. **Blood pressure** (BP). Normally your BP decreases by the second trimester. If your BP increases during the second trimester, it may be one of the signs of preeclampsia, a dangerous disease for both you and the baby.

2. **Weight.** Your pattern of weight gain is important to your baby's growth. Unusual weight gain, more than 2 pounds in 1 week, may be the first sign of preeclampsia.

3. **Uterine size.** Your doctor measures the distance from your pubic bone to the top of your uterus. The measurement indicates if the baby is growing appropriately and helps detect the small

for gestational age (SGA) and intrauterine growth retardation (IUGR).

4. **Fetal heart rate.** Your doctor does this test routinely to reassure you and entertain the siblings. It's a nice touch, but it doesn't provide reliable information regarding the baby's well-being. There's no validity to predicting sex according to heart rate, which tends to be faster in early pregnancy and slows as the central nervous system matures. Usual heart rates are between 120 to 160 beats per minute.

5. **Fetal movement.** An active baby is usually a healthy baby. Try to become acquainted with your baby's wake and sleep cycles (activity patterns). Your doctor will routinely ask if the baby moves a lot.

6. **Urine testing.** Your *urine* is traditionally tested every visit for protein and sugar. Many normal pregnant women spill sugar into their urine. A blood sugar test is the preferred way to screen for diabetes. Protein is checked to detect preeclampsia, but weight gain and BP are earlier indicators of the presence of the disease. Refer to the "Preeclampsia" section in Chapter 13.

OTHER TESTS

Chlamydia

Chlamydia is a common sexually transmitted disease, with 3 million new infections occurring annually in the United States. There are no known adverse effects on pregnancy. Occasionally, the mother contracts a postpartum pelvic infection from chlamydia. The newborn baby whose mother has the chlamydia virus in her cervix can contract eye infections or pneumonitis after birth. Chlamydia, detected during pregnancy, can be treated effectively before delivery to eliminate the risk to the baby and mother.

Chicken Pox

Five percent of the adult population escaped contracting chicken pox as a child. Only one-fourth of adults with no history of having the virus are susceptible. A lab test will detect immunity if you're uncertain whether you've had it. Chicken pox can be very serious in pregnancy. If you aren't immune and you're exposed to the virus, you can be treated with zoster immune globulin (ZIG) while pregnant. Talk to your doctor.

Cytomegalovirus (CMV) and Parvovirus

CMV exposure may occur in health care workers, school teachers, and day care providers. Parvovirus causes "Fifth disease," which is a fairly common viral illness in schoolchildren. If the mother contracts the infection during pregnancy, the risk to the baby is very small. If you're exposed to either virus, tell your doctor who'll advise you.

Human Immunodeficiency Virus (HIV)

HIV is a sexually transmitted disease that causes AIDS (acquired immunodeficiency syndrome). The virus attacks the body's immune system, resulting in a loss of resistance to various infections. The virus may be present in the blood many years before symptoms of AIDS develop. Ninety percent of AIDS cases have occurred in homosexual or bisexual men, intravenous drug users, and those who've received HIV-contaminated blood or blood products. In cities with a high rate of IV drug users, HIV in pregnant women is becoming more prevalent.

Obstetricians are concerned about HIV because the pregnant woman can unknowingly transmit the virus to her unborn child. If you've had sexual contact at some time with someone in the high-risk groups for carrying the AIDS virus, discuss your concerns with your physician.

Hepatitis B (serum hepatitis)

It's possible to carry the hepatitis B virus and not have symptoms. The virus can be transmitted to the pregnant woman's baby during delivery. When a pregnant woman is identified as a virus carrier, treatment can be given to the baby at delivery to prevent infection.

Health care workers and Southeast Asians are considered at higher risk for being carriers of the virus. In some areas, hepatitis B testing is routine for all pregnant women. If you're in the high-risk category, talk to your doctor.

96

Toxoplasmosis

If you're a cat owner or work in the veterinary field, this one's for you. Toxoplasmosis is an infection resulting from contact with airborne protozoa from cat feces or from eating contaminated raw or rare meat. The infection isn't serious unless it's the first occurrence and you're pregnant. If you're in the at-risk category, tell your doctor so she can test to see if you've had a previous infection. It's nice to have reassurance that there's no risk to your baby. Ideally, you should be tested before you become pregnant.

ΔΔΔ

12

When to Call the Doctor

Two kinds of women drive doctors crazy: those who call for every little twinge and those who wouldn't call if they were staked to an ant hill because "I didn't want to bother you." Here are some hints to help you avoid falling into these two categories.

ANY VAGINAL BLEEDING

Vaginal bleeding doesn't automatically mean disaster, but the source of the bleeding needs to be investigated. Panic usually follows if you're on the toilet when you discover the bleeding because even a few drops will look like gallons as soon as they hit the water. Wipe with toilet paper and make note of the color—bright red or more reddish-brown? Did the bleeding start after some activity, such as intercourse or moving furniture? Is it associated with cramping or localized pain anywhere? Your doctor will ask you these questions and how much blood you think you lost. Just remember the difference between bleeding and hemorrhaging: If blood isn't running down your leg and filling up your shoe, you're not hemorrhaging. Keep calm and call your doctor.

SWELLING OF FACE AND FINGERS—GENERALIZED SWELLING

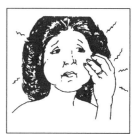

Swelling of feet and ankles is common in pregnancy, so it's no cause for alarm. Swelling of face and fingers along with feet and ankles may be a sign of preeclampsia (toxemia) and needs some follow-up with your doctor. (See the "Preeclampsia" section in Chapter 13.)

SEVERE OR CONTINUOUS HEADACHE

Headache that is severe or continuous is another possible sign of preeclampsia. Dimness or blurring of vision may accompany this type of headache. Migraine headaches also have these symptoms.

ABDOMINAL PAIN

Aches and pains are so common in pregnancy that you sometimes need help in deciding if your abdominal pain is something to be concerned about. Before calling your doctor, think about what kind of pain you're having. Where is it? What does it feel like? Do you have any other symptoms besides abdominal pain, such as bleeding? Have you noticed an increase in your vaginal discharge? Does the pain come and go, or is it constant? It may just be the old round ligament pain again, but call your doctor and check it out.

PERSISTENT VOMITING

You need help with this one so you won't become too dehydrated and upset your body's chemical balance. Don't wait until you're so dried out that your tongue looks like the sands of the Sahara. Call your doctor.

CHILLS OR FEVER

This could be old garden variety flu that no one can do much about, BUT, it could also be a kidney infection, which is serious. If your temperature is over 101 degrees, call your doctor. If you have a fever lower than 101 degrees but pain in the area of your kidneys and/ or frequency and burning on urination, call your doctor; you may have a kidney infection.

The garden variety flu with temperatures below 101 degrees with no other symptoms usually resolves itself within 24 hours. Try Tylenol and fluids. If your symptoms don't resolve within 24 hours or you're concerned, call your doctor.

PAINFUL URINATION

Most women don't have to be encouraged to call the doctor for this one. You feel like your bladder is going to burst, but all you can manage are a few drops that feel like razor blades. A bladder infection, besides being painful, is a common cause of preterm labor symptoms and needs to be treated because you can't cure it yourself.

ACCIDENTAL INJURY

Generally, the baby is well protected from blunt trauma to the abdomen in early and middle pregnancy by the cushioning effect of the amniotic fluid. In late pregnancy, injury to the baby is more likely to occur when the head is fixed in the pelvis and amniotic fluid is normally decreased.

Seven percent of women experience some type of injury during pregnancy. The vast majority of these accidents don't harm the baby. Occasionally, injury to the abdomen can seriously decrease oxygen to the baby. Premature separation of the placenta from the uterine wall and high stress levels associated with an auto accident or other trauma are thought to be contributing factors.

If you have an accident, and your abdomen receives a blow, call your doctor. Some reassuring tests can be done in the hospital. In addition to examining you, the medical staff can evaluate the baby. A contraction stress test and fetal monitor can detect signs of fetal distress. The Kleihauer-Betke blood test is done to detect fetal bleeding. The tests may take 2 or 3 hours to complete, but you'll have some peace of mind to go with your bruises.

An ounce of prevention: Wear your three point seat belt restraint. The lap belt should be positioned on your thighs. Seat belts significantly decrease injury to both mom and baby.

△△△

Complications in Pregnancy

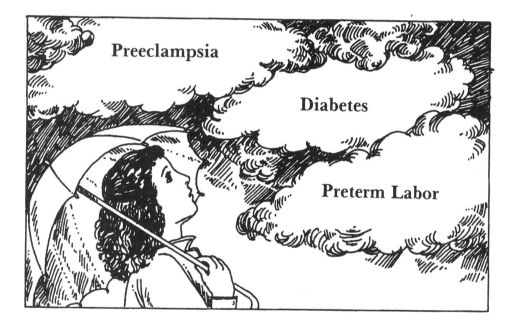

RAIN ON YOUR PARADE

For the majority of women, pregnancy is a normal and physiologically uneventful process. You count on breezing through pregnancy with no problems, looking and feeling great. When complications arise, you're forced to make adjustments in your idyllic pregnancy plan. It is not an easy adjustment for most women. Your self-esteem suffers. Disappointment and anger are common emotions as you struggle to deal with the unexpected events. You add anxiety and fear for you and your baby to the witch's brew of unknowns facing you. You need expert care, added emotional support, and accurate information to cope effectively with the changes.

This chapter discusses the more common complications in pregnancy. When you understand the basics, your anxiety decreases. When you're calm, you're better able to hear and understand what your doctor communicates to you. You'll find that you can cope and maintain some control over the unanticipated events which altered your pregnancy plans. You don't have to junk your original blueprint for your pregnancy; you just have to do some remodeling. For example, you can still enjoy and revel in the normal aspects of your pregnancy. You can feel the baby move, take childbirth classes, and shop for baby furniture. You'll still experience those "normal" aches and pains of pregnancy along with every other pregnant woman. Only part of your pregnancy is complicated, not all of it!

GESTATIONAL DIABETES

Approximately 1 to 4 percent of pregnant women develop the condition known as gestational diabetes. What happens?

Pooped Pancreas

During the second trimester, the hormones of pregnancy are in full force. These hormones inhibit the effectiveness of insulin in the body. The pancreas, which produces insulin, has to work harder to produce more insulin to keep up with the increased demand. Most women are able to meet the increased demand; for those who can't, a temporary state of diabetes results when the demand is greater than the supply of insulin.

Banking on Your Body

In the diabetic state, your body can't effectively transact the business of converting the food you eat into energy. The food you eat can be considered energy checks that you deposit in your body bank. Insulin acts as the bank teller who converts your checks into available energy. Simple sugar is like cash for immediate energy; fat is stored as savings for emergencies; other sugar is stored as an easy access checking account. Insulin is the key to the system running efficiently and keeping you in funds. Without insulin, your assets are frozen. Your deposits don't make it into your accounts, and

you don't have access to what's already there. Your blood develops high levels of sugar but isn't able to use it. It's similar to having $1 million in a safety deposit box but not having the key to open it.

Good News

Unlike the type of diabetes that requires insulin, gestational diabetes is a temporary condition. After delivery, when the pregnancy hormones are gone, your body returns to its regular metabolism. Also, your baby doesn't run the increased risk of developing congenital anomalies since gestational diabetes doesn't develop until the second trimester. Let's discuss some potential problems that do need to be anticipated.

Fit or Fat

The higher blood sugar levels you experience with gestational diabetes present some problems for you and your baby. Your baby's prime fuel is sugar. By 12 weeks she's making her own insulin to handle the sugar you give her. Your blood sugar crosses the placenta very easily. When you have excess amounts in your bloodstream, it gravitates to the baby. Uncontrolled blood sugar levels that are chronically elevated pose big risks for your baby.

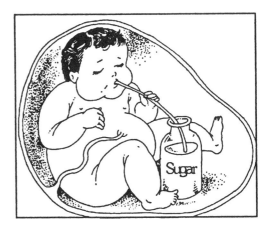

The chronically elevated blood sugar levels force-feed the baby; excessive weight and size result. The more your baby weighs, the more potential problems for both of you during labor and delivery. For example, you may have no problem delivering an 8-pound baby, but at 9 to 10 pounds there isn't enough room. Birth injury to you and the baby is a possibility. Your chances for a cesarean birth increase. Jaundice and low blood sugar (hypoglycemia) are also common complications for the baby when blood sugar is uncontrolled during pregnancy. Detection and management of the condition are crucial for a successful pregnancy.

Detection and Treatment

The American College of Obstetrics and Gynecology (ACOG) recommends screening all pregnant women 30 and over, and those who have risk factors for diabetes. Many experts believe that all pregnant women need screening at 24 to 28 weeks of pregnancy. Screening includes either ingesting a 50-gram sugar drink or eating a meal high in carbohydrates. A blood sample is taken 1 to 2 hours later. Some doctors have sugar meters in their office and offer this test to their patients; it's worth doing. These days, with early detection and appropriate management, many potential problems can be avoided.

Treatment of gestational diabetes is fairly simple. Your doctor will prescribe a diet from the American Diabetic Association (ADA). The diet controls your blood sugar, keeping it within safe levels. Most pregnant women are able to maintain their blood sugar with just the diet. It's important to follow the diet if you want to avoid the problems discussed earlier. A reasonable exercise program also helps control blood sugar. If your blood sugar can't be controlled with diet and exercise alone, insulin will be prescribed also. Remember, this metabolic condition is only a temporary one; with just a little extra effort on your part, you can assure that your baby will be healthy.

106

After Delivery

Half the women who develop gestational diabetes during pregnancy are at increased risk for diabetes in later life. So even if your metabolism returns to normal after delivery, you need follow-up. Developing diabetes in later life is associated with a family history of the disease, obesity, lack of exercise, and inappropriate diet. After pregnancy, resolve to continue the good eating habits you learned from your ADA diet, and continue exercising to lose unhealthy pounds. It will pay off in the future.

INSULIN-REQUIRED DIABETES

For those of you who are diabetics and regularly use insulin, there's also good news. The outcomes for women with diabetes and their babies is the best it has ever been. With well-controlled sugar levels during pregnancy, you can expect and have a healthy baby!

Management of insulin-required diabetes in pregnancy has become more efficient, less costly, and less disrupting to your life-style than it used to be. Monitoring sugar levels at home gives you more control and the consistent feedback you need to keep your blood sugar levels consistently within safe limits.

To assure the best outcome possible for your planned baby, see your internist, obstetrician, or perinatologist **before** you get pregnant. Achieving the best control possible before conception lowers the risks for congenital anomalies. By the time you realize you're pregnant, it may be too late since the anomalies occur in the first trimester. **Get an early start on prevention.**

HERPES

Not So Simplex

Herpes simplex used to be just a plain old "cold sore." In the 1980s it became the dread virus that threw a wet blanket on the fires of the sexual revolution. The herpes hysteria grew because medicine had neither prevention nor cure.

Even the admonition "Hey, let's be careful out there!" didn't help. The herpes hysteria has diminished because of the more serious threat of AIDS.

The herpes virus is the Greta Garbo of sexually transmitted diseases—elusive and mysterious. The true incidence of herpes isn't known since it's not reported to public health agencies. Even trying to confirm whether or not you have herpes can be maddening. Let me count the ways.

Blood Test

A blood test only proves exposure to the virus, not whether you've had herpes. Most adults will have a positive test that only shows a universal exposure to the virus.

Cultures

The *only* way to prove the diagnosis of herpes is to use a swab and dab the suspected area and have the specimen tested to see what grows (culture). Problems arise with false positives (the test says you have it but you don't) because of other viral infections. False negative culture (virus present but doesn't grow) occurs even if you have lesions but they aren't "shedding" at the time. It's also possible to contract the virus and not have it show up as an infection for years. No one knows for sure what triggers the infection. Some marriages have met an untimely and unnecessary end over who gave what to whom. Remember, a clinical diagnosis, where the doctor just looks at the lesion and says "Yep, you've got it," is subject to error. Cultures must be done to be certain.

Contracting herpes creates havoc with both your body and psyche. Common feelings are shame and guilt. You may feel like a sexual leper. Your pregnancy will probably dredge up those old feelings you thought you had worked through, especially the guilt. Now you have your baby and the possible consequences to consider. The facts should reassure you and allow you to enjoy your pregnancy without the gloom and doom.

Just the Facts

One percent of pregnancies are complicated by herpes. The risks to pregnancy differ between the primary infection (your first) and any recurrence. In early pregnancy with a primary infection, there's a greater risk for miscarriage but not birth deformities. Herpes generally isn't an indication for terminating pregnancy. In the last 6 weeks of pregnancy, there's an increased risk for preterm labor and infecting the baby after birth. Recurrences of herpes during pregnancy don't offer any risk to the baby; very rarely does the virus cross the placenta to the baby. The number of babies who actually become infected with herpes after birth is very small, 1 in 4000 or 5000. Unfortunately, those babies who acquire herpes have a mortality rate of 40 percent. Two-thirds of those who survive have serious neurological problems or eye damage. To help ensure your peace of mind, here are a few simple guidelines to follow:

- If you've already been proven as having herpes, no cultures are needed during pregnancy.

- If you haven't previously had herpes and you discover lesions (sores), you need to be cultured while the virus is still "shedding." The best time to do a culture is when you feel the tingling or burning right before the outbreak and the first or second day after the outbreak. Make an appointment with your doctor and show him exactly where your suspected lesion is.

- During outbreaks, be sure not to spread the lesions to other parts of your body. Soap and water are good disinfectants. Corn starch on the sores and drying them with your hair dryer work as well as anything.

- There's but one cardinal rule: The baby and the virus shouldn't meet. If lesions are present when you go into labor, you'll most likely have a cesarean.

- If no lesions are detected at the time of labor, you'll have a vaginal birth.

Delivery Management

When lesions are present at delivery, a cesarean birth is done to try to prevent transmission of the virus to the baby, but there are no guarantees. When there are active lesions and the membranes are ruptured, the role of cesarean is unclear. Some doctors won't do a cesarean if the water has been broken for more than 4 hours because they feel that the infection has had ample time to travel upward into the uterus. Other doctors prefer to do a cesarean regardless of the length of time the membranes have been ruptured. It's a tough decision because no one knows for sure which is the best approach.

The Good News

Even if you deliver with active lesions, remember that more than 90 percent of babies don't become infected. Most babies appear to be protected from infection by the mother's antibodies.

After delivery, even if you have lesions, the only precaution you need to observe is good handwashing. Isolation procedures or a private room aren't necessary. The nursery may insist you room with your baby, depending on their policy. You can breast-feed if you wish.

PREECLAMPSIA

Facts and Fallacies

Preeclampsia has probably been around for as long as women have been getting pregnant. It's also known as toxemia, pregnancy-induced hypertension, or EPH gestosis. Preeclampsia is the most misunderstood and myth-ridden disease in pregnancy. Let's clear up some of the more common myths with some facts.

- Preeclampsia isn't related to obesity or excessive weight gain during pregnancy.

- It isn't caused by salt (sodium chloride). Women with preeclampsia actually have normal sodium levels. **Salt restriction isn't recommended.**

- The condition isn't cured or alleviated by taking water pills (diuretics) for the swelling.

- Preeclampsia isn't caused by a diseased placenta, poisons, or toxins in the body. The term "toxemia" is still used, but it isn't an accurate one to describe the disease.

- It isn't prevented by vitamin therapy or high-protein or other special diets. **There's no known prevention.**

Preeclampsia is one of the most studied diseases in pregnancy. In spite of all the research, we still don't know what causes the disease or how to prevent it. The only cure at this time is to deliver the baby.

110

The Computer Goes Kaput

Preeclampsia usually occurs during a first pregnancy. Five percent of pregnancies develop preeclampsia. In addition to the first-time mother, women with diabetes, chronic hypertension, and multiple pregnancies are at risk for developing the disease. Preeclampsia seems to result from a number of interacting factors that affect the response of the mother's immune system. Her immunological system may short-circuit because of poor nutrition plus exposure to placental hormones for the first time. Genetic factors may play a part . . . some unknown incompatibility between mom and dad. Who knows for sure? The body's immunological computer, because of some unknown variable, doesn't "program" the body's response to the pregnancy in a normal way and preeclampsia results.

Software Snafu—What Goes Wrong

Preeclampsia has important effects on you and your baby. Your vascular system, which holds and carries blood throughout your body, changes in shape with this disease. Instead of being straight hollow tubes with unrestricted blood flow, your vessels look more like sausages. Some areas are very narrow and others very wide. The increased pressure inside the blood vessels forces fluid out into the tissues, to relieve the pressure. Your blood becomes thicker without the fluid. Your blood pressure (BP) rises because of the areas of constriction in the vessels. The changes in the vessels produce the three symptoms used to diagnose preeclampsia: edema (swelling), hypertension (increased blood pressure), and protein in the urine.

The blood flow to the baby is decreased due to the decrease in fluid volume inside your vessels and the increase in blood pressure. These "short rations" produce a small baby whose physical growth potential isn't reached. Intrauterine growth retardation (IUGR) is the term used to describe the condition.

Signs and Symptoms

Preeclampsia is similar to a computer virus. It's present long before you realize something is wrong. The disease makes its appearance some time after the twentieth week of pregnancy. The first sign is usually a weight gain of more than 2 pounds in 1 week. Generalized swelling (edema) appears next. It's normal to have swelling of the feet and ankles, but it isn't normal for the face and hands to swell. Pay attention if you can't get your rings off and your face seems fuller than usual.

111

After the swelling, your blood pressure starts rising. A BP of 140/90 is abnormal in pregnancy. You can still have preeclampsia even if your blood pressure doesn't reach that level. If the top number of your BP rises 30 points above your early or prepregnancy BP and the bottom number rises 15 points, it's still possible to have preeclampsia. For example, if your first trimester pressure was 90/60 and now you consistently register 120/75, you need to be evaluated, particularly if you have swelling also. With mild preeclampsia, you may not have protein in your urine.

Downtime—Treatment

Since delivery is the only cure for preeclampsia, your doctor tries to slow the progress of the disease until your baby's lungs are mature enough for safe delivery. There are no advantages to waiting if it isn't necessary—the disease doesn't get better with time.

Preeclampsia is classified as mild or severe. Each category is managed differently. With mild preeclampsia, you may have generalized swelling and your BP is elevated but under 160/110. You probably have no protein in your urine. You feel fine, which is misleading. With this disease, you can rapidly progress from the mild to the severe form in a matter of hours. It's very unpredictable. Listen to what your doctor tells you and cooperate fully. Your doctor may let you stay at home instead of hospitalizing you if you have mild preeclampsia. Your doctor's instructions usually include lots of rest while lying on your side. This position helps the edema fluid be reabsorbed back into your vessels. Your blood pressure usually decreases, and your baby benefits from the extra blood flow. You can enjoy catching up on your favorite soap or reading a romantic novel for the third time. Strict bed rest usually isn't necessary, but cooking, cleaning, shopping, and bouncing babies around are off limits. If you try to continue your normal activities, your preeclampsia will only get worse and you'll end up in the hospital.

Besides rest, your doctor will have you take your BP several times a day. Check your BP in the same arm in the same position each time for consistency in the readings. She may also have you check your urine for protein with a dipstick.

Your trips out of the house will be short. You can go to the doctor's office or hospital to have stress or nonstress testing to monitor how the baby is handling the effects of the preeclampsia. You may have blood tests done weekly to monitor the progress of the disease. Ultrasound exams may be done to reassure everyone your baby is growing on schedule. If you aren't getting better despite the decreased activity, hospitalization may be necessary.

With severe preeclampsia, your BP will be 160/110 or higher on two or more checks 5 minutes apart after resting. Your urine will show 2+ or more protein. You probably won't feel well. You may have what you think is heartburn and a headache. The treatment is hospitalization. The decision to deliver your baby will depend on what your doctor decides is the best course of action for both you and your baby.

With severe preeclampsia, your doctor is worried about convulsions. She'll give you magnesium sulfate, the drug used to prevent seizures, usually administered intravenously. When the drug is first administered, you may develop a stuffy nose, headache, and feel very flushed. These common side effects subside within a short period of time.

Your doctor will discuss the available options and help you understand the best course of action for both you and your baby. Remember, with delivery comes the cure. Preeclampsia has no long-term effects, you get well, and everything returns to normal. You're soon feeling better and getting acquainted with your newborn baby.

PRETERM LABOR

Six to eight percent of all babies born arrive before 37 weeks' gestation. These small numbers, however, account for 75 percent of all the neonatal deaths—a significant statistic. It costs as much to care for 5 preterm babies as it does 150 pregnant women. Everyone agrees that prevention is the best approach since Mother Nature provides the best incubator. But this is easier said than done.

An Obstetrical Stew

It's extremely difficult to prevent something when you aren't sure of the exact cause, as in 50 to 60 percent of preterm labors. The current strategy is to identify in advance those women most at risk for preterm labor. A look at a risk-assessment guide reveals an obstetrical stew of social, physical, and pregnancy factors that contribute to preterm labor. The following is a sample list.

Major factors for preterm labor:

Previous preterm labor

Multiple pregnancy (twins or more)

Abdominal surgery during pregnancy

Two second-trimester abortions

Cervix less than 1 cm long

Cervix dilated more than 1 cm

DES daughter

Cone biopsy of cervix

Incompetent cervix

Irritable uterus

Polyhydramnios (excessive amniotic fluid)

Uterine anomaly (double uterus)

Minor factors for preterm labor:

Bleeding after 12 weeks

One abortion in the second trimester

Three or more first-trimester elective abortions

Febrile (fever) illness

Pyelonephritis (kidney infection)

More than 10 cigarettes per day

Prevention

The earlier preterm labor is diagnosed, the sooner treatment can begin. Once the cervix has started to dilate, it's difficult to stop the progress of labor for very long. Intensive education of women in the high-risk group is one method being used to prevent preterm labor. The women are shown how to assess themselves for signs of preterm labor. The education is reinforced by frequent telephone contact with nurses who provide support and information.

Ambulatory home monitoring is an investigational technique that may help identify preterm labor. The woman wears a uterine contraction monitor several times a day. The recorded contractions are transmitted by phone to a central unit where doctors or nurses evaluate the strip. Some feel that the home monitoring system is effective, but others feel that education and self-assessment by the pregnant woman combined with frequent nurse contact work as well and are also less expensive. Time will tell.

What's Cooking: Symptoms

Symptoms of preterm labor are often very subtle; they may go unrecognized until the cervix has dilated. You can suspect preterm labor if you have:

- An increase in your usual clear, mucousy, vaginal discharge

- Noticeable tightening of your uterus, every 10 minutes or less

- Backache different from the type you usually have

- Feeling of pressure in your pelvis

Urinary tract infections are a common cause of preterm labor symptoms. Call your doctor if you have one or more symptoms (frequency and burning on urination). It's easier to check it out than to deal with a preterm baby in the neonatal intensive care unit (NICU) for a month or two.

Treatment—Your Interventions

If you experience uterine contractions before 37 weeks of your pregnancy, lie on your left side and drink a quart of water. The combination of rest and fluids often quiets the irritable uterus. Call your doctor and tell her how often your contractions are occurring and what you're doing to quiet your uterus.

Treatment—Your Doctor's

If contractions continue in spite of your interventions, hospitalization is required to observe and treat preterm labor. Half the women treated will respond to bedrest on the left side and an IV to increase their fluid level (hydration). The fetal monitor documents the uterine activity and ensures that the baby is doing well. If after an hour or two the contractions are getting closer and/or the cervix is changing, the decision to try to stop labor has to be made. Labor usually won't be stopped if:

- You're 35 weeks or more pregnant

- The baby's lungs are mature

- You're 4 or more centimeters dilated

- Your bag of water has ruptured

Contraindications to suppressing labor include fetal distress, poorly controlled diabetes, severe preeclampsia, intrauterine infection, and bleeding.

Several drugs are used to stop labor if you're between 26 and 35 weeks pregnant. They buy time to allow the baby's lungs to mature. The more your cervix is dilated, the less time you can buy. The decision to use the drugs rests with you and your doctor.

If you're less than 34 weeks pregnant and your hospital doesn't have an NICU, you'll probably be transferred to a hospital that can provide the expert care your baby needs. This is in the best interests of your baby. If the receiving hospital has a highly trained transport team, you may be allowed to deliver in your hospital. After delivery, your baby is then transferred.

The Crisis

The delivery of a preterm baby precipitates a major emotional and financial crisis. Important developmental tasks have been interrupted. You're plunged into motherhood before you're emotionally ready—you have no time to savor the anticipation. You have to work through the formidable emotions of disappointment and guilt. Disappointment is painful and acute—you didn't have your fantasy-perfect birth experience. Instead of a picture-perfect, full-term baby, your preemie is skinny, red, wrinkled, and frighteningly fragile looking.

Disappointment is minor compared to the guilt you feel. You're convinced somehow that you're responsible for your baby being born early. Emotionally, you have a lot of grieving to complete. You find yourself stumbling through the grieving process with stops along the way. Anger follows shock and can be directed outwardly to those around you or inwardly expressed as depression. Anger comes from fear. Communicate your feelings and fears to each other, your doctor, and the nurses caring for you and your baby.

Then, there's your baby. Instead of euphoria, there's fear for the fate of your very little new one. You're expected to begin the attaching, loving process when there may be no guarantees she'll survive. You may try to protect yourself, after all you've been through, by delaying the attachment process. You wonder if you'll have to say goodbye before you really have the chance to say hello. The situation can seem overwhelming. What do you do now?

Coping

You and your husband need as much love and support as your new baby does. This isn't a time to tough it out alone. Gather around you all the emotional support you can. Use the hospital social worker, chaplain, or other professional to help you work through that difficult but necessary grieving and adjustment process.

The development of the NICU has had a tremendous impact on the survival rates for the very preterm baby. Babies as young as 28 weeks, in the hands of a neonatologist and highly trained nurses, have very good survival rates.

The personnel in the NICU know the value of having you touch, spend time with, and nurture your baby right from the start. Liberal visiting hours provide the opportunity to hold and cuddle your baby. You can still develop that important attachment. It won't take long before you no longer notice the tubes and machines. You only have eyes for your "little one" as he grows into that regular-sized baby you expected.

Read the books in Appendix 3, "Recommended Resources." It helps to realize that with half of all preterm labors, nobody knows why it happened. You can't hold yourself responsible for what you don't know. The fates have handed you a difficult test, but from adversity comes strength.

TWINS

Pass The Smelling Salts!

The possibility of more than one baby lurks somewhere in the dark recesses of every pregnant woman's mind. Twins occur once in every 100 pregnancies. The thought may delight some and provoke horror in others.

Head Start

Before ultrasound, as many as 30 percent of twin pregnancies were surprises. The smelling salts weren't needed until delivery. Early diagnosis of the twin pregnancy is critically important; plans must be made. In the first or early second trimester, an ultrasound exam can eliminate surprises. You can see two babies in there—no guessing. For the duration of your pregnancy and definitely after, you'll need to make adjustments in your life-style.

Double Trouble

Twins may double your fun after birth, but there are potential problems during pregnancy that your doctor will want to anticipate and avoid. The twin pregnancy is high-risk. Careful attention to detail and planning help ensure a happy landing for your double duo. Listing some of the potential problems for you isn't done to scare you but to give you a good idea why you need skilled care during your pregnancy.

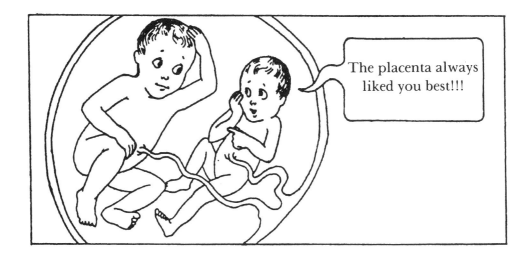

Potential Problems for Twin Pregnancy

- Significantly higher infant mortality rates than single pregnancies.

- Low birthweights.

- Preterm labor. Twins deliver on the average about 3 weeks early.

- Discordant growth—intrauterine sibling rivalry. One twin receives more nourishment from the placenta, and the other one is "underfed." "The placenta always liked you better" kind of thing.

- Preeclampsia.

- Maternal anemia.

- Placental problems such as premature separation and placenta previa.

- Complicated labor. If one twin is breech, a cesarean birth is often done.

Now you know why many obstetricians have gray hair. Guiding your twin pregnancy to a successful, uneventful completion is a real challenge for both you and your doctor. There are five important things you can do for yourself:

- At about 28 to 32 weeks, your doctor may ask you to quit work and spend a fair amount of time lying on your side to increase placental blood flow. This also helps the babies gain weight.

- Learn the signs of preterm labor. Pay attention to what your body is telling you.

- **Don't hesitate to call the doctor or the office nurse if you think you're having contractions.**

- Eat a well-balanced diet with adequate calories.

- Take your vitamins, the ones with the iron and folic acid.

Your doctor will perform several ultrasound exams during pregnancy to follow the growth patterns of both babies—remember the sibling rivalry.

Nonstress testing might be added weekly at 32 weeks, if it's indicated, to evaluate how well the babies are doing.

Delivery may add a few more gray hairs to your obstetrician's head. He'll want you to deliver in a hospital with equipment and personnel trained to care for you during labor and your babies at birth. Talk to your doctor about your options. If preterm labor strikes, a perinatal center is usually your best bet. It's less anxiety-provoking if you plan ahead for all possible situations. Have a game plan. You've had enough surprises.

BLOOD INCOMPATIBILITIES

Erythroblastosis Fetalis (EBF)

EBF is the result of blood incompatibility between the mother and her fetus. Understanding how the negative and positive blood incompatibility occurs can be confusing, but here goes.

When the mom's blood type is negative and the baby's father's type is positive, the baby has a 50/50 chance of being positive too. Being positive is what causes the problem between mom and baby. The mother's body normally views the baby as a friendly, harmless parasite. In the Rh negative mom whose baby is Rh positive, the mother's body views the fetal blood cells as dangerous intruders and takes action. Mom becomes sensitized and develops antibodies (weapons) to destroy the red blood cells in the baby. As the red blood cells are being destroyed, the baby becomes anemic. More

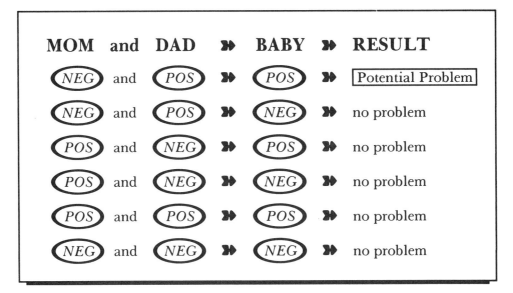

MOM	and	DAD	⇒	BABY	⇒	RESULT
NEG	and	POS	⇒	POS	⇒	Potential Problem
NEG	and	POS	⇒	NEG	⇒	no problem
POS	and	NEG	⇒	POS	⇒	no problem
POS	and	NEG	⇒	NEG	⇒	no problem
POS	and	POS	⇒	POS	⇒	no problem
NEG	and	NEG	⇒	NEG	⇒	no problem

problems develop as the baby tries compensating for the anemia. In severe cases, the fetal heart and liver can fail from trying to keep up, although with current treatment 70 percent of even severely affected babies survive.

A Stitch in Time

Prevention is always the best approach to any problem. This is no exception. Once the mother is sensitized, the sensitivity is lifelong and irreversible. It doesn't help to lock the barn door after the horse has escaped.

Blood typing, Rh determination, and antibody screening are routinely done at the first prenatal visit. All Rh negative mothers have the antibody screen repeated at 28 weeks of pregnancy. If there are no antibodies to indicate she's sensitized, a prophylactic injection of Rh Immune Globulin (RhIG) should be given. After delivery, if the baby's blood type is positive, another injection of RhIG is given within 72 hours, locking the barn door to sensitization. Even if you're having a tubal ligation, you need RhIG because occasionally tubal ligation fails, or at a later time you might want your tubes reconnected.

Other Indications for RhIG

- Spontaneous abortion (miscarriage) occurring more than 6 weeks after the last menstrual period.

- Induced abortion

- Ectopic pregnancy

- After amniocentesis

There's always great optimism that EBF will be wiped out in our lifetimes. Do your part; there are always inadvertent slipups. If any of the above situations occur, remind your doctor to order the RhIG injection. Don't assume you don't need it—you do.

ABO Incompatibility

Occasionally, blood incompatibility can result when mom has type O and baby has either AB, A, or B type blood. Only 2 percent of births are affected by ABO incompatibility. This type of EBF is different from the Rh problem. ABO isn't as serious and doesn't become more severe with each pregnancy. The baby doesn't die before birth, and the sophisticated technology, such as amniocentesis and ultrasound, isn't necessary. Preterm delivery isn't necessary. ABO incompatibility is more a pediatric disease than an obstetrical one and can usually be treated with little difficulty after the baby is born.

The Overdue Blues—Postdates Pregnancy

You're now 2 weeks past your due date and officially considered postdates by your doctor. You're afraid to be seen in public because you're tired of people asking "Haven't you had that baby yet?" You stop answering the phone because your mother calls every 3 hours to ask "Is anything happening?" You've stopped speaking to your husband, your doctor, and the rest of the world. You don't want to be pregnant anymore. You want your doctor to do *something*! You may be miserable, but your doctor isn't having any fun either. She has to worry about your "aging" placenta providing enough oxygen and nutrients to your baby. Your doctor has to weigh many factors in order to make the appropriate decision in your particular case. If your actual due date is really uncertain, add more gray hairs.

I've got those overdue blues

The state of your cervix is usually the critical factor in whether or not labor can be induced. With an unripe cervix, some doctors prefer to leave Mother Nature alone if the fetal well-being tests are reassuring, the baby is growing appropriately, and there's an adequate amount of amniotic fluid. Some obstetricians start fetal testing at 41 weeks.

The more unripe the cervix, the less chance of a successful induction of labor. There are no guarantees the oxytocin will work. In some cases with an unripe cervix, doctors try the serial induction technique: The first day is spent just trying to ripen the cervix, another day is spent "priming" the uterus, and on the third day efforts are made to establish true labor—sometimes it works, sometimes not.

If your cervix is ripe and ready to go, most doctors feel comfortable inducing labor. Everybody can breathe a sigh of relief. If you and your doctor opt for inducing labor, skip to the induction section—your prayers have been answered.

ΔΔΔ

HEALTH CARE OPTIONS AND PERSONNEL

Health Care Options

Particularly if you have a complicated pregnancy, you need to be aware of the different options open to you for your health care. Many states have regionalized perinatal health care. Areas within state boundaries are divided into regions. Hospitals within the regions are classified according to the level of services they're able to provide.

A **level 1** center is usually a small community hospital that offers basic obstetrical services to the woman with a low-risk pregnancy.

A **level 2** center has a larger number of deliveries than the level 1 center. It has an NICU and the ability to care for more complicated pregnancies. It offers services to the low-risk mother as well.

The **level 3** center is the designated perinatal center for the region. The perinatal center must have perinatologists, neonatologists, and the necessary trained personnel to care for the very high-risk mother and her baby. All necessary services are offered on a 24-hour basis, including genetic counseling, maternal/fetal transport, education, and research. While a level 3 center specializes in high-risk care, they usually offer services to the low-risk mother as well.

Personnel

Obstetricians specialize in caring for the pregnant woman. A board-certified obstetrician is one who has passed a rigorous written and verbal examination administered by a board of peers for ACOG. A doctor is eligible to take the exam after being in obstetrical practice for 3 years. The certificate isn't required to practice, but it's considered a badge of honor—going the extra mile to demonstrate competence.

Perinatologists are obstetricians with added training. They specialize in the care of complicated and very high-risk pregnancies, such as diabetes requiring insulin. Most of the time, perinatologists are found in perinatal centers. Their practice base is mainly referral from obstetricians. In addition to direct care of the high-risk mother, they offer consultation services to the obstetrician if needed.

Neonatologists are pediatricians with added expertise who specialize in the care of the new baby with medical problems or conditions that require intensive care, such as the preterm baby. Neonatologists work closely with highly skilled and trained nurses in the NICU to provide the highest quality care for the baby who needs it.

When you're investigating hospitals in which to deliver, ask if they're a level 1, 2, or 3 for future reference. For instance, if you're a diabetic who requires insulin, a level 1 center wouldn't be able to provide the services you need.

124

14

Fetal Well-Being Tests

Complications can occur during pregnancy. When the complications have the potential to affect the health of your baby, certain tests can provide important information regarding your baby's well-being. This chapter discusses the various tests currently used to assess the fetus at risk. The information the tests provide allows your doctor to reassure you the baby is doing well in spite of the existing problems, or they can indicate if the baby is better off being delivered. Keep in mind that the various tests are immensely helpful to your doctor but aren't fool proof.

STRESS AND NONSTRESS TESTS

These tests determine if the baby is receiving enough oxygen and nutrients from the placenta. They provide a way for the baby to tell us if he's "rich" in oxygen and nutrients or if he's so "poor" that he can barely make ends meet. These tests, often used in conjunction with others, help the doctor identify the "poor" baby and allow time to make appropriate decisions regarding the best plan of action.

Contraction Stress Test (CST)
Oxytocin Challenge Test (OCT)

Oxytocin is a natural female hormone that, when released, stimulates the uterus to contract. During contractions, the flow of oxygen to the baby temporarily decreases. The process is similar to you holding your breath. The baby rich in oxygen has no problems coping with the temporary decrease. The baby poor in oxygen reserves will show subtle but detectable changes in his heart rate when the oxygen flow decreases even temporarily.

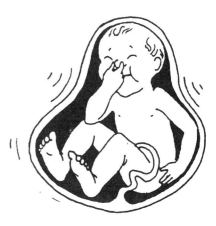

Both the CST and OCT are intra-uterine physical fitness tests. They evaluate the placenta's ability to deliver adequate oxygen to the baby. The baby's heart rate is observed and evaluated through three contractions occurring in a 10-minute period. The fetal monitor records and evaluates any changes in the baby's heart rate that may indicate potential problems with oxygenation.

The body releases oxytocin through stimulation of the nipples by rubbing or rolling. This method is less expensive than the OCT because it doesn't require an IV and is less time consuming. The nipple-stimulation method is successful about 75 percent of the time.

With the OCT, an IV is placed in the hand or wrist, infusing oxytocin until the three contractions in a 10-minute period are produced. This method may take 1 hour to complete.

The contractions produced by either method are painless. Once the stimulation or medication is discontinued, the contractions subside within 1 hour in most cases. The chances of initiating actual labor are very remote. OCT testing usually begins at 34 weeks' of pregnancy and continues weekly until delivery.

NONSTRESS TEST (NST)

Many doctors prefer the NST since it's less complicated and cheaper to perform and can be done in the doctor's office. No medication or IV is required. The NST is a test of the baby's central nervous system and, indirectly, placental function. If the central nervous system is functioning adequately, it is assumed adequate oxygen is being supplied to the baby from the placenta. The fetal monitor identifies the relationship between the baby's movements and accelerations of the heart rate. A normal response to movement from the baby should produce an increase in the heart rate. If the baby moves at least twice in 20 minutes, and the heart rate accelerates by 15 beats for 15 seconds, the test is reassuring that the baby is currently doing well. The NST is done weekly or biweekly at about 34 weeks in pregnancy and continues until the baby is delivered.

Common Indications for Stress and Nonstress Testing

- Diabetes (insulin needed)

- Preeclampsia (toxemia)

- Chronic hypertension

- RH disease

- Previous stillborn

- Postdates pregnancy (more than 2 weeks overdue)

- Cardiac disease

- Hyperthyroidism

- Intrauterine growth retardation (IUGR)

BIOPHYSICAL PROFILE

The biophysical profile is a complex assessment of a combination of fetal well-being tests. The nonstress test assesses fetal heart rhythm and reactivity. Ultrasound is used to observe and evaluate fetal movements, breathing motions, baby's muscle tone, and the amount of amniotic fluid present. The biophysical profile has become an important assessment tool for your doctor, especially when additional information is needed to make important decisions.

FETAL ACOUSTIC STIMULATION TEST (FAS)

The FAS also tests the baby's reactivity. A vibratory device that produces a sound at 80 decibels is applied to the mother's abdomen for 3 seconds. The healthy baby is startled by the sound and vibration into increasing her heart rate. The test is reassuring if the baby can accelerate her heart rate 15 beats per minute above her resting pulse twice within 10 minutes for at least 15 seconds.

PRENATAL GENETIC TESTING

With amniocentesis and/or chorionic villus sampling, an ever-increasing number of genetic disorders can be detected, including Duchenne muscular dystrophy, alpha and beta thalassemia, hemophilia, sickle cell anemia, cystic fibrosis, and polycystic kidney disease.

A prenatal genetic screening history, adapted from and developed by the American College of Obstetricians and Gynecologists, can help you and your doctor determine if you're at risk for any of the disorders listed (see Appendix 4).

AMNIOCENTESIS

Amniocentesis is done by withdrawing 1/2 to 1 ounce of amniotic fluid from one of the pockets of amniotic fluid that surrounds the baby in the uterus. An ultrasound examination with the amniocentesis shows the doctor precisely where the baby, placenta, umbilical cord, and pockets of fluid are located.

The procedure is relatively painless. Local anesthetic numbs the skin before the doctor inserts the long, thin needle into the uterus. Most women say they just feel pressure as the needle goes in, but not pain. The procedure takes 10 to 15 minutes to complete.

Intermittent cramping may be felt after the amniocentesis, but it usually subsides within a couple of hours. Occasionally, a small amount of amniotic fluid leaks from the vagina. The small leak quickly seals over, and newly manufactured amniotic fluid replaces the lost fluid without harming the baby. If the leaking continues, call your doctor. Refrain from douching, intercourse, and use of tampons until your doctor can evaluate the leaking.

The incidence of complications for amniocentesis is 1 percent—extremely low. The potential risks, such as preterm labor or sticking the baby, cord, or placenta with the needle, are more hypothetical than real, particularly when used with ultrasound guidance. Amniocentesis is widely used and considered an important tool to help your doctor make an appropriate and a safe obstetrical decision for both you and your baby.

128

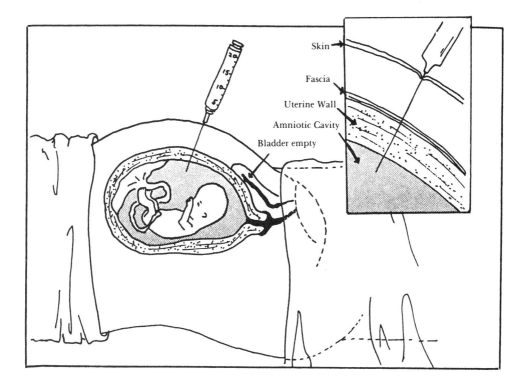

Skin

Fascia

Uterine Wall

Amniotic Cavity

Bladder empty

Common Uses for Amniocentesis

Genetic studies and counseling that indicate inherited diseases such as Tay-Sachs disease or chromosome disorders such as Down's syndrome (mongolism). Testing can be done at 15 to 18 weeks when there's sufficient amniotic fluid for a specimen.

Neural tube defects suspected—spina bifida (spinal cord not covered and anencephaly (deformed head with exposed brain). See the "Serum Alpha Fetoprotein (AFP)" discussion later in this chapter.

Fetal lung maturity. If your due date is uncertain or if preterm labor threatens, amniotic fluid analysis can determine whether or not the attempt should be made to stop labor.

Rh disease where blood incompatibility is a factor. The test can determine the amount of bilirubin (decomposed red blood cells) in the amniotic fluid. High rates of bilirubin may indicate that the baby is severely anemic and needs to be delivered.

CHORIONIC VILLUS SAMPLING (CVS)

CVS is a new technique devised to detect certain genetic abnormalities. Testing is done between the ninth and eleventh week of pregnancy, in contrast to an amniocentesis, which is done after the fifteenth week of pregnancy.

A small slim tube or catheter is directed into the cervix under ultrasound guidance. A small sample of the baby's placenta is retrieved for analysis. Results are obtained in approximately 1 week. The additional biochemical studies amniotic fluid offers can't be done since amniotic fluid isn't obtained with CVS.

The advantages of the test are the earlier results and answers to the questions of abnormalities. Anxieties can be relieved earlier. The disadvantages are a slightly higher infection and pregnancy loss rate over amniocentesis. CVS isn't, at this time, widely available; only a few designated medical centers offer this service.

SERUM ALPHA FETOPROTEIN (AFP)

This maternal blood test done at 15 to 16 weeks of pregnancy is used to screen for neural tube defects, particularly anencephaly or spina bifida. An elevated AFP level doesn't automatically confirm anencephaly or spina bifida since a number of other conditions can produce the same elevation. Levels of AFP that are higher than normal can be further evaluated with amniocentesis and ultrasound to confirm or rule out those abnormalities.

There is increasing support in the United States to offer routine serum AFP testing to all pregnant women, as is done in Great Britain.

ULTRASOUND/SONOGRAPHY (USG)

Before USG, doctors had to work largely in the dark where the baby was concerned. USG has provided an illuminating window to the womb, a way to see and examine the baby inside the uterus. The internal organs, placenta, and umbilical cord can be seen as well as movements such as the heart beating and the baby sucking his thumb.

USG isn't an x-ray. Instead, it operates the way sonar does in a submarine. Short pulses of intermittent, low-intensity sound waves are sent from the scanner placed on your abdomen. The sound waves "echo" off the baby.

The returning electrical signal is converted into a picture of the baby.

Reproduction of Sonogram

How USG Is Done

For an unobstructed view of the uterine contents with the USG exam to be obtained, you must have a full bladder. You'll have to drink several large glasses of water before the procedure. The exam is done while you're lying on a table. Be sure the head of the table is raised slightly to avoid compressing major vessels. A lubricating gel is used on your abdomen, and the doctor or technician moves a hand-held device (scanner) over your abdomen. The exam is painless and requires no medication. You should be able to see the pictures on the screen. If your husband and/or children are along, you can all be thrilled to see the baby for the first time. You might even get a picture to take home.

Is It Safe?

USG has been around for about 30 years, but consumers still have questions regarding its safety. The risks are hypothetical. Well-controlled studies by reputable researchers report no evidence that ultrasound has any ill effects on babies.

Women commonly have at least one ultrasound exam during pregnancy. The National Institute of Health (NIH) lists 27 approved uses for USG but doesn't recommend its use routinely for bonding or determining the sex of the baby. If your doctor recommends an USG exam, fair questions to ask are why you need the exam and what benefits or answers will it provide.

In the last decade, ultrasound has had the greatest impact of any diagnostic testing method on the practice of obstetrics. Those obstetricians who use USG in their practices couldn't imagine practicing without it.

Uses for Ultrasound

First trimester

Diagnose pregnancy. This is helpful if you're bleeding. Seeing your baby's heart is very reassuring. A tubal pregnancy can also be evaluated or ruled out.

Date the pregnancy. USG is often used to pinpoint your due date. If done before the second trimester, it can be accurate to within 1 week. This is an important baseline to establish if you previously had a pregnancy complicated by such conditions as cesarean birth, stillbirth, small for dates baby, preterm labor, twins, high blood pressure, diabetes, kidney or heart disease. If there's any question as to when to deliver you, an accurate due date makes the decision decidedly easier.

Second trimester

Date the pregnancy. It can be fairly accurate within 1 to 2 weeks of your due date when done in the second trimester.

Genetic counseling. If you're in the high-risk category, have a family history of anomalies, or you're 35 or over, your doctor may recommend that genetic studies be done. Amniocentesis may be done by your doctor, or you may be referred to the nearest regional high-risk center. Chorionic villus sampling, used in the first trimester, can also be done.

Third trimester

Measure fetal growth. If your baby is suspected to be small or large for the dates of gestation, the pattern of growth can be evaluated. Intrauterine growth retardation (IUGR) refers to the baby's physical size and development, not to mental development. With IUGR, the placenta isn't able to provide optimal nutrition; the baby may be chronically underfed. If IUGR is diagnosed, the baby can be delivered early, if necessary.

Determine fetal position. If a breech presentation or other abnormal position is diagnosed, there's time to discuss and plan the best method of delivery.

Amniocentesis guide. It's essential to use USG as a guide to minimize the risks of the amniocentesis procedure. The amniocentesis procedure may be done in the doctor's office or the hospital under ultrasound guidance.

MAGNETIC RESONANCE IMAGING (MRI)

MRI is one of the newest technologies being used in obstetrics. MRI is a safer replacement of x-ray diagnostic studies and an adjunct to USG to provide data on fetal structure, development, and growth. MRI confirms fetal anomalies and visualizes maternal abdominal or pelvic structures when USG scanning isn't possible because of obesity or gas.

ΛΛΛ

PART III

The Experience

15

Special Delivery

PREGNANCY AFTER 35—
THE LATE BLOOMER

In the not so distant past, physiologically speaking, the obstetrical ideal was a 20-year-old cheerleader. It was all downhill after that. The field of obstetrics traditionally has been very age conscious and very conservative. It was unwise to be too old or too young for pregnancy. For instance, teenagers were automatically considered at high risk, but age isn't the critical factor. When teenagers receive proper prenatal care, they have no more complications than do any other pregnant women.

THIRTY SOMETHING

Obstetricians are reconsidering another age myth: pregnancy after 35. The previously pessimistic belief that in pregnancy "You're only getting older, not better" isn't necessarily true. Don't start shopping for a wheelchair to go with your maternity wardrobe. The news is really positive.

Attitudes and Outcomes

When you look in the mirror and see a perfect example of the results of eating right and exercising, it's hard to convince yourself that your biological time clock has hardening of the arteries. Hold onto that thought when you find yourself referred to as "obstetrically senescent" or an "elderly" gravida. It's enough to make your yogurt curdle! Attitudes change slowly, *but*, they do change. All you maternal late bloomers out there can take heart. There are more women currently in the 30 to 35 and over age group than the 20 to 29 age group. The proportion of babies born to women 35 and over will double by the end of the century. You're no longer an obstetrical oddity but part of a mighty majority.

If you're age 35 to 44 and *healthy*, here's what you can anticipate based on the recent studies. You have **no increased risk** for

- Preterm delivery

- Intrauterine growth retardation (IUGR)

- Low Apgar score baby

- Infant death

Your risks during pregnancy **increase slightly** for:

- Gestational diabetes

- Preeclampsia

- Bleeding during pregnancy

- Placental abruption (bleeding from premature separation of the placenta)

- Placenta previa (low-lying placenta)

The cesarean birth rate is higher in the 35 and over mother. It isn't quite clear why that is, but it may be related to a more conservative obstetrical approach and a slightly higher incidence of fetal distress in labor. After all, you waited a long time for this baby, and doctors may be more willing to throw in the towel sooner if the labor of the more mature mother-to-be isn't progressing.

Each year, after the age of 35, the risk for a baby with Down's syndrome (mongolism) increases. The following chart shows the risk of Down's syndrome according to maternal age:

Maternal Age at Delivery	Frequency of Down's Syndrome
35	1 in 365
36	1 in 287
37	1 in 225
38	1 in 176
39	1 in 139
40	1 in 109
41	1 in 85
42	1 in 67
43	1 in 53
44	1 in 41

Women of 35 are offered the option of amniocentesis to detect Down's syndrome.

You may have waited a while to start your family, but studies report that the mature mother seems highly motivated when it comes to the pregnancy experience. One study reported that "thirty-something" moms used less medication during labor and delivery; more tended to breast-feed (95 percent) compared to 42 percent in other age groups.

The Bottom Line

If you've no health problems—such as high blood pressure, diabetes, kidney or heart disease—extensive, expensive studies of your various organs and body parts to see if you can withstand the "stress" of pregnancy are unnecessary. As one front porch philosopher said, "If it ain't broke, don't fix it." The healthy woman 35 to 44 *isn't* at high risk; there are no significant differences in outcomes for either mom or baby.

How do you feel when all is said and done? One mom, when interviewed, reported the experience of motherhood as "overwhelmingly rewarding." That's a nice endorsement in itself.

INDUCTION OF LABOR

Babies by Appointment

The inability to predict and conveniently time delivery makes the practice of obstetrics a relatively inefficient business. A time analyst would go nuts! Doctors eventually give up birthing babies, not because they don't like to but because the stress and lack of sleep take their toll. So why not induce all labors routinely for convenience? Babies by appointment? Life would be so simple. Let's review the options of induced labor.

Famous Last Words

Women naturally have great faith in their doctors. Doctors are generally optimistic souls. Unfortunately, optimism and success aren't synonymous when it comes to inducing labor. Many misunderstandings have occurred and hopes dashed (yours) over unrealistic expectations.

If you want to guarantee performance anxiety for your labor nurse, sweep into labor and delivery like a movie star on location with your entourage (35 relatives and 10 pillows) and announce "My doctor sent me in to have my baby *today*." Nurses tend to be more cautious and somewhat less optimistic in these matters than either you or the doctor. It's no fun being a wet blanket, but somebody has to be.

To Be or Not to Be

Successful induction of labor for vaginal delivery requires a compliant cervix—soft and yielding. Just as fruit isn't easily picked from the tree unless it's ripe, babies can't be easily "plucked" from the womb unless the cervix is ripe. A ripe cervix is soft, thinned (effaced), and partially dilated (opened). Trying to get an unripe cervix to dilate can be as hard as trying to blow open a bank safe with a firecracker.

Shaking the Tree

You're considered a candidate for induction if you have a medical indication that threatens either you or the baby. Conditions that warrant induction of labor include

- Intrauterine growth retardation (IUGR)

- Preeclampsia (toxemia)

- Insulin-required maternal diabetes

- Prolonged rupture of membranes (water broken) at or near term

- Rh disease

- Prolonged pregnancy (42 or more weeks)

The Federal Drug Administration (FDA) "prohibits" elective or convenience inductions of labor. In reality, elective induction is still done but not as widely as before the prohibition.

The most widely used method for inducing labor is the drug oxytocin, also called pitocin, given intravenously (IV). The idea is to duplicate *normal* labor. Two things happen during contractions: The uterine muscle works hard, and the baby holds her breath from being squeezed by the contractions. You don't want to tire your uterine muscle; you want to pace it just as you would for a marathon. The uterus doesn't need to be whipped into exhaustion with too frequent contractions. Neither does the baby need the added stress of too frequent episodes of decreased oxygen.

Contractions should be 3 to 4 minutes apart, lasting about 40 to 60 seconds for maximum efficiency and safety. Contractions closer than 3 minutes are usually weaker. Force, not just contraction frequency, dilates the cervix.

Along with the IV oxytocin, you'll have a fetal monitor to evaluate the baby's response to the oxytocin. The oxytocin is started with a very low dose calculated in milliunits per minute (mU) and gradually increased every 30 minutes. Induced labors ARE NOT MORE PAINFUL, if the dose is kept below 16 mU per minute; 75 percent of women have adequate contractions with 8 mU and 90 percent with 12 mU. Very rarely, 20 mU are needed. Usually, when you reach higher doses, you can forget it—it isn't going to work because your uterus becomes overstimulated from the drug and won't work properly.

After 8 to 10 hours of oxytocin, the uterus may get tired. A fatigued uterine muscle can initially increase its activity when the dose is increased, but it soon tires. The response is similar to that of the exhausted work horse: Even a whip will coax only a few more steps before the horse collapses. You can't make any progress that way. Just like the horse, the only remedy for an exhausted uterus is rest. The oxytocin is turned off and restarted in a few hours or the next day, depending on the circumstances.

Risks and Complications—Too Much, Too Soon

The most common complication with oxytocin is overstimulation of the uterus. Some women are so very sensitive to the drug that even minute amounts make their uteruses "quiver" instead of contract. Contractions that occur closer than every 2 minutes and/or last longer than 90 seconds are considered hyperstimulated. Fetal distress can result. (Try holding your breath for 2 minutes!)

Luckily, oxytocin wears off very quickly. Once it's stopped, the contractions start to decrease in frequency within 3 minutes. Most babies recover rather quickly from the temporary distress of too frequent contractions. The usual intervention for hyperstimulation is to turn off the oxytocin, turn you on your side, and give you a few minutes of oxygen by mask to help your baby get back on an even keel.

The Bridge Burner

Breaking the water bag (amniotomy) is also used to induce labor. It's a "bridge burning" commitment to delivery. For this reason, it is generally inadvisable to rupture membranes if the cervix is unripe. When the cervix is unripe, the interval to delivery time can be significantly lengthened, increasing the chances for infection and cesarean birth. Only oxytocin or Mother Nature will ripen a cervix, not rupturing membranes.

Under certain circumstances, amniotomy alone does a good job of starting labor:

- The cervix is ripe

- Not the first baby

- Baby's head is fitting snugly against the cervix

142

When an induction of labor is skillfully managed by specially trained personnel, the risks of an induced labor are minimal. Many hospitals now provide training and certification for staff performing inductions. Training adds greater measures of safety and success to the procedure.

FORCEPS

Deliveries by forceps are done less frequently than in the past. The use of forceps became less prevalent with the increased interest in the natural method of childbirth. Many women rejected regional anesthesia such as caudal, epidural, and spinal. The higher doses of anesthetics routinely used affected their ability to push. Currently doctors are more willing to let the mother push for more than the traditional 2 hours. Also, labor nurses have become attuned to different positions for pushing instead of relying on the old flat on the back routine. Squatting or sitting while pushing often adds that extra little bit of space to the pelvic outlet and allows gravity to help push the baby down.

Forceps do have a place in obstetrics. They can be very useful in the second stage of labor when, for example, there's evidence of fetal distress. Sometimes, after a long labor, the mother is just too pooped to push and needs a little help. If the baby's head is well down into the pelvis, a properly performed forceps delivery isn't dangerous for the mother or baby.

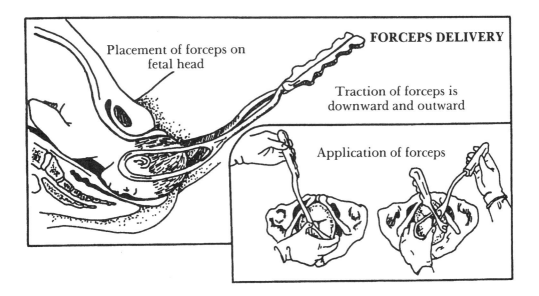

Placement of forceps on fetal head

FORCEPS DELIVERY

Traction of forceps is downward and outward

Application of forceps

VACUUM EXTRACTOR

In some instances, an alternative to forceps is the vacuum extractor, widely used in Europe for years and now finding favor here. A soft silicone cup is attached to the baby's head by suction. Gentle traction is used to deliver the baby's head. Anesthesia isn't necessary, as it is with forceps. It isn't any more uncomfortable than pushing. The baby's scalp swells at the site of the suction cup, but the swelling disappears within 24 hours.

CESAREAN BIRTH

Current Trends and Approaches

The first cesarean birth in this country was performed in 1827. The procedure didn't set the medical world on fire or make the doctor rich and famous. Until 25 years ago, the cesarean birthrate remained at less than 5 percent. Current figures run around 20 percent in most hospitals. Something obviously happened. Contrary to popular belief, there's no direct correlation between the higher cesarean rate and the number of Mercedes Benz being sold to obstetricians.

The increased cesarean rate actually reflects some important changes in obstetrics. Surgery has become very safe, and there's an increased degree of concern for the baby's safety. Parents are delaying childbearing and having fewer babies. They're also much less accepting of less than perfect outcomes. A positive factor to the rising cesarean rate is that the number of babies dying or injured from delivery-related causes has decreased.

The indications for cesarean birth have also increased. Everyone agrees that the rate is high and something should be done about it. The following approaches are among those being examined to decrease the rate without increasing the perinatal mortality rate.

Bottom down. Three percent of babies are breech (bottom first). When delivered vaginally, breech babies have a higher incidence of complications and neurological problems—those less than perfect outcomes. Most doctors recommend that all first babies, if breech, be delivered by cesarean. The complications and mortality of vaginal birth are higher in this group. Women who've already had one baby or more may be at less risk since at least one baby has been through the birth canal. Not everyone agrees with this theory.

Some doctors are willing to attempt a vaginal delivery, but the decision must be made carefully. After eliminating various high-risk factors such as

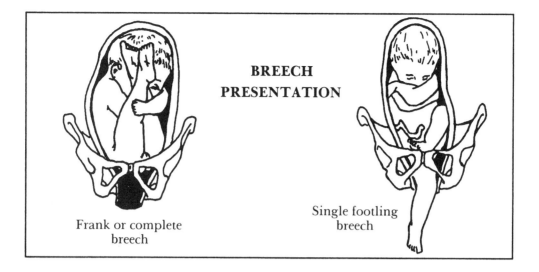

BREECH PRESENTATION

Frank or complete breech

Single footling breech

double footling (feet first), large baby, and small pelvis, only 20 percent of breeches are acceptable candidates for a vaginal delivery. Such small numbers aren't going to make a large impact on the cesarean birthrate.

Performing a breech delivery requires loads of experience, great skill, and nerves of steel. A number of things can go wrong. Delivery can be obstructed if the baby's arms become "locked" over the head. The cord can drop into the vagina if the baby's bottom isn't wedged against the cervix. The head must be delivered within a few minutes to prevent brain damage and/or suffocation. Things get very tense if there's difficulty in delivering the head; hearts sink as seconds tick away into minutes.

If you have your heart set on a vaginal delivery and you're an acceptable candidate, ask your doctor how many breech babies he has delivered. You need skill here, not optimistic bravado. Since most breeches are delivered by cesarean, there isn't enough practice to go around. Delivering breech babies vaginally is a dying art.

Bottoms up—external version. External version is a new look into an old bag of tricks—a golden oldy being streamlined for a comeback. External version is the term for the procedure of turning the baby from bottom down to head down. The technique, done near term, involves manipulating the pregnant abdomen to turn the baby into the normal position of head first.

External version isn't without some risk and expense. Since there's the possibility of the umbilical cord becoming entangled and/or the placenta separating from the uterine wall, the procedure is performed in the hospital for safety. It's understood that an emergency cesarean may have to be performed for fetal distress. External version is expensive because you need a full ultrasound exam, fetal monitoring, IV with medication to relax the uterus, and the doctor to perform the manipulation.

There's no guarantee that the procedure will work, but it's successful about 75 percent of the time. The success rate depends upon the skill of the doctor and favorable circumstances. It's always worth a try. Check your insurance; it may pay for the procedure.

Fetal distress. In the old days before electronic fetal monitoring, the labor nurse listened to the baby's heartbeat once an hour for 15 seconds. The technique didn't provide a wealth of information. As a result, some cesareans were done for fetal distress that wasn't there. Some babies who were distressed were missed because a stethoscope couldn't pick up subtle clues.

Our knowledge of fetal monitoring and heart rate patterns has increased dramatically. Much is still to be learned, but more than a few cesareans have been avoided because the fetal heart rate pattern on the monitor was reassuring. In many cases, fetal monitoring also lets personnel head off disaster by detecting early signs of fetal distress.

The fetal monitor has very little overall impact on the cesarean birthrate. Fetal distress accounts for only a small percentage of the increase.

The three P's: Passenger, pelvis, and power. The three common reasons for cesarean birth are lack of contractions powerful enough to dilate the cervix, a large baby, and a small pelvis. One or all of these situations may work together to stall progress in labor.

Cephalopelvic disproportion (CPD) describes a baby who's too big to fit through mom's pelvis. The labor that doesn't progress because of inadequate or dysfunctional uterine activity becomes "failure to progress," which leads to the diagnosis of CPD.

The true incidence of CPD is undoubtedly much less than previously thought. Numerous studies have now demonstrated that half of women previously delivered by cesarean for CPD and/or failure to progress will deliver vaginally in a subsequent pregnancy if given a trial of labor.

The major reason for failure to progress in labor is abnormal uterine activity. The contractions don't effectively dilate the cervix. When you aren't progressing according to schedule, your contractions need evaluation. The most effective way to measure the strength of the contractions is with an internal uterine catheter. If your contractions are measuring less than 50 millimeters mercury (mmHg), your uterus needs some encouragement. Oxytocin, given IV, is the drug of choice to enhance ineffective contractions so you can make progress and deliver the baby some time before the next century. Most women would prefer not to have to resort to artificial means. But if you don't use the oxytocin, the only other alternative may be cesarean birth. This is one of those situations in which you have to adjust your labor plan. Just in case, read the "Induction of Labor" section to familiarize yourself with oxytocin and what you can expect. In most cases, you need only small doses of oxytocin to stimulate your labor.

Experts agree that more cesarean births could be avoided with closer evaluation of cases of failure to progress and stimulating labor with oxytocin.

VAGINAL BIRTH AFTER CESAREAN (VBAC)

The repeat cesarean is the number one culprit in the dramatic increase in abdominal delivery. Historically, even if the original reason for the first cesarean wasn't likely to recur, the belief that the uterine scar would separate during labor was sufficient reason to repeat the cesarean procedure.

Enlightening studies have shattered some long-held beliefs. The old dictum "Once a cesarean, always a cesarean" has been dramatically revised. It seems that CPD may not always be what it seemed. True CPD is rare, and the uterus is tougher than everybody thought. Here's a fresh look at some old scars.

Incisions and Decisions

The type of incision made into the uterus determines the difference between a repeat cesarean and a vaginal delivery the next time around. The two types of incisions are the classical and the low transverse.

The *classical uterine incision* is vertical—up and down. The scar that results from this type of incision often isn't strong enough to withstand labor. There's no disagreement on this one: it's an automatic repeat cesarean. The classical incision may be used when the baby is lying transversely (sideways), or if the baby is preterm.

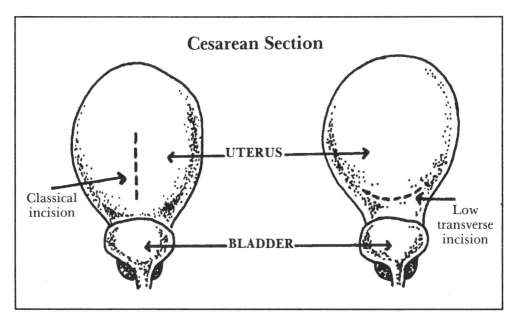

Cesarean Section

Classical incision

UTERUS

Low transverse incision

BLADDER

The *low transverse incision* is in the lower segment of the uterus. The incision withstands the stress of uterine contractions very well. The incidence of uterine scar separation is half of 1 percent—extremely low.

Beauty and the Bikini

The title doesn't refer to the latest swimsuit but one type of *skin* incision used. Most women and doctors prefer the bikini incision for various reasons: The bikini is less painful, heals better, rarely results in hernias, and keeps open the options in swimwear. The other type of skin incision goes up and down from the pubic bone to just below the belly button. Doctors rarely use this type of incision except when speed is important (fetal distress, bleeding, and so on) or to deliver a large baby.

Keep in mind that your skin incision can be different from your uterine incision. The incisions can be mixed or matched, depending on the circumstances.

Sweet Smell of Success

Once the safety of the low transverse uterine incision was established, it seemed reasonable to allow those women without a recurring problem to attempt a vaginal delivery if they so desired. Success rates were more than encouraging: two-thirds or more of the women delivered vaginally.

The American College of Obstetricians and Gynecologists encourages their members to be more liberal in performing VBAC. Hospitals have relaxed the previous rigid rules so doctors don't have to be present during the entire labor. More doctors are offering VBAC as an option. The VBAC rate could be still higher, but some women just don't want to go through labor. Some doctors still aren't comfortable with the whole idea of a trial of labor, so it may be a few more years before VBAC makes a bigger dent in those cesarean birthrates.

△△△

16

Labor and Delivery

COPING AND HOPING

How you feel about your birth experience will depend to a great extent on your expectations and how realistic they are. Setting impossible goals for yourself can result in disappointment and negative feelings afterward. If you're the type who gets hysterical over a hangnail, don't expect anyone to guarantee you a painless labor without an epidural anesthetic. It's all right to have expectations; just build in some flexibility so you can modify your plan when necessary and not feel guilty.

We all have different perceptions of pain. You won't be able realistically to evaluate yours until the time comes. For some, the old silver bullet clenched tightly between the teeth, Lone Ranger style, is sufficient. For most, active labor is the time to dip into that bag of support "souvenirs" you acquired in childbirth classes. Before labor is the time to start packing your bag of birth aids. The operative word for labor is *coping*, not *competing*. If one method of coping doesn't work, try something else.

Following are some tricks of the trade you can learn to help you during labor. Some you learn in childbirth classes, and the others are for you to sample, if you choose. Use the ones that suit your style.

GO WITH THE FLOW—RELAXATION

Fear and tension create pain and block your ability to flow with the birth process. Childbirth education techniques can help you develop cooperation between your mind and your body to avoid the fear and tension trap. You train and program your mind for a successful labor and birth process through meditation and visualization. Breathing techniques, massage, and stimulation of acupressure points fine-tune the body to relieve pain and keep the energy flowing. Your mind and body learn to work together and develop a partnership that can be mutually beneficial for the rest of your life.

Let's review the various methods that you can pack in your traveling bag for birth—besides the pillows.

IT'S ALL IN YOUR MIND

The mind is an awesome tool that can be either a help or a hindrance. Fear, which creates tension, produces pain and is a major handicap in labor. You need to train your mind for the big event. A positive, confident attitude is a valuable key to success.

Because the subconscious mind is much like a computer, it gives out the same information in response to old input until it's reprogrammed to accept something new. We need to revise and rewrite any program that prevents us from attaining important goals. Visualization is a tool that many people are discovering as a way of reaching into the subconscious to reprogram it. Relaxation, meditation, and visualization open the door to any subconscious and unpleasant past experiences. It allows us to learn new positive ways of experiencing—whether it be improving a golf game or having a baby.

The first step to self-programming is to learn relaxation techniques to banish tension. You learn to listen to cues from your body. The progressive relaxation method includes slow deep breathing and visualization. Start at the top of your head and end at your toes. Become aware of the difference by alternately tensing and relaxing each part of your body (neuromuscular exercise). Tapes are an excellent way of learning the progressive relaxation technique. Try some, or all, of the tapes in the Recommended Resources section. In time, your new techniques provide cue cards for your body to automatically relax. Along with the deep breathing, you think of relaxing sensations such as floating on a cloud or the feeling of warm water flowing over you—any situation or feeling that helps you relax.

Once you can put yourself into the relaxed, meditative state, you can begin programming your subconscious.

GUIDED IMAGERY

When we were children, we effortlessly daydreamed the most wonderful fantasies. Anything seemed possible; it still is—through guided imagery. A little practice gets the old creativity going again. You can clean your mental computer of any old, outmoded, emotional data that inhibit you. Some people call it "self-Gestalting." Here's how it works.

Let's say this is your second baby. Your last birth experience wasn't exactly perfect. Put yourself into your most relaxed state, without falling asleep, and daydream yourself back to that birth experience. From start to finish, fantasize exactly what you wanted to happen that didn't. Be creative, extravagant! Your subconscious doesn't know the difference. It's your program. Your subconscious accepts the emotions you feel *now*. You can replace fear, pain, disappointment, and anger with joy, confidence, and happiness. Now with this pregnancy and birth your emotions are positive and geared to success. You've removed the blocks to a happy outcome, instead of repeating the old program from the last experience.

Practice your dream scenario for this labor and delivery. Positive expectancy works wonders. See yourself relaxing on cue. Feel your serenity and confidence. Visualize the energies in your body as free and flowing. See your uterus working efficiently and in perfect rhythm and harmony with your body. Imagine your baby happily enjoying those farewell hugs from your uterus. Watch your baby help dilate the cervix by pushing down and working with the contractions . . . anxious to be out and about. Concentrate on each detail. Practice your relaxation and visualization every day, if possible.

LEARNING TO RELAX

Sit comfortably in a chair, your feet flat, spine straight, hands relaxed at your side, palms turned up, or sit in bed with your spine straight

LEARNING TO RELAX

First Level

1. Take three slow, deep breaths. At the height of the inhalation breath, pause for about 2 seconds before releasing the air. Breathe naturally and rhythmically in through your nose and out your mouth with lips slightly pursed. Imagine a balloon inflating and deflating in your belly.

2. Close your eyes tightly and frown. Relax the tensed muscles.

3. Grit your teeth and then relax, letting your tongue drop from the roof of your mouth.

4. Bend your neck forward, and then drop your chin onto your chest.

5. Raise your shoulders at attention and then let them droop forward into a comfortable slump.

6. Clench your right hand as if squeezing a ball and then relax. Repeat with your left hand.

7. Take a very deep breath. Fill your lungs and hold your breath for 2 to 3 seconds and then exhale fully.

8. Pull in your stomach muscles as tightly as possible and let go.

9. Squeeze the muscles in your buttocks and perineum (Kegel's exercise) and then relax.

10. Tense the muscles in your right leg and then relax. Repeat with your left leg.

11. Flex your right foot. Point your toes toward your body and then relax. Repeat with your left foot.

12. Feel the feeling of having your whole body relaxed.

Second Level

1. Do slow, rhythmic breathing.

2. Tense face muscles and then relax.

3. Tense neck and shoulders; relax.

4. Clench your hands and tense your arms and then relax.

5. Tense your abdomen and buttocks and then relax.

6. Tense your legs and feet and then relax.

Third Level

1. Use rhythmic breathing.

2. Relax your face.

3. Relax upper body.

4. Relax lower body.

and knees bent, tailor fashion. Use pillows to support your knees for comfort. Some New Age music can help you relax. The sounds of waterfalls, birds, and ocean waves combine with instruments such as harps and flutes. "Eastern Peace" by Steven Halpern is an example. "Healing Journey" by Emmett Miller, M.D., provides step-by-step guidance to relaxation and visualization.

When you're comfortable, close your eyes and take three deep breaths; inhale and exhale, slowly. Beginning at the top of your head, progressively tense and relax each part of your body. Concentrate on the difference you feel between being tensed and relaxed. Use the "Learning to Relax" chart as your guide.

Use visualization to aid in relaxing. See relaxation as a white light of energy flowing in through the top of your head. As the white light advances downward, see the tension being pushed out of your body through your fingertips and toes until it disappears.

The only difference in the three levels of relaxation is practice. As you become more aware of your body and learn to relax, you can hasten the process to reach the relaxed state.

BREATHING EXERCISES

Rhythmic breathing and concentration can aid relaxation. Everyone has a comfortable breathing pace. When you become attuned to your own breathing rhythms, you help avoid hyperventilation. Anxiety precedes hyperventilation, not the reverse. With hyperventilation, your fingers and face feel numb and tingly, and you feel short of breath. It's very uncomfortable and distracting, especially during labor. We used to think rebreathing your air in a paper bag would reverse the results of hyperventilating, but new research shows it only makes it worse. The best intervention for hyperventilating is to halt the anxiety attack and slow your breathing.

Concentrating on a focal point will provide distraction during contractions to alter your perception of pain. Your focal point can be external if you prefer to keep your eyes open. Place an object or picture at eye level to keep you in a comfortable position. If you prefer to keep your eyes closed, focus your mind's eye on your favorite relaxing vision. It can be a place, like a mountain or a still lake. You could be in a forest or standing under a warm waterfall. Imagine warm water cascading over you, relaxing your whole body.

Childbirth instructors teach three types of breathing techniques. There are no specific times to use each technique during labor.

156

It's best not to start using the breathing exercises until your contractions definitely demand your attention as they become regular and intense. If you start them too early in labor, you wear yourself out. Try the exercises at various stages to see which one of the three works best for you at the time. You may find yourself switching back and forth, but return to exercise 1 as quickly as possible. Some women prefer to use a deep inhalation and full exhalation (cleansing breath) to signal the beginning and end of contractions.

1—Slow-Paced Breathing

This exercise is the most relaxing and helps avoid hyperventilation. Slow-paced breathing is the type you used during your relaxation exercises. The rate is usually half of your normal breathing pace. You use both your chest and abdominal muscles with this technique, which is less tiring than the other techniques and enhances the calm, relaxed state you want.

2—Modified Paced Breathing

With this technique, you breathe no faster than twice your normal rate. You can try this one when your contractions become more intense. The danger with this exercise is that it can lead to hyperventilation if you aren't careful. When the contraction is over, return to exercise 1.

3—Patterned Breathing (Pant-Blow)

This type of breathing has the same rate as exercise 2, but combines a pattern of inhaling and slow blow exhaling. When you exhale, pretend you're softly blowing out a candle. The blowing technique can be useful to avoid pushing; the inhalation breath in this technique is shallow. If you take a deep breath, you have an uncontrollable urge to push. By concentrating on exhale blowing, you can refrain from taking that deep breath which makes you want to push.

THERAPEUTIC TOUCH

The holistic approach to healing is gaining more and more attention. Eastern philosophy believes in the mind and body relationship, where everything is an interrelated part of one "whole"—each part affecting the other. In

contrast, Western philosophy believes that everything is separate and distinct—the old "parts is parts" routine.

Therapeutic touch is a method of holistic healing taught by Dolores Krieger, a professor of nursing at New York University. Her students have used the technique effectively to relax patients before stressful events such as surgery and to relieve cancer pain. Relief from pain may be caused by the profound relaxation that occurs with the treatment. Whatever the reason, the results make therapeutic touch a worthwhile tool—and the technique doesn't cost anything.

Proponents of the technique are enthusiastic. A few pioneering midwives, nurses, and childbirth educators are using hands-on to ease pain in childbirth. Anyone can learn the technique. This is another potential helping aid for the "coach" to add to his bag of balms if he chooses.

The theory of therapeutic touch relates to flow within an energy field. In this case, the energy field is the body. When energy is blocked or depleted within the body, the affected area can't function effectively. The person applying the treatment gives or directs energy to needed areas, reestablishing the flow.

There are easy-to-follow, basic steps to using therapeutic touch. The person giving the treatment begins by achieving a relaxed state (centering) in order to concentrate and focus on the treatment.

The next step is assessment. Place your hands several inches above the body (energy field) and move down the entire surface to detect any disturbances in energy flow. Flowing energy feels warm or wavelike. Some areas feel hot; that's where there's an overabundance of energy flow. Blocks in the flow feel like cold, tingling congestion or pressure to the hands. Being able to perceive the various sensations may take some practice. You learn to tune into the sensitivity of your hands. When you find blocks, eliminate them by using a sweeping motion above the area of congestion, similar to smoothing bedsheets. After you clear the blocked areas and the hot spots, you balance the energy flow to the entire body (modulation). You then repattern the energy flow to the hot spot by visualizing a cool color such as blue. Warm cold spots by imagining the color yellow or any other hot color. The process is similar to adjusting the vents in the rooms of your home to assure even flow of heat to all parts of the house. A treatment can last 20 to 25 minutes.

During labor, rhythmic downward stroking above the abdomen induces relaxation and reminds the laboring woman to direct her energy to her lower body. Facilitate energy flow by smoothing out the abdomen before and after each contraction. See the Recommended Resources section for further information on therapeutic touch.

MORE SOOTHING TOUCH— ACUPRESSURE MASSAGE

For centuries, the people of the Orient have practiced the art of zonal therapy, called acupressure or reflexology. They believe that imbalances within the body cause blocks in the natural flow of energy carried through the nervous system. The blocked areas can't function properly without the flow; tension and pain result. You restore energy flow by pressure-massage on specific

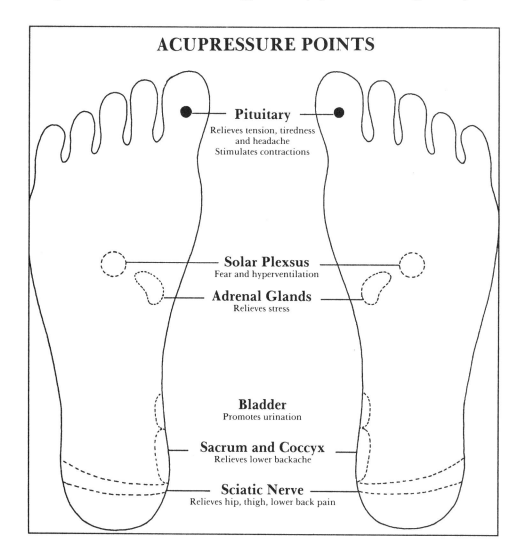

ACUPRESSURE POINTS

Pituitary
Relieves tension, tiredness and headache
Stimulates contractions

Solar Plexsus
Fear and hyperventilation

Adrenal Glands
Relieves stress

Bladder
Promotes urination

Sacrum and Coccyx
Relieves lower backache

Sciatic Nerve
Relieves hip, thigh, lower back pain

points, or meridians, on the body to relieve the tension and pain. If you choose to use the acupressure techniques, practice them the last 2 months before delivery and intensively the last week.

Therapeutic touch and acupressure aren't mainstream techniques. They're interesting additions to the other techniques you may want to use.

TRAINING FOR TWO—
DIRECTION FOR THE COACH

It doesn't take long to learn or become comfortable with acupressure techniques. No matter how you do them, she'll love it. Who can resist having their feet massaged? After all your hard work, you can have your wife turn the tables and do your feet. You'll both love the relaxed feeling you have after a session.

You become familiar with the flow of energy between the two of you by experimenting with the various acupressure points (APs). Stimulating the various APs incorporates firm pressure with soothing massage. The amount of pressure you use is similar to pushing a thumb tack into a piece of wood: firm but not painful. You move from one point to another smoothly and with rhythm, returning to those areas where you felt hard or crunchy bumps like lumps of sugar under your fingers. The bumps represent crystal deposits that block the energy flow.

THE TREAT AND TREATMENT

Have your wife recline semipropped on the bed with her arms outstretched and palms facing upward. She begins by putting herself into a relaxed state with the techniques she has been practicing. Follow the directions and corresponding illustrations beginning below. Start with the left foot and move through the exercises. Repeat on the right foot.

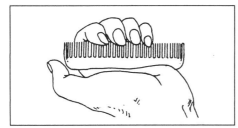

1. Have your wife tightly grasp an aluminum comb in each hand to stimulate all APs in her body.

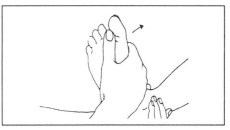

2. Grasp her foot and flex it toward her stomach (dorsiflex) briskly 20 times to stimulate the circulation.

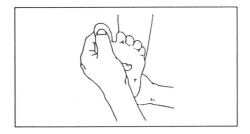

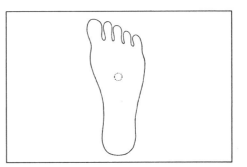

3. Massage the entire big toe to relieve tension and tiredness.

4. Massaging the inner aspect of the toe (pituitary) may stimulate the uterus to work more effectively during labor.

5. Grasp both feet with your thumbs pressed into the solar plexus region. Visualize calm, peaceful energy, flowing between you. You may feel tingling in your hands. Add this to the cleansing breath at the end of contractions. Keeps you both calm and centered.

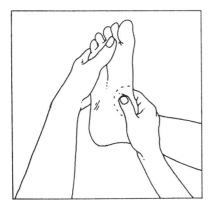

6. Massage adrenal glands to relieve stress.

7. Do this technique to stimulate urination; can be done hourly during labor to encourage her to empty her bladder.

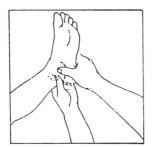

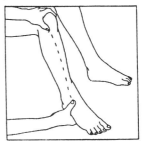

8. Massage the inner aspect of the lower ankle to ease back pain and help the uterus to work efficiently. Smooth any bumps you feel. This one is important for labor; do it as often as possible.

9. Massage the lateral aspect of the leg from the knee down to stimulate her circulation.

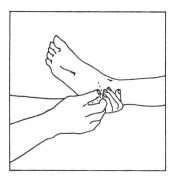

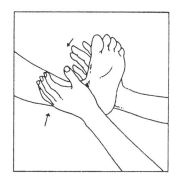

10. Massage the lower heel to relieve sciatic nerve and hip pain, which is common during labor.

11. Promote relaxation by placing her heel between both your palms and rubbing vigorously back and forth—a good way to end a contraction.

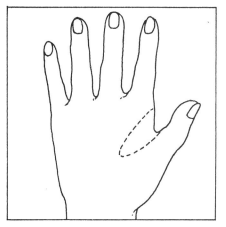

12. For a very calming effect, place your finger on her forehead with your middle finger in the hollow of her throat. This may help if she starts to lose control during labor. With practice, she can condition herself to think calmly when you do this.

13. To control nausea during labor, massage the top side of her hand between the thumb and first finger. Keep this one in mind for the transition stage of labor.

If you really get into the acupressure techniques and want some feedback, consult a reflexologist, who'll be happy to give you some further tips. Reflexologists suggest two to four professional treatments before labor to enhance your home treatments. Usually the cost is relatively inexpensive.

THE FULL MOON AND OTHER MYTHS

When you find yourself at the point where you're sick of being pregnant, you can get a little crazy. You start looking for good omens such as a full moon to pin your hopes on. Scientific analysis hasn't found the lunar phase to have any bearing on the numbers of deliveries. Sorry.

More labors tend to start during the nighttime hours, but the actual deliveries are equally divided between days and nights.

Your mother might offer to help by giving you a therapeutic dose of castor oil to start labor. Just say no; all you get is intestinal cramps and diarrhea. It takes your mind off being pregnant temporarily, but it won't put you into labor.

If it has been 7 years or more since you last had a baby, you may be told that your labor will be like a first one. Not exactly joyous news. Luckily, that old belief hasn't panned out. Generally, you can plan on getting credit for previous time served—hopefully with a shorter labor than the first one.

Many women worry when their water breaks before labor starts. You've heard all those tales about "dry birth." Not to worry—there's no such thing. Labor usually starts within hours, and you make new amniotic fluid all the time.

THE EGO AND I—MIND AND MATTER

Labor and delivery bring psychological as well as physical stress. In the last few weeks of pregnancy, the irrevocability of the coming event of labor crowds out the usual everyday concerns. You'll find yourself becoming more

and more preoccupied with thoughts of labor and babies. Don't be alarmed if you have dreams in which you just delivered puppies instead of a baby or you had a baby but somehow seemed to have misplaced him. Most pregnant women have rather weird dreams those last few weeks. Your preoccupation will center on the inevitability of the birth, the unknown, and fear of losing control during labor. It's a very sobering thought to realize that your uterus has a mind of its own and is in control, not you. You're along for the ride. You find yourself hoping your uterus knows what it's doing and can do it right.

SIGNS AND SYMPTOMS OF LABOR

Whether you're having your fifth baby or your first, deciding whether or not you're in labor can be confusing. There are only two real signs of labor:

1. Regular, strong contractions lasting 40 to 60 seconds.

2. Cervical dilatation (the cervix opening to let the baby pass through). Dilatation is measured in centimeters, from 1 to 10.

Contractions

The only sign *you* can actually use to evaluate your labor is the regularity of your contractions. When you get to the hospital, the doctor or nurse will confirm your "diagnosis" by examining you vaginally to see if your cervix is dilating. Is this the *real thing*? To decide, look for three things in your contractions. These are exactly the questions your doctor will ask when you call:

1. How far apart are they?

2. How strong are they?

3. How long do they last?

How far apart? Measure the time between your contractions from the beginning of one to the beginning of the next. Your contraction begins when you feel your abdomen tightening, not when you first feel it start in your back.

How strong? Everyone's pain tolerance is different. Some people become hysterical over a hangnail, while others can smile from a bed of nails. Gauging

165

your contractions by the degree of discomfort you feel can be unreliable. To determine how strong your contractions are, which means how hard your uterus is working, follow these simple guidelines:

1. Place your hand at the top of your abdomen, which is where your uterus contracts, even though you feel the sensation in your lower abdomen.

2. With your fingertips, press on your abdomen to feel how firm it is.

Mild contractions. These contractions are slightly uncomfortable. They're probably not unlike the false contractions you probably experienced during your pregnancy. An easy way to measure their strength is to put one hand on your abdomen and the other on the end of your nose to compare the resistance. A mild contraction feels similar to the end of your nose. There's something there, but you can still push it in.

Moderate contractions. These contractions make you frown and pay attention, but they're not too bad. When you check your abdomen for resistance, it feels more like your chin than your nose. It feels a little firmer, but not that much.

Strong contractions. These contractions are toe curlers, unless you're the bed of nails type. You definitely have to stop what you're doing until they go away. They feel as firm as your forehead, just like a rock. You can't push your abdomen in at all.

How long? To determine how long your contractions are lasting, start counting the seconds when you feel your abdomen tightening, not when you start feeling the discomfort in your back. Stop counting when your abdomen starts to relax, not when the contraction is totally gone. Errors in timing are common. You want to count only the number of seconds during which the baby's head is being pushed against the cervix and trying to dilate it. Backache doesn't count because the contraction hasn't started working yet. When the uterus starts to relax, the pressure of the baby's head is also relaxing. The contraction isn't working anymore. Even at their longest and strongest, contractions usually last only 60 seconds.

POPULAR—AND LESS RELIABLE— SIGNS OF LABOR

The following signs of impending labor are highly variable and unreliable. Only one, the rupture of membranes, requires a call to the doctor.

Bloody Show

Slight, bloody discharge is a highly unreliable indication of labor. The small blood vessels in the cervix become very fragile as your pregnancy progresses. Some common causes of bloody show are:

1. **Vaginal exam.** You can count on some bloody discharge whenever your doctor checks your cervix. The discharge may even last several days, turning from bright pink to dark brown. Worry not.

2. **Intercourse** may do the same thing to your cervix as the vaginal exam.

3. As your cervix thins and "ripens" during the last several weeks of pregnancy, some of the small, fragile vessels within the cervix rupture and produce the **bloody tinged mucus** you find in your underwear.

It's common to mistake the bloody show for true bleeding, which is an obstetrical emergency. True bleeding is bright red. If it gushes out, runs down your leg, and fills your shoe, that's bleeding. If you have any doubts, call your doctor. Be ready to describe the color and estimate the amount you lost in teaspoons, or cups. If you're wearing a sanitary pad, is it soaked through?

Mucus Plug

You can lose your mucus plug several weeks before your labor begins. It's an absolutely useless indicator of labor. Forget you even have one.

Water Bag Breaks—Rupture of Membranes

Usually, when your water breaks, whether it's a gush or a trickle, your contractions aren't far behind. If you aren't having contractions but you're losing watery fluid, call your doctor. Amniotic fluid has a very distinctive smell, and a sensitive nose can distinguish it from urine.

Once the membrane surrounding your baby breaks, the barrier to infection is gone. It's standard practice to have you go to the hospital to await labor. If you're at term, the goal is to see you in labor before 24 hours elapse, which tends to lessen the chance of infection. *Remember:* Once your water breaks, absolutely no intercourse, tub baths, or douching.

WHAT TO EAT

Once you think you're in labor, *don't eat.* During labor, your stomach takes much longer to digest food. The heavier the food, the better your chance of vomiting during the transition phase at 8-centimeter dilatation. If you succumb to temptation and make the forbidden pit stop for a chiliburger, you won't have to ask "Where's the beef?" You'll be wearing it. Have pity on your labor nurse and any other innocent bystander.

Instead, stick to light soups (chicken broth), crackers, Jello, apple juice, natural sodas, and weak tea. You're going to be working hard. You need to replace the fluids and energy you expend during labor. Dehydration can keep your uterus from working efficiently and make you even more fatigued. After delivery, you can indulge yourself shamelessly with any kind of food that strikes your fancy—you earned it.

THE WARM UP: PRELABOR

There are three stages to labor. The beginning of the first phase of the first stage is called prelabor, prodromal labor, or latent phase. It's the warm-up for the real thing, called active labor. Contractions actually begin several weeks before you get to the point where you realize something is going

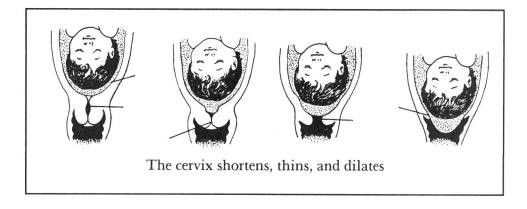

The cervix shortens, thins, and dilates

on here. This is the "false" labor people talk about. You may have contractions irregularly for a few hours at a time over several days, but they keep going away. This time they don't. The contractions are mild to moderate. The cervix continues to thin out, shorten, soften, and move to a more forward position. For primiparas (first baby), cervical dilatation will still be less than 3 centimeters. Multiparas can be running around dilated 2 to 3 centimeters without contractions. Mother nature gives you points for reenlisting. On average, multiparas complete the latent phase in less than 14 hours, primiparas in less than 20 hours.

During the latent phase, the tendency is to get very excited because you're on the verge of the big event. Try to contain yourself. At this point, it's best to carry on as usual. Don't jump the gun and alert all your support troops yet. Be aware of your contractions but not fixated on them. Keep a balance between activity and rest. This is the time to read, meditate, and visualize your cervix getting ripe and ready. Alternate between walking and sitting. *Calm, centered* and *patient* are your operative words. Eat lightly and drink fluids so you don't get dehydrated.

Sometimes the latent phase lasts longer than normal and you find yourself becoming exhausted, discouraged, and feeling like a failure. Mild panic sets in. As the hours go by, you become more anxious. Your cervix just refuses to "open sesame." What's happening?

Several factors set up a vicious cycle that sabotages your progress. Anxiety produces two hormones whose effects on contractions oppose each other. One hormone stimulates the uterus; the other inhibits it. The result is frequent but mediocre contractions, although they won't feel that way to you. Exhaustion knocks out your coping mechanisms. If dehydration sets in, that also decreases contractions. What do you do for a prolonged latent phase? As a general rule, this isn't the time to get aggressive by breaking your water or starting oxytocin to stimulate labor. Amniotomy before 4-centimeter dilatation may even lengthen this phase. Not all doctors agree on the best approach. It only makes sense, if you're exhausted, that you and your uterus need some rest. One approach that works is to give you some demerol or morphine to knock out your anxiety, which spaces out your contractions. You can rest and maybe even sleep for a while. Even though you sleep, your uterus doesn't. Demerol stimulates the uterus to work more efficiently. It's not unusual to wake up and find you're in booming labor. With a few hours of much needed rest or sleep, you're ready to lick your weight in wildcats—and finally have this baby!

IT'S THE REAL THING—D DAY

This is it! You're probably excited, anxious to get it over with, and wondering if you really want to go through with it after all. If you've had childbirth classes, you might feel as if the final exam is here. You mentally review all those exercises you wish you'd practiced more diligently. You've got performance anxiety.

What to Expect

If this is your first baby, the nurses will refer to you as a primip. After the first baby, you're a multipara or multip. During labor, there are a lot of "usuallys" but no guarantees. For instance, multips usually have shorter labors than primips. The different phases and stages of labor move along at a quicker pace for the multip. Mother Nature gives you points for experience.

Your progress is compared against averages. A multip usually shows cervical progress of 1.5 centimeters per hour and a primip 1.2 centimeters per hour once you're in active labor. The averages are a way of alerting those entrusted with your care if you've "fallen off" the normal labor curve and your lack of progress needs further evaluation. Usually, everything moves along on schedule, with variations on the main theme. Keep in mind that everyone, and every labor, is different. If you're extremely compulsive and try to ensure that your labor fits the textbook picture of "normal labor," you could make yourself crazy—and everyone around you. The key word is "progress." Be optimistic and go with the flow as long as you're progressing, however quickly or slowly. Practice what behavioral psychologists call "positive expectancy." If you believe you'll do well, you will.

Routines and Rituals

Tribal and cultural rites have been an important part of the birthing process since recorded time. The laboring woman has been the subject of a multitude of bizarre and occasionally (to others) humorous practices. Here's a look at some historical routines and rituals for childbirth.

Preps and enemas.   In the childbed fever days of the early 1900s, the routine admission for the mother-to-be was like a holdover from the Spanish Inquisition.

- Women were stripped of their personal belongings.

- Heads were cleansed with kerosene, ether, or ammonia.

- Charity patients had their heads shaved. The rich got clipped.

- Vaginal douches of bichloride of mercury were given during and after labor.

As if that weren't enough, nurses had to bathe regularly and change their uniforms once in a while.

You've come a long way.   By the 1960s, things had improved very slowly. Preps and enemas were still routine. Everyone was shaved balder than a billiard. The 3H enema (high, hot, and a hell of a lot) was the sacred ritual. It supposedly had magical powers to speed up labor. Actually, it was a two-for-one deal: You had intestinal cramps to go along with uterine cramps. But it didn't speed up labor.

In the 1970s, people began questioning the need for routine preps and enemas. It seems shaving didn't prevent infection after all. Enemas scaled down to a trickle compared to the old 3H. Studies proved that fecal contamination was fairly common, regardless of enemas. It didn't make any difference anyway.

Eighty years have gone by and things are improving. Some doctors still order preps and enemas, but every year fewer and fewer doctors do so. Most women recall the enema as the worst experience of labor. If you don't want an enema, and your doctor forgot and ordered one, utter the magic word: "diarrhea." The enema will disappear quicker than smoke on a windy day. Doctors and nurses aren't fond of being sprayed by liquid leftovers during delivery. If you do want an enema, they give very small amounts of fluid now, just enough to clear the lower bowel. They no longer clean everything from the tonsils on down. That's progress.

To avoid being shaved, clip your pubic hair very short before you go into labor. Most doctors don't order preps anymore.

Chips and sips. The only hors d'oeuvres you get in labor are ice chips and sips of water. Your stomach empties very slowly during labor. If you guzzle lots of liquids, they just sit in your stomach waiting for 8 centimeters. You'll be busy enough without having to worry about where the emesis basin is kept.

Snip and stitch—episiotomy. An episiotomy is an incision made in the perineum, the skin and tissue between the vagina and rectum. Episiotomies make more room for the baby's head and can hasten delivery. Of the three types of episiotomies, the most common is the midline, a straight incision extending from the vagina to, but not into, the rectum. As a rule, the midline episiotomy causes very little discomfort as it heals.

The mediolateral incision, which was popular about 30 years ago, gave episiotomies a bad name. This type of episiotomy, which is at an angle from the vagina, has fallen into disfavor with good reason: It's very painful while healing. You could always tell who had a mediolateral—she walked stiff-legged and needed three pillows just to sit.

The third type, the episioproctotomy, is the midline incision that goes into the rectum. Perineums are like people: Some are short, some medium, some long. If you have a midline incision or tear, your chances of having it extend through your rectum are greater than with the mediolateral incision. Certain situations predispose you to an episioproctotomy: a large baby and a short perineum; a breech delivery, where you need all the room you can get; and the baby's shoulder getting stuck coming out—you need more room in a hurry. This type of incision isn't routine, but sometimes it's necessary.

The stitches used to repair episiotomies usually dissolve in 10 to 14 days. Don't bother asking how many stitches you have; you won't get a straight answer. Doctor's don't count them. He puts you back together in layers—muscle, fascia, and skin; each layer has stitches.

The issues and your tissues. In years past, deliveries and episiotomies were like love and marriage; the two always went together. In the last two decades, consumers questioned the need for routine episiotomy. Consumer pressure resulted in the medical establishment rethinking their position.

172

There have been many mythical arguments in favor of episiotomy. Doctors believed that if you delivered without an episiotomy, your vagina would be permanently stretched and intercourse would be less satisfying.

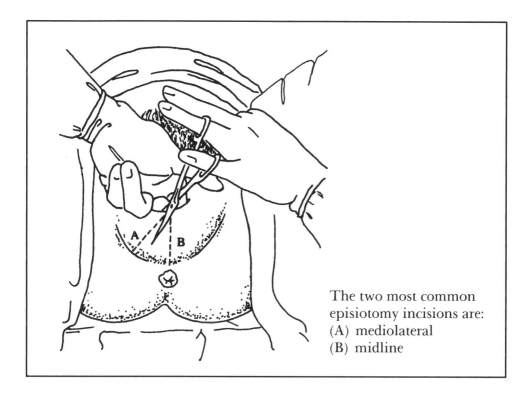

The two most common episiotomy incisions are:
(A) mediolateral
(B) midline

We've all heard about the famous "husband stitch" that transforms you into a virgin again and gives your husband something to look forward to after the postpartum checkup. No one really proved these old dictums true, and the experts agreed that routine episiotomy wasn't necessary. Keep in mind that the emphasis is on routine, not episiotomy.

There's agreement that some situations warrant an episiotomy. The preterm baby is better off not battering his head against the perineum. His soft head doesn't tolerate the process very well. When you're too pooped to push anymore, an episiotomy is a welcome relief. If your perineum looks like it will tear from here to Texas, an episiotomy is the humane thing to do. When there's evidence of fetal distress and the baby needs delivering in a hurry, episiotomy does speed things up.

In the final analysis, the real issue isn't the episiotomy but whether you have stitches. Not having an episiotomy doesn't guarantee that you won't have stitches. Delivering a baby over an intact perineum requires infinite patience for both you and your doctor. With your first baby, you may have to push for an extra hour to stretch your perineum enough to deliver without an incision. At that point, you may not be willing to spend the extra time pushing. If the baby's heart rate decreases as a result of the prolonged pressure on his head, everyone becomes anxious to get you delivered.

Discuss your preference with your doctor. What is her routine, and how does she feel about the issue? If it's really important to you, a few essential factors will increase your chances of delivering without stitches or an episiotomy. Ask your doctor if it'll be possible to deliver without having your legs in stirrups. With your legs in the air and shoved back, your chances of tearing and/or having an episiotomy increase. In that position, your perineum stretches upward, which doesn't allow much "give." You can further decrease your chances by pushing without holding your breath or bearing down strenuously. A more gentle pushing eases the baby down, letting the tissues stretch gradually and lessening the chance of a tear.

Realistically, it's impossible to predict what will happen because too many variables are involved. The size of your baby and the ability of your tissues to stretch and relax are unknowns until the time comes. Your ability to push diminishes with fatigue if you have a long labor. The circumstances are too numerous to list. It all boils down to being flexible and trusting your doctor to make the appropriate decision at the time. Most women who have a regular midline episiotomy agree that it's no big deal. The incision heals rapidly and the discomfort is minimal—you don't need pillows to sit.

With or without an episiotomy, a good way to strengthen your perineal muscles is the Kegel's exercise, also known as the perineal squeeze. You do this isometric exercise by alternately contracting and relaxing the pubococcygeal (vaginal/perineal) muscle. This is the muscle that lets you stop the flow during urination. Contract your vaginal muscles to the count of 10 and then relax them for several seconds. Repeat the process two or three times several times a day. An alternative to the Kegel's exercise is the Vagette,* a plastic electrical device you can order through your doctor. Inserted into the vagina, it causes your muscles to contract rhythmically. You can set the amount of stimulation and increase it over time to tighten those muscles. The Vagette isn't recommended during pregnancy, but it can be used after you deliver.

---

* Vagette 76, Mfg. Myodynamics, Inc.: Carson, California.

The perineal squeeze promotes healing of your stitches by improving circulation. Vaginal tone will bounce back more rapidly. As years go by, it may help prevent the "dribbles" (urinary incontinence) when you cough or sneeze. Last, but not least, it will improve your sex life even without the husband stitch. Kegel's exercise is beneficial during pregnancy, after delivery, anytime.

I'VE GOT YOU UNDER MY SKIN

Intravenous Fluids (IVs)

IVs aren't a routine with most doctors. They reserve them for special occasions. If you show up in labor with your tongue looking like a baked Alaska and your urine the color of molasses, you're dehydrated. Lack of fluids can affect your labor. You need an IV to fill your tank and keep your uterus humming along. Bleeding, labor induction, regional anesthetics, and fetal distress are other reasons for starting an IV.

An IV is much easier to tolerate these days. A needle still goes through the skin and into the vein, but a fine plastic tube slips over the needle and stays in the vein. The needle comes out. You don't have the discomfort or worry about the needle. Once the tube is in the vein, you don't feel it. You can use your arm with comfort.

FETAL MONITORING

A Farewell Hug

One function of the placenta is to act as the baby's lungs. Blood, carrying oxygen, travels from the placenta through the umbilical cord to the baby. Uterine contractions force blood out of the placenta. For 40 to 60 seconds, the baby is being squeezed by the uterus. Tolerating the intermittent lack of oxygen is stressful to the baby. Most babies handle the stress very well, but those who can't tolerate even the short periods of decreased oxygen become distressed. The fetal monitor is a way to evaluate how well the baby is handling the effects of the contractions.

I'm O.K., You're O.K.

The fetal monitor provides an ongoing chronicle of the relationship between the baby's heartbeat and the uterine contractions. When the monitor tracing is normal, it's 99 percent predictive of a good outcome—very reassuring to all. However, if the baby is having difficulty tolerating the contractions, then early intervention to prevent further problems is very important. Early, subtle clues from the heart rate pattern can often be identified and therapeutic measures taken to counteract the problem.

It's important to know what the monitor can and can't do. Fetal monitoring tells us if the baby's central nervous system is functioning adequately as reflected by the heart rate pattern. It only tells us that right now the baby is receiving adequate oxygen for the central nervous system to function normally. Fetal monitoring can't prevent or detect neurological problems such as cerebral palsy (CP). Most cases of CP aren't preventable or related to labor and delivery events.

Accurate interpretation of the baby's heart rate pattern can prevent an unnecessary cesarean when the tracing is reassuring. Fetal distress accounts for less than 5 percent of the cesarean birthrate. The monitor does just what it intends to do: identify the babies who need help and those who don't.

External Monitoring Method

The baby's heartbeat and the uterine contractions are recorded by two belts, with small sensors, fastened around your abdomen. The information records continuously on a strip of paper from the machine. The ultrasound transducer picks up the movement of the baby's heart and transforms it into a heartbeat sound. The monitor shows the heart rate as a jiggly line at the top of the tracing paper. The transducer may "lose" a signal temporarily if the baby moves out of the range of the ultrasound beams. If the heart rate suddenly isn't recording anything or seems to be jumping all over the paper, it just means that the transducer needs readjusting. Call the nurse, who'll relocate to the best spot for recording.

The toco-transducer is a simple pressure device that records the contractions. The "toco" can accurately measure the time between contractions and their length but not their strength. If you tighten the belt, the contractions look like whoppers. If the belt is loose, even the toe curlers look like mild contractions. The contractions record on the bottom of the tracing paper and look like little hills.

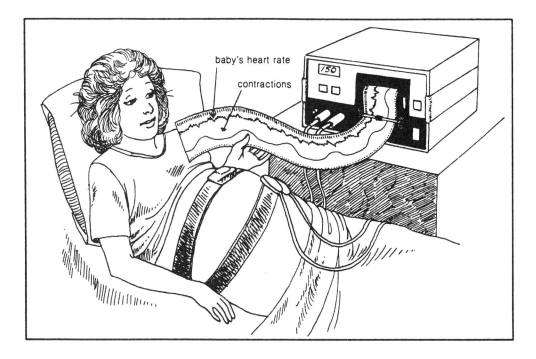

baby's heart rate

contractions

The technology for the external monitor has vastly improved over the last few years. The newer monitors can produce a tracing that closely resembles the information you can obtain from an internal tracing. The improved quality of the external tracing reduces the need, in many cases, for artificially rupturing membranes to apply the internal electrode to record the baby's heart rate.

The major drawback to the external method is the discomfort of the belts. They need frequent readjusting if you or the baby moves. On the positive side, no risks have been associated with the use of the external monitor.

Internal Monitor Method

The internal method accurately records the baby's heart rate and moment-to-moment changes in each heartbeat. A thin, wire electrode is inserted just under the baby's scalp (much like sticking a straight pin into a callus on your finger). The procedure probably is no more uncomfortable for the baby than the contractions.

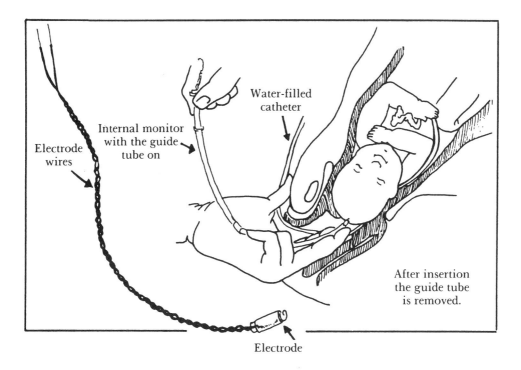

Electrode wires

Internal monitor with the guide tube on

Water-filled catheter

After insertion the guide tube is removed.

Electrode

The strength of the contractions can be electronically measured with a soft pliable tube (catheter) placed in the cervix beside the baby's head. During contractions, the monitor records the amount of pressure exerted on the sensitive diaphragm. The internal catheter can be used when the water bag is broken. Evaluating the strength of contractions is particularly important if your labor isn't progressing at a steady rate and/or your labor must be augmented by oxytocin.

In addition to providing more accurate data, the internal method is more comfortable . . . no belts. Internal monitoring alone doesn't cause uterine infections. The original concern is unfounded. Women with prolonged rupture of membranes and a long labor are at higher risk for infection. They're more likely to be examined more often and end up with an intrauterine catheter to evaluate labor. The culprit is prolonged rupture of the membranes, not the catheter.

Who Needs It?

Pregnant women fall into two categories: low- and high-risk. The low-risk woman has no preexisting medical or pregnancy-related problems. During labor she doesn't develop any unforeseen complications such as prolapse of the baby's umbilical cord or premature separation of the placenta.

The high-risk pregnancy includes a number of maternal conditions that could potentially affect the baby's ability to tolerate labor, including

- Preeclampsia (pregnancy induced hypertension)

- Diabetes

- Chronic hypertension

- Postdates pregnancy (42 plus weeks)

- Preterm labor (less then 37 weeks)

- Breech presentation

Among the situations during labor when the baby's heart rate needs closer surveillance are meconium staining of the amniotic fluid and suspicious changes in the heart rate detected with a stethoscope.

Continuous fetal monitoring doesn't seem necessary for the low-risk mother who remains in that category for her entire labor. The ACOG feels that just listening to the fetal heart rate with a stethoscope is acceptable monitoring for the low-risk pregnancy. That sounds simple enough, but they require the nurse to listen so often that she becomes a continuous human monitor. The vast majority of obstetrical units don't have the one-on-one nursing personnel to adhere to those standards.

Many labor departments do what is called a baseline strip for the low-risk clientele. A 20-minute monitor tracing is done on admission and repeated every hour or so. This seems like a reasonable approach.

Excuse the Intrusion

The use of the fetal monitor isn't incompatible with an intimate, harmonious birth experience. A monitor won't ruin your experience, but insensitive personnel can. If monitoring becomes necessary, the reason for its use should be explained in advance. The nurse should show you and your husband how it works and keep you informed of the information the monitor is providing. Being confined to bed is unnecessary. You can be monitored standing at the bedside or sitting in a chair by the monitor. The monitor can also be disconnected long enough for you to go to the bathroom.

When properly informed of the necessity, and educated regarding its use, expectant couples have a positive experience with the fetal monitor. It's a help, not a hindrance.

WATER, WATER, EVERYWHERE— AMNIOTOMY

The status of your water bag (membranes) can affect your labor. There doesn't seem to be much doubt that after 4 centimeters, an ineffective contraction pattern can be improved by artificially rupturing membranes (AROM). When the contraction pattern is already effective and normal progress is being made, AROM serves no real purpose. It may speed up labor slightly. Are there any benefits to a slightly faster labor? There don't seem to be any for the baby. The baby tolerates labor better when the water cushions his head and umbilical cord during contractions. After delivery, the babies who had their membranes unruptured had higher oxygen levels, but this isn't a serious difference.

TIPS FOR THE COACH

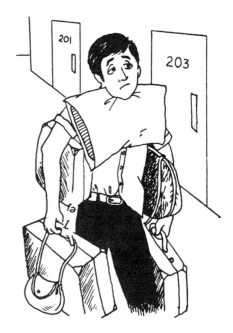

Fathers at one time were trained in the Butterfly McQueen/Blanche DuBois school of support for mom during labor. They paced the waiting room wringing their hands and mumbling "I don't know nothin' bout birthin' babies, Mizz Scarlett!" Their wives had to "rely upon the kindness of strangers" for their comfort and support during labor. Things have improved since comedian Bob Newhart described the role of the expectant father as being "the lowest form of life," where "even maintenance men will have nothing to do with you." Attitudes and rules change. In the 1960s if you wanted to be present during the birth of your baby, you were accused of being a "pervert." Now, if you don't want to be there at the moment of birth, you're an insensitive clod. Not true!

180

Labor is stressful for you too. Your role has become one of protector, comforter, and coach. Prepared childbirth classes help but can't totally allay your own fears and anxiety. You have to deal with your own feelings as you watch your wife in pain. Involving yourself in your role helps you keep your perspective. Don't be surprised if you find yourself, initially, a little embarrassed to coach your wife in the breathing exercises you both learned. You wonder how you're going to remember everything they taught you in class. Performance anxiety is normal.

Your role as coach actually begins well before labor. Read this entire section on labor and become familiar with the acupressure, relaxation, and visualization techniques and the various positions and medications available during labor. Study the illustrations and learn the acupressure techniques you think you might use. Practice them for at least 2 months before her due date—every day, if possible. Become familiar with her visualization and relaxation techniques so you can recall them for her during labor if she needs the help. It can be your way of helping her select those coping aids at appropriate times. Bring her favorite relaxation tapes along. Whatever works! For those times when she seems to be losing her cool, use the pressure points that promote a calm and peaceful feeling.

During the active phase of labor, as her concentration becomes more intense, you may feel as if she doesn't need you. Be assured that she does; she just isn't interested in small talk. She won't be able to cope with anything but limited conversation and direction. Keep your sentences brief, and use

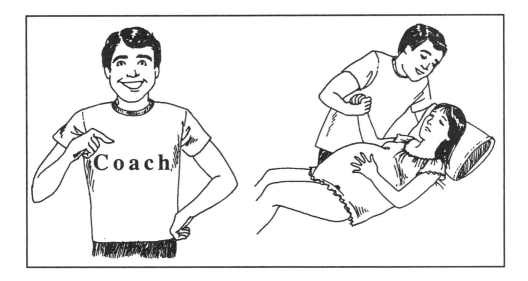

positive words for directions. For instance, say "Relax," instead of "Don't tense up"; "Blow," not "Don't push." Keep your voice soft and your head cool if she flies off the handle with some undeleted expletives. Even the most fragile flower of womanhood can temporarily develop the vocabulary of a truck driver at this time, much to her husband's horror.

You can help keep her calm by ensuring that only one person at a time is providing verbal direction. Too much input from too many sources can confuse and distract her, especially during the second stage. When you have a lot of support people, they can get excited. Everyone can be trying to cheer her on at the same time. Check with her periodically to see if she's still comfortable with more than just you in the labor room. She may decide that she can't cope with too big an audience. You can run interference for her and send everyone out for snacks. If you find yourself in the situation where she isn't progressing, that may be the signal for the snack break for the support group. She can get performance anxiety, which affects her labor.

Most importantly, what she needs from you is support and understanding, not goal setting. This isn't a championship game. If she finds she needs medication, don't try to talk her out of it, or worse, tell her she can't have it. She's depending on you to look out for her.

These days, everyone expects you to be present at the moment of birth. Some men just can't handle the intensity of the experience and would rather not be there. It doesn't mean you're insensitive or don't love your wife. If you're one of those who'd rather go 10 rounds with the heavyweight champ than watch a delivery, tell her. You can still be there for her in labor, but when the big moment arrives, you can step outside or close your eyes— whatever seems most suitable at the time. You can always change your mind, but at least you have the option if you want it.

Don't forget to be good to yourself. Periodically, you may need a break after hours of coaching. Ask her labor nurse, or other support person, to give you a break. They can stay with her while you take a much needed breather. Try some relaxation techniques on yourself and eat something. You convey peace and confidence to your wife through your sense of well-being and soothing touch. Consider having a support person present for *you*, someone who's optimistic, upbeat, and calm to cheer *you*.

GETTING SERIOUS: ACTIVE LABOR

During labor, your body and psyche head in opposite directions. As your body opens up to allow the baby to move into the world, your ego heads for cover. It closes itself to the outside world like a flower. You withdraw into yourself more and more as labor advances, into an altered state of consciousness. Some women describe the sensation as feeling like being at the bottom of a well. When people talk to you, you feel very removed. Your concentration on the task at hand is very intense. You become very irritable if someone interferes with that concentration, particularly during a contraction. You find yourself attaching to one voice for support or direction and excluding all others. That one voice provides a psychological anchor amid the storm of uterine activity and intense physical sensations. You're quite willing to delegate decision making for less important details to those around you.

Physical Changes

The second part of the first stage is the active phase of labor. By now your cervix will be at least 3 centimeters dilated. Your contractions have graduated from the menstrual-like cramps and backache to a more rhythmic regularity and strength. There are no drums rolling or trumpets playing to announce your progression to the active phase; it's just more of the same, only more so. Your contractions are longer, stronger, and more predictable in timing, occurring anywhere from 3 to 5 minutes apart and lasting 45 to 60 seconds. Bloody mucus (show) tells you your cervix is changing.

Contractions increase in intensity during the active phase. If you're curious about the feeling and mood of labor, listen to Ravel's "Bolero" for a preview; it best captures the symphony of uterine activity. The same basic melody repeats over and over with increasing intensity and tension. In the same way, contractions become more demanding and intense as they continue methodically toward culmination—the expulsion of the baby.

ALTERED STATES—ANALGESIA

Thirty years ago, when you came through the labor room door, you got a sleeping pill, a tranquilizer, and a narcotic, usually demerol. A touch of scopalomine added to your labor "cocktail" drove you over the edge. It was a nightmare called "Twilight sleep," where drugged women lost all inhibitions, battered their nurse, and ripped off their bedclothes during labor. Scopalomine induces amnesia, so the women forgot the previous events of the drug-induced haze. The bruises on the nurses were the only telltale evidence.

In these modern times, the approach to pain relief in labor has changed. The use of narcotics hasn't disappeared, but it has declined. Only the

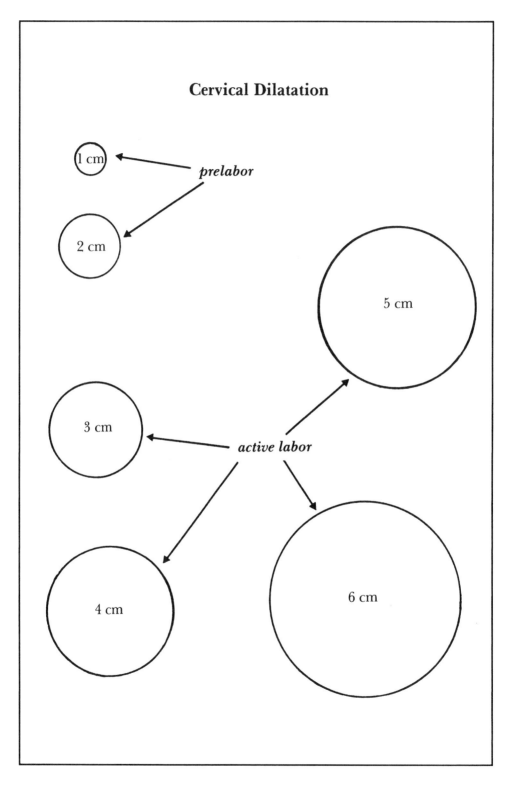

old-timers remember scopalomine. You don't have to worry about being forced into a drug-induced stupor today.

During the "natural" childbirth era, pain medication acquired a bad name, unjustly. Doctors now order much smaller amounts of narcotics so that you and the baby can stay alert. Use of sleeping pills and tranquilizers is infrequent, if they're used at all. They really don't have any advantages in labor; they make both you and the baby groggy, and they don't help the pain.

Pain-relief drugs such as demerol and stadol are given intravenously (IV) or intramuscularly (IM). With the IV route, smaller amounts (see Summary of Labor Medications table) avoid the risk of respiratory depression for both you and the baby. The IV route also avoids prolonged drug effects. Generally, respiratory depression isn't a problem for either of you unless you receive large amounts, such as 50 milligrams of demerol every hour for more than 6 hours or a 100-milligram IV in one big dose. Doses of 25 to 50 milligrams given, even within 1 hour of delivery, don't depress the baby, as previously thought. Another important myth to dispel: narcotics *don't* slow labor. They actually have no detectable effect on contractions. Demerol may have a slightly stimulating effect if you receive oxytocin at the same time. Some narcotics can't be "mixed and matched." For instance, you can't give stadol and then administer demerol for the next dose because they cancel each other out and you get no pain relief.

DO-IT-YOURSELF DRUGS

The newest development in pain management for the laboring woman is intravenously self-administered demerol, called PCA (patient-controlled analgesia). PCA has been used for some time for the management of postoperative pain. It should work as well during labor. Some obstetrical units are testing the safety and effectiveness of this method, and so far, the results look good. The amount of drug left in the baby's circulation after birth was significantly lower in the self-infused group. Patient satisfaction scores for this group were also higher than the ones for the groups using traditional methods.

AVOID ANXIETY

Anxiety and tension are your greatest enemies in labor. They have a negative effect on contractions, which in an anxious mother may be frequent but not effective enough to promote normal progress in labor. See how it goes

SUMMARY OF LABOR MEDICATIONS

Type/Name/Dose	Benefits	Precautions
Narcotics		

Demerol
  25–50 mg IV
  every 2 hr
  50–100 mg IM
  every 3–4 hr
	Does not slow labor.
	Good pain relief.
	Decreases anxiety.
	Allows sleep between
	  contractions.
		Nausea and vomiting if
		  given too rapidly.
		Possible respiratory de-
		  pression if given in
		  large doses.

Stadol
  1–2 mg IV
  or IM
	Less respiratory
	  depressant effect
	  than other
	  narcotics.
		Cannot be given before
		  demerol (makes it
		  ineffective).

Morphine
  2–3 mg IV
  10–15 mg IM
	Good pain relief.
	No effect on labor.
	Used to treat
	  prolonged latent
	  phase of labor.
		Respiratory depression
		  with high doses.
		Not routinely used
		  for active labor.

Nubain
  10 mg IM or
  IV
	Good pain relief.	Can produce respiratory
		  depression in baby.

Talwin
Ketamine
		Not recommended. Poten-
		  tial psychotic reac-
		  tion and dream
		  disturbance.

Antianxiety		

Vistaril
  50–100 mg IM
  50–100 mg
  orally
	Enhances relaxation
	  in early labor.
		IM injection painful.
		  Oral administration
		  preferred.

SUMMARY OF LABOR MEDICATIONS

Type/Name/ Dose	Benefits	Precautions
Antianxiety Valium Sparine Phenergan Largon	Decreases anxiety.	Not recommended for labor. Causes depression in newborn.
Sedatives Seconal Nembutal Chloral hydrate	None.	Drowsiness. Depression in newborn.

for you in labor. If you're able to keep on top of the contractions and feel good about how you are doing—great! If you're giving it your best shot but feel as if you're losing control, ask for a little medication. It doesn't indicate failure; it's just one of those coping aids in your birthing bag. It's there if you need it.

TOTAL RELIEF: REGIONAL ANESTHESIA

Regional anesthesia during labor numbs particular areas of your body to relieve pain. The epidural and spinal blocks for labor and delivery generally numb you from the waist down. The medication is the same type your dentist uses to numb your gums. In labor, it numbs the other end of your anatomy. You no longer feel contractions or pressure from the baby's head on your bottom (perineum).

In past years, epidural anesthesia, while still used, lost some favor with both consumers and doctors. The desire to labor without drugs led to a decline in use by the consumer. With the higher doses of medication used then, complete anesthesia resulted. The mother was unable to push effectively, and delivery with forceps was common. It took several hours for the anesthesia to wear off. You had to stay in bed. Bladder dysfunction was a common problem.

A new approach to epidural anesthesia eliminates some of the previous problems. With low-dose, continuous epidural infusion, lack of motor control isn't a problem. Now you can be numb but still move your legs and push when the time comes. There's much less need for forceps. A new twist to the epidural is to inject a narcotic such as morphine or fentanyl instead of the local numbing agent into the epidural space. You get good pain relief without all the systemic side effects to you and the baby.

If you have no interest in experiencing labor pain from start to finish, epidural is the only way to go because it provides wonderful relief when it's effective. That's the upside. Here's the downside.

If you have an epidural, you'll also have an IV, the epidural tube taped to your back, a fetal monitor, continuous pulse and blood pressure monitors, a blood-measuring device (oximeter) attached to your finger like a clothespin, and possibly a urinary catheter. It's a high-tech trade-off. You get total relief most of the time, but a bunch of tubes to go with it. It's also not uncommon for contractions to decrease temporarily after an epidural. You might have to add oxytocin stimulation to your list. If you don't want any pain, you probably won't care about the tubes. It's your decision.

Usually, you can have your epidural at 4-centimeter dilatation. It can be very uncomfortable to sit up and hold still while the needle and tube are being placed. It's possible to have the anesthesiologist put the tube in earlier in labor and administer only the test dose. Once you receive the loading dose, you get pain relief in about 15 to 20 minutes. First labors are the best candidates for this type of anesthesia; after that, labor often progresses too quickly for the anesthetic to take effect.

If you think you want an epidural, let your doctor know in advance. Some hospitals offer 24-hour service, others don't. It can also be expensive. Check out the possibilities in advance so you can make your plans.

Spinal anesthesia was very popular in the 1960s. It works well, but you can't have it until delivery is a push or two away. It may not be worth it at that stage. If you need a forceps delivery, however, it offers much welcome relief.

188

LOCAL AND PUDENDAL ANESTHESIA

If an episiotomy is necessary, the doctor uses a local or pudendal anesthetic. A local anesthetic involves injecting the numbing medication into the skin of your perineum where the incision is made. With a pudendal block, the doctor injects the anesthetic around the nerves inside the vagina. You experience relief from pain in the lower half of the vagina and in a wider area of the perineum than with a local.

POSITIONS FOR LABOR

Your position in labor has a definite and important effect on your contractions. While you're lying on your back in a semipropped position, contractions are more frequent but less painful and *not as effective.* If you feel more comfortable lying down, turn on your side. Contractions in this position will be further apart but much stronger. The blood flow to the placenta is best in this position also. Contractions closer than 3 minutes apart decrease in strength. Force dilates the cervix more efficiently than frequent contractions. Given the choice, most women in labor will choose to sit or stand, not lie down. Labor in the upright position is more comfortable and requires less medication. The force of gravity aids in dilating the cervix. Labor can be monitored electronically, if need be, while you're standing or sitting. How about if your water breaks? Do you have to stay in bed? *No!* If your baby's head is fitting snugly against the cervix, there's no reason to stay in bed. The possibility that the baby's cord might fall through the cervix and cut off the oxygen supply is remote. Once you stand up, gravity keeps the baby's head down. Unless the head isn't in the pelvis (floating), there's no logical reason for you to be confined to bed. Having to use a bedpan, especially during labor, is cruel and unusual punishment.

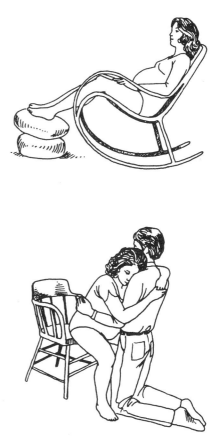

During labor, change position frequently. Many women find sitting on the toilet about as comfortable as anything. Pillows placed behind the back provide even more comfort.

LAZY LABOR

If you're having contractions but aren't setting any speed records in dilating, your doctor will probably want to give you some oxytocin to stimulate closer, stronger contractions. See the "Induction of Labor" section in Chapter 15, "Special Delivery." Some temporary alternatives to oxytocin are worth trying first. Walk! Ask your doctor if you can try some nipple stimulation by gently stroking one nipple through your gown for no more than 2-minute intervals with a rest period of 5 minutes between sets of stimulation. During a contraction, stop stroking until it goes away. Releasing your own natural oxytocin encourages stronger contractions. Don't get carried away with the nipple stimulation because it can hyperstimulate the uterus and your baby's heart rate can temporarily decrease. As a precaution, your nurse will most likely want to use the fetal monitor during nipple stimulation to detect any decrease in heart rate. Follow the guidelines carefully. Nipple stimulation isn't a good idea for long periods because your nipples get too sore. Try some therapeutic touch or acupressure exercise 4. Whatever works!

SUNNY SIDE UP— PERSISTENT POSTERIOR

A small percentage of women experience "back labor." The baby's head is down, but she's looking at the ceiling instead of the floor. This position puts more pressure on your back and it also makes your cervical dilatation slower. The occiput posterior (OP) position can add 3 to 5 hours to your labor. The trick is to get the baby's head to rotate so there's more efficient

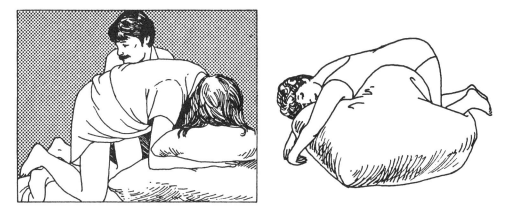

dilating of the cervix. A position on your hands and knees helps the baby's head rotate. If you don't have a beanbag chair to drape yourself over, use pillows in bed. Try to simulate the sleep position of a baby: Tuck your knees under your abdomen, keep your rear end in the air, and have your shoulders and face touch the bed. Stuff pillows under your chest for comfort.

THE TURNING POINT—TRANSITION

The transition stage of labor occurs at 8 centimeters. You feel a difference in the contractions, and you have the sense that something is about to happen. The contractions are at the height of their intensity. It's very common to feel emotionally scattered and irrational at this time. More than one woman has found herself saying "I've changed my mind. I want to go home, *now*!" That's a little extreme, but you feel that you just can't cope anymore and nothing is working right. You want your mother! The urge to push becomes stronger. Nausea may overcome you. Luckily, this phase is short.

THE FINISH LINE: SECOND STAGE

You're soon completely dilated, and the contractions mercifully feel less intense even though they're actually stronger. You no longer have to deal with the pain of cervical dilatation. Now you feel more pressure as the baby's head moves down.

In the second stage of labor the hardest part is over, but there's still work to do. Amid exhaustion, euphoria overtakes you. Somehow, you find the energy to finish the job. The adrenalin is flowing, and you feel like pushing. As you're pushing, your pelvic organs become more and more engorged with blood. Some women describe experiencing an orgasm while pushing or at the moment of birth. A fine line twixt pleasure and pain!

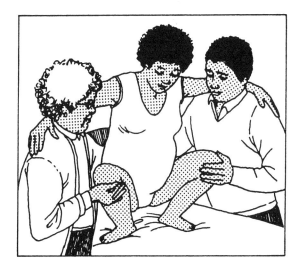

There are two ways you can push your baby out. Most doctors and nurses still favor the traditional way. Childbirth educators teach both the traditional and "natural" methods. Here's a crash course on both methods.

The Big Push

After all the waiting around, your doctor and labor nurse are ready for some real action and speedy results. They want you to push, and they think that the longer and harder you push, the faster the baby will be born. The usual instructions are to grab your legs and pull them back. Take two deep breaths and blow them out as the contraction starts. With the third deep breath, hold it and push for a fast count of 10, as hard as you can. The smell of victory is in the air and everyone is yelling, "*push*!!!" Your face turns red and your eyes pop. It's very tiring and unnecessary most of the time.

The Little Push

With the natural method of pushing, you listen to your body. You don't hold your breath or push hard. You do what feels natural. Your pushes are short and grunting. This method doesn't unduly prolong the second stage of labor. It may take a little longer, but not much. Your baby has higher oxygen levels because you aren't holding your breath every 2 minutes and pushing for 10 to 40 seconds. Again, it's not a serious difference, but

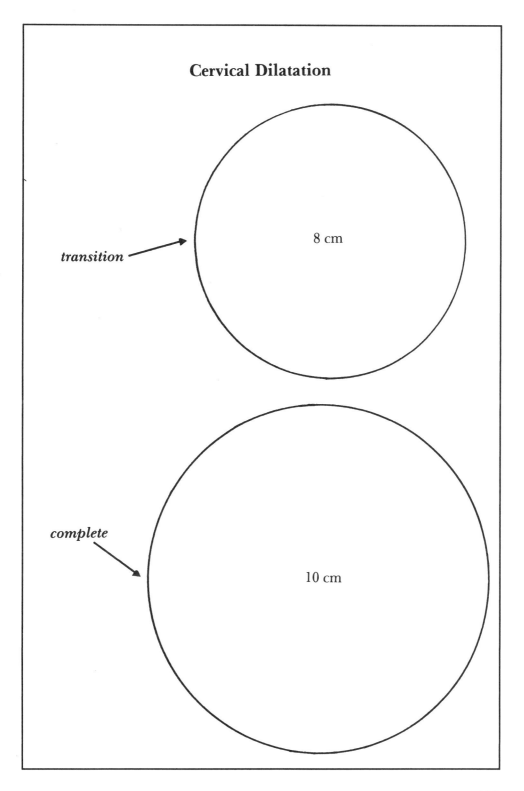

Cervical Dilatation

transition → 8 cm

complete → 10 cm

why wear yourself to a frazzle. Your body knows what to do, so just listen and do what comes naturally.

Sound Effects

It's normal, natural, and usually rather satisfying to make noises during labor, especially when you're pushing and working hard. Moaning, groaning, and grunting are perfectly acceptable. If it makes you feel better, do it! And it's music to your labor nurse's ears because the sounds tell her that you're completely dilated.

How Now?

You can use several positions to push. To the more reticent or uninitiated, squatting looks pretty primitive, but it gives your baby the most room in which to move down the birth canal. Your pelvic outlet is the widest in this position. When the time comes, you won't be spending much time thinking about how you look; all your concentration is on helping your baby out.

You can squat on the bed, the floor, the toilet—whatever is handy and gives you the most comfort and support. The illustrations give you some idea of what's possible.

Sitting up in bed will work until the baby's head needs room under your bottom to extend upward and start crowning (you can see the baby's head). When you're sitting on the bed, the mattress prevents the baby's head from extending further. At this point, squatting is a good position, or turn on your side. Birthing chairs have the advantage of using gravity and letting the head descend and extend without interference. Try several positions until you decide which one works best for you.

The average pushing time for primips is 25 to 75 minutes. If you have to, you can push for an hour or two if everything remains normal. Babies just don't fall out the first time; you have to work hard to stretch those tissues. Sitting on the toilet to push is pretty safe and fairly comfortable.

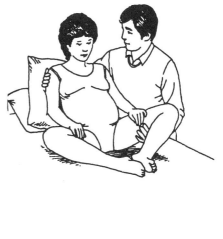

Multips usually have a faster second stage and not as much pushing to do. A good average pushing time is 13 to 17 minutes. If you choose to squat while pushing, do it by, or in, your bed. Your labor nurse should stay with you in case things move along quickly. Squatting on the toilet, for you, is risky—babies don't come equipped with water wings.

The side-lying position is comfortable and keeps the baby better oxygenated by not compressing large vessels. Your husband can support your upper leg or prop it on the side rail of the bed.

For the actual delivery, most doctors prefer the traditional flat on your back, legs in the air position. The disadvantages to you in this position include a higher incidence of episiotomy. The entrance to the vagina tightens and narrows as you flex your knees and draw your legs back. Contractions also become weaker and irregular. You also have to push uphill against gravity, which isn't very efficient.

For the uncomplicated delivery, the side-lying position has distinct advantages. Extension and expulsion of the head are easier. Episiotomy isn't required as often, and shallower incisions are possible. Some doctors and midwives use this technique and really prefer it once they use it for a while. This is an especially convenient position if you deliver in your labor bed.

If you have to use a regular delivery table, it can be modified into a pseudobirthing chair with some adjustments. The table tilts the head up. The stirrups are lowered to support your legs in a sitting position—anything to keep your legs from being stretched back toward your abdomen. Delivery time can be shortened with any position that simulates the squatting position. Everybody can be in a comfortable position, even your doctor.

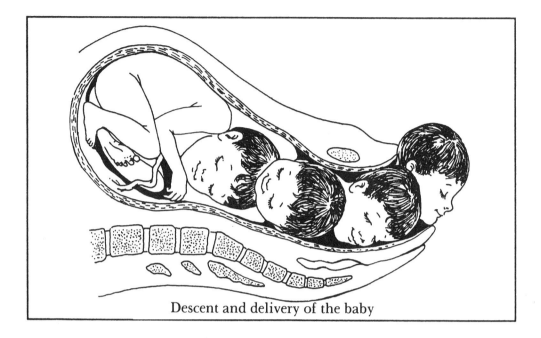
Descent and delivery of the baby

THE PAUSE THAT REFRESHES

It's over. The deed is done. Your baby has just been born. Relief washes over you. Your body is tired but tingly. You automatically close your eyes and pause. You take a silent moment to say a quick goodbye to the old you before plunging into motherhood—at last.

Now you want to know if your baby is all right, if all the crucial parts are in the right places. You have shared your body with this little intimate stranger for what seems like forever, and now you want to get even better acquainted. As you hold your baby, you gaze into her eyes. Don't be surprised if you find those brand new eyes staring right back. Babies can see rather clearly the first hour of birth, and they love looking at faces the best.

Keep in mind that newborn babies don't look like the ones you see on the front of baby food jars. Newborns are more dusky blue at first than pink, and they're messy. Your newborn has blood from the placenta and the cheesy white coating of vernix all over her. Her head is a little elongated and misshapen. Don't worry; a baby's head molds to the shape of the vaginal canal. Within a day or two, she'll look perfectly normal.

As you hold her, you gently explore her face with just your fingertips—lightly, tentatively. You draw her closer to you and brush her cheek with yours. As thoughts of germs flit merrily in your head, you throw caution to the winds and plant a big kiss on her cheek. You can't help yourself. This whole process is what behavioral psychologists call attachment and bonding.

Your curiosity satisfied for now, you turn her over to her daddy for inspection. He holds her and stares at her with rapt attention. He conducts his own inspection as he begins his attachment process.

A PERFECT 10—APGAR SCORE

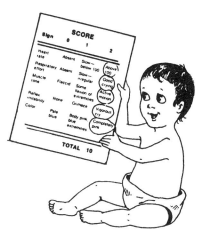

Your baby isn't even a minute old and already she's taking her first exam. At 1 and 5 minutes after birth, babies are evaluated by the Apgar scoring method. This isn't an IQ test but a test of cardiopulmonary function to see how well the baby is adapting to life outside. Most babies are in great shape and receive a score of 7 or better.

The delivery doctor usually gives a higher score, the pediatrician a lower score, and the nurse is close to being on target. Don't feel bad if your baby doesn't score a perfect 10. It's almost impossible because it takes more than 5 minutes to pink up her hands and feet. Settle for a 9.

OH, SAY CAN YOU SEE? EYE DROPS

For years, silver nitrate was the preventive measure against blindness from gonorrheal infection. Treating the newborn's eyes is a hospital requirement and a law in some states. Couples started objecting to the routine because they didn't want their baby's vision distorted in that first hour after birth. They didn't want anything to interfere with eye-to-eye contact. Some objected to the suspected gonorrhea part. The reasons for the routine seemed antiquated and unnecessary.

Many hospitals are delaying the prophylactic treatment so baby can have that clear look at mom and dad. Antibiotic ointments have replaced the use of silver nitrate. The concern now is for chlamydia transmission.

Chlamydia is a bacteria found in the cervix of some women. It doesn't produce symptoms in the mother, but it can infect the baby's eyes at birth. Since chlamydia is more prevalent than gonorrhea, it makes more sense to use the antibiotic ointment.

FUNNY FEELINGS

Mingling with your feelings of ecstasy and relief is, maybe, a tinge of disappointment! How can you possibly be disappointed when you made it through your labor and had a healthy baby? It's easy if you wanted a girl but got a boy. If you got a girl but she has brown hair instead of blonde. If you planned an unmedicated labor but had just one little shot. The possibilities are endless. If you decide to verbalize your disappointment, you run the risk of hearing a chorus of "Just be thankful you have a healthy baby!" That may be true, but that's not the point. You spent 9 months fantasizing about this baby: hair color, eyes, sex. Your dream baby rarely looks like your real baby. You had certain expectations for your labor. You can be a little disappointed if you want. With a little time, the picture of your dream baby and labor will fade away, as will the disappointment.

Meanwhile, your body is reminding you how pooped it is. It's common to experience chills that shiver your timbers. Your labor nurse heaps a few blankets on you as your teeth chatter away. No one has figured out why you get chills. Probably muscle fatigue, along with a touch of low blood sugar and lowered body temperature from the normal blood loss, are the culprits. Maybe it's just your body jumping for joy because it isn't pregnant anymore. Take your pick.

CLOSING SHOP—THE THIRD STAGE

The third stage of labor is when the placenta delivers. This is the official end of pregnancy. As soon as the placenta plops out, the uterus starts closing down the baby shop. It starts contracting, anxious to get back into its old shape. Your doctor may have the nurse give you a shot of oxytocin or add some to your IV bottle if you have one. Doctors agree that most women don't need it, but they can't seem to help themselves. If your uterus isn't staying firm and you're bleeding more than is expected, it really helps. If you aren't bleeding a lot, it just gives you painful cramps that strike every couple of minutes like labor pains. You might want to discuss your doctor's routine in advance and reach an understanding. If he feels you need it— great. If not, forget it.

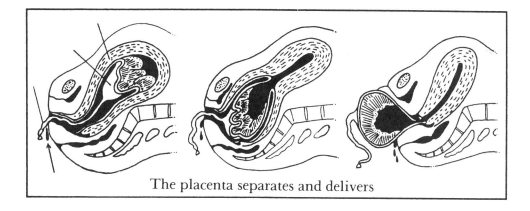

The placenta separates and delivers

Usually, at this point you're feeling so euphoric you won't pay much attention to such details. You don't feel the need to sweat the small stuff. You just want to bask in the glow of a job well done.

A FEW MORE ROUTINES AND RITUALS

Circumcision

Circumcision has been a tribal and religious rite in various cultures for centuries. Circumcision consists of removing all or part of the foreskin of the penis. Currently, most circumcisions are done because of parental request. The complication rate of 1 percent relates to bleeding and infection.

In consideration of new data, which reports a much higher rate of urinary tract infections in the uncircumcised baby, the American Academy of Pediatrics is reviewing its previous stand against routine circumcision. It probably won't make any difference because the reasons for parents having their babies circumcised don't have anything to do with medical reasons; they're based on cultural factors. The majority of newborn males are still circumcised.

Painless is possible. Newborn circumcision is the only elective surgery routinely performed without anesthesia. Anyone who tries to tell you it doesn't hurt the baby is deaf, dumb, blind, and lying through his teeth. It's painful and very stressful for the baby—and anyone who's within earshot as it is being done.

Fortunately, many doctors are now using local anesthesia to perform the procedure. Studies show that when doctors use local anesthesia, babies are quiet during circumcision and don't exhibit the typical restless, fussy, and crying behavior seen in babies without anesthesia.

Discuss any questions you have about circumcision with your doctor before you make your decision. Some insurance companies don't cover the cost of the procedure since they consider it cosmetic surgery. Ask your doctor if he uses local anesthetic. If the answer is no, call your hospital nursery and ask the nurses which doctors do use a local for circumcision. Your baby will thank you.

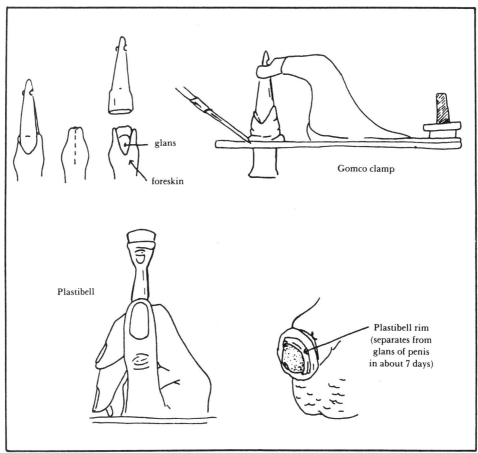

Hold the Milk—Lactation Suppression

If you plan to bottle-feed your baby, you hope to avoid engorged breasts. Most women count on their doctors to provide quick, easy potions or pills to take care of the problem. Magical medicine! There are some medicines available, but they aren't magical.

The available "drying" medications to suppress lactation are a clearcut case of the cure being worse than the disease. Their use is overkill, like using a bomb to kill a mosquito. Mosquitoes and engorged breasts have one thing in common: They're an annoyance, nothing more. Bombs and drying medications have one thing in common: They're dangerous to your health.

Drying medications have some potentially harmful side effects. The estrogen-based medications such as Tace carry warnings regarding the possibility of phlebitis (blood clots in the legs). The alternative to the estrogens is the drug bromocriptine (Parlodel). Doctors use Parlodel to treat hormone disorders in women. As a side effect, Parlodel inhibits lactation.

Parlodel must be taken for 7 to 14 days. The expense ranges from about $35 to $115. The side effects are unacceptable. In addition to your other postpartum aches and pains, you don't need nausea, vomiting, headaches, dizziness, more fatigue, diarrhea, or more cramps. The incidence of these adverse effects varies from study to study, but the manufacturer cites 28 percent. Parlodel has been associated with postpartum hypertension, seizures, and strokes. Engorged breasts may be temporarily uncomfortable, but they won't incapacitate you. Think about it.

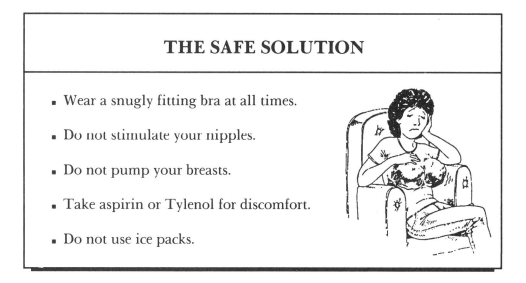

THE SAFE SOLUTION

- Wear a snugly fitting bra at all times.

- Do not stimulate your nipples.

- Do not pump your breasts.

- Take aspirin or Tylenol for discomfort.

- Do not use ice packs.

Should you decide to use the available drugs, what kind of results can you expect? The estrogen-based drugs only delay lactation, not prevent it. With Parlodel, you can expect an 18 to 40 percent engorgement rate after you finish taking the drug. Since Parlodel promotes ovulation, you need to use a reliable method of birth control.

Even the drug manufacturers agree that engorged breasts aren't a fate worse than death. It is a self-limited condition that responds to these simple supportive measures:

If your breasts become full and feel like two hunks of granite perched on your chest, jump into a hot shower for relief. The milk already in your breasts will drip out and relieve the engorgement and discomfort. They won't fill again if you don't pump them or stimulate your nipples. In a day or two it will all be over and done with.

THE CESAREAN BIRTH EXPERIENCE

Family Centered Surgery

It took a while for hospital personnel to graciously accept "aliens" into the hallowed walls of the operating room. Most hospitals now allow fathers to be present during the cesarean birth of their baby. Some even allow other support people and video cameras. How times have changed—for the better.

Most hospitals offer cesarean birth preparation classes to couples to acquaint them with the process and hospital policy. You find out what you can and can't expect. Rules and regulations vary from hospital to hospital. It's advisable to take those hospital tours, make those phone calls, or attend those classes to find out who offers what.

Getting Ready

Whether planned or unplanned, the process to prepare you for your cesarean birth is pretty much the same. Your abdomen is shaved and, probably, part of your pubic hair that would be close to the incision. A soft, pliable, rubber tube (catheter) will be placed in your bladder to keep it from ballooning up with urine during the surgery. Being catheterized is only mildly uncomfortable as the tube goes in. It stings slightly, but it's over with quickly. An IV is started. You commonly take an antacid to neutralize your stomach acids. Preoperative sedation with narcotics and tranquilizers isn't done. Your doctor and anesthesiologist will discuss the procedure with you and answer any of your questions.

Once you're in the cesarean birth suite, you lie on the operating table with a wedge or sandbag placed under your right hip to prevent the uterus from compressing your abdominal vessels, which can cause a drop in blood pressure. A nurse scrubs your abdomen with antiseptic solution that feels cold. The anesthesiologist busily checks your IV and attaches you to blood pressure, pulse, and cardiac monitors. This is a good time to practice your relaxation and visualization techniques. Ideally, your husband will be there to hold your hand and help you relax.

Anesthesia

Do you prefer to be awake or asleep? Discuss your preference and options with both your doctor and anesthesiologist. A number of factors must be considered because each type of anesthetic has advantages and disadvantages. For example, if you wish to be awake for the birth, your doctor needs time to arrange schedules with an anesthesiologist who's proficient and willing to do that type of anesthesia. Most anesthesiologists are agreeable to doing a regional (awake) anesthetic.

Psychologically, the advantage to being awake is the ability to share the experience with your husband, see your baby right away, and begin the attachment process. You're able more quickly to make the transition from pregnant to nonpregnant status. There are no gaps missing in your memory.

Some women, however, don't want to be awake during the surgery. If you feel that way, have your husband be present for the birth anyway. He can begin his attachment to the baby right away and fill you in on the important details of events you missed. Some women find themselves in a time warp. They go to sleep pregnant and wake up not pregnant anymore. Large gaps are missing in the memory bank, the Rip Van Winkle syndrome. They need someone to fill in the missing blanks. What time was the baby born; how long did it take; how much did he weigh; how long is he; what was his Apgar score? If your husband isn't interested in being present during the cesarean, have one of the nurses fill you in.

Cocktails for Two—General Anesthesia

Before you adjourn to the birthing suite, your anesthesiologist will discuss what will happen and answer any questions. When you're ready for your anesthesia, the anesthesiologist will start with something like sodium pentothal, which immediately turns your lights out—instant sleep. The process is pleasant. Pentothal doesn't produce the scary, psychedelic dreams that ether did. Penthothal does cross the placenta to the baby, but not in large amounts, and delivery is done within a few minutes. Your next IV cocktail is a muscle relaxant and blocker because surgery can be difficult if your muscles are tense and rigid. Good relaxation is a must. This drug doesn't cross the placenta. Anesthetic gas and oxygen go through an airway tube placed in your throat. The cocktail "chaser" is usually nitrous oxide, to keep you comfortably asleep and unable consciously to remember the surgery. After the baby is born, a narcotic alleviates the pain after you wake up.

The advantages of general anesthesia are mainly speed and ease of administration. If your cesarean is unplanned or an emergency, the doctor may prefer general anesthesia, which is easier and faster to do and gets the baby out quickly. The biggest potential problem is vomiting under anesthesia, which is always a possibility because of the delayed gastric emptying time during pregnancy.

Regional Anesthesia

Two common regional anesthetics are spinal and epidural block. This type of anesthesia numbs you from the waist down, leaving you awake and alert for the birth of your baby. Although you still feel pressure and pulling during the surgery, you feel no pain. Nausea and vomiting are uncommon. The anesthetic wears off in an hour or two, and you don't have that groggy, drugged feeling. Postoperative pain can be controlled with a narcotic injected into the epidural space (morphine epidural).

There are several contraindications to using a regional anesthetic. A regional can lower your blood pressure (hypotension). If you're bleeding, it makes a bad situation worse. If there are any abnormalities in the spinal column, it may not be possible to place the needle properly. If the woman is obese, placing the needle in the proper space can be difficult.

Spinal Block

Spinal block gives reliable and predictable pain relief, usually within minutes after administration. A small-gauge needle is placed between the vertebrae in the back and inserted into the spinal canal. Complications are infrequent, but postspinal headache can result from the leakage of spinal fluid from the puncture site of the needle. If untreated, the headache will improve by the third day and be absent by the fifth day. Different methods for treating spinal headache are used. Lying flat in bed for 8 hours isn't particularly effective. A procedure known as "blood patch" provides relief: A small amount of the patient's blood is injected into the same needle space as the spinal.

When it works, relief is usually immediate. An abdominal binder also helps. The incidence of spinal headache decreases significantly when a small-gauge needle is used.

Epidural Block

The epidural block works similarly to the spinal block but doesn't enter the spinal canal. Headaches aren't usually a problem unless the needle is inadvertently placed in the spinal canal.

The epidural block has several disadvantages. Even with an expertly administered epidural, pain relief can be unpredictable, with some areas not fully anesthetized. In expert hands, the failure rate is about 3 percent—fairly low.

Many hospitals have moved cesarean birth from the operating room to the obstetrical unit. Labor and delivery staff are trained to do cesareans. It's a nice touch to have the same staff who know all about babies be with you throughout the whole experience.

Cesarean birth isn't usually a first choice for most couples, but you can still have a happy and satisfying birth experience. You try to combine what you really want versus what's available. If you're able to check out options in advance, you're more likely to have more of what you want.

It's Never Too Late

A ton has been written about attaching, bonding, entrainment, engrossment . . . entrapment (that happens if you can't pay your hospital bill). Many couples have the mistaken notion that if they can't immediately go through all the motions of bonding described previously, they're doomed to a second-class relationship with their baby. Attachment is supposed to be a unique relationship between two people that endures and grows over *time*! There's a vast difference between a cow that'll abandon her calf if she misses those "sensitive" early minutes after birth and a human who misses them for whatever reason. There are those circumstances where early interaction isn't possible, such as when you have a general anesthetic with your cesarean birth or you promptly go to sleep after a long and difficult labor. You just make adjustments.

If fate intervenes and you have to start the getting-acquainted process a few hours later than planned, remember, **all the important, necessary rituals**

you go through to get to know and love your baby will still occur. Bonding should be synonymous for loving, and love is never static; it grows and changes over years. The events of one day aren't going to alter forever your potential to develop a loving relationship with your child. Keep the event and the experience in perspective.

Good Grief

If you had your heart and mind set on a vaginal birth and ended up with a cesarean, you both undoubtedly have some strong feelings to resolve. Husbands share, to some degree, the same feelings as their wives. How about confusion, anger, disappointment, and let's not forget guilt? You may feel, somehow, inadequate because you couldn't do it the "normal" way. You wonder why you had to go through all those hours of labor. Why couldn't your doctor have done the cesarean to begin with, instead of putting you both through all that misery? It isn't always possible to tell in advance who won't be able to deliver vaginally. As long as labor progresses, however slowly, the standard policy is to hang in there. Only when the cervix stops dilating, or the baby's head doesn't descend, does cesarean birth become an alternative. Most doctors find themselves between a rock and a hard place, but every effort is made to avoid surgery as long as you and the baby aren't in danger.

Discuss your unresolved feelings with your doctor or anyone else who can help you work through your disappointment. It's important for the future to put the experience in proper perspective. You don't want unfinished business hampering your joy of motherhood or coming back to haunt you with the next baby.

Recovering

Don't be surprised if for at least the first couple of days after your cesarean you're only able to muster brief episodes of euphoria for motherhood before you slip back into exhaustion. You're busy coping with stitches in your abdomen and just trying to make it back and forth to the bathroom. Trotting down to the nursery can seem like an insurmountable task. Your natural, instinctual drive is to let your body recover adequately before you can throw yourself headlong into being supermom or even plain old mom. Give yourself a break. If you spend more time focusing on your aching body than your baby at first, it's OK—you're normal.

How Do You Spell Relief?

There are more options available for postoperative pain these days. You used to have to depend on the nurses to bring you regular pain shots every 3 hours the first day or two to keep you comfortable, but now you can have the same patient controlled analgesia (PCA) mentioned earlier in the labor section. You can hit the switch on your PCA unit and get a pulse of painkiller when you need it. If you had an epidural, morphine or fentanyl can be injected into the tubing; the effects can last 24 hours or more. Ask your doctor about these options before your cesarean, if possible.

However you get your pain relief, narcotics won't affect your baby because the amount of narcotic that passes into your breast milk is negligible.

Once you're home, you definitely need some help. If you try to carry on alone, you'll find yourself crying as often a the baby does. You have all the same postpartum adaptations and stresses, only they're more magnified and intense. You aren't going to bounce back as fast as you would from a vaginal birth; but you will bounce back.

∆∆∆

LABOR GUIDE

EARLY LABOR—1-3 cm DILATATION

Physical changes	Emotional changes	Activities and support
Contractions mild, irregular, of short duration (30-40 sec).	Anxious but excited.	Drink fluids, eat lightly, continue normal activities.
Cramps and low backache.		Use relaxation exercises. Wait to start breathing exercises. Don't focus on contractions.
May have bloody show and mild diarrhea.		Visualize cervix ripening and thinning.
		Use acupressure points (APs) 2, 3, 5, 6, 9. Start AP 1 when needed.
		Call doctor when contractions occur every 10 min for multip and every 5 min for primip.

ACTIVE LABOR—4-7 cm DILATATION

Physical changes	Emotional changes	Activities and support
Contractions every 2-5 min. More intense. Lasting 50-60 sec.	Anxious for progress.	Change position often. Keep upright as long as possible.
Bloody show may increase.		APs 1 and 8 with each contraction.

ACTIVE LABOR—4-7 cm DILATATION

Physical changes	Emotional changes	Activities and support
Water may break.	Tendency to be tense.	Visualize baby pushing on cervix; uterus working well; your calm peaceful place; everything working in harmony and flowing.
		Can use therapeutic touch after each contraction.
	Needs encouragement.	Praise her. Have doctor or nurse tell how much progress she's making.
	More withdrawn, less talkative.	Speak softly. Keep sentences simple and brief.
	More difficult to remain calm and centered. Very irritable if disturbed during contractions.	Delay caretaking activities during contractions.
		APs 5 and 11 to restore calm between contractions.
		AP 12 if she loses control.
		Alternate between breathing exercises 1 and 2.
May hyperventilate.	Can feel panicky.	AP 5 to slow breathing and relieve anxiety. AP 12.

ACTIVE LABOR—4-7 cm DILATATION

Physical changes	Emotional changes	Activities and support
Pain with contractions.	May worry about being able to cope with contractions.	APs 1 and 8 with contractions.
Pain in hips and thighs.		AP 10.
May need to urinate.		Help her to bathroom every hour. Ask nurse to help.
		AP 7 to encourage urination.
Lips may become chapped.		Apply glycerine. Offer ice chips.
If progress slows or stops, may become discouraged.		AP 4 to increase contractions.
		Walk and stimulate nipples per guidelines.
		Discuss other options with nurse or doctor (oxytocin or medication).

TRANSITION—8-10 cm DILATATION

Physical changes	Emotional changes	Activities and support
Contractions 1-2 min apart, lasting 60-90 sec at their strongest and most intense.	May become irrational and paranoid. Common to want medication.	Continue AP massage. Breathing exercise 3 to keep from pushing too soon.
May feel intense pressure in perineum and urge to push.	Can feel overwhelmed with physical sensations.	Use positive directions. Say "Blow," not "Don't push."

TRANSITION—8–10 cm DILATATION

Physical changes	Emotional changes	Activities and support
		Remind her that this stage is short.
		Try semisitting position to help baby move down.
Face is flushed.		Apply cold cloth to face.
Leg cramps may strike.		Grasp toes and push ball of foot backward to stretch calf muscles. Hold position until cramp is relieved.
May become nauseated.		Use AP 13 and grab emesis basin.

SECOND STAGE

Physical changes	Emotional changes	Activities and support
Contractions stronger, but she feels some relief from pain.	Exhausted and euphoric.	Assume squatting or side-lying position.
Feels pressure and urge to push.	Finds energy to push.	Push with urge.
Perineum bulges as baby's head descends. Crowning occurs when you see part of baby's head.	Peaceful and sleepy between contractions.	Visualize baby moving down with each push. Feel your perineum relaxed and yielding. Think—calm and confident. APs 5, 6, and 11 between contractions.

17

The Postpartum Experience

AND BABY MAKES THREE

You made it! You survived labor and delivery. Your reward, badge of honor, and living purple heart is your baby. Your prevailing mood is probably euphoria. You're on a honeymoon with your baby and the whole idea of motherhood. This is going to be great, you think. Psychologically, what you're feeling is called "taking in," or accepting the new role of motherhood.

THE EARLY DAYS

At first you focus on yourself and your battle-fatigued body. You're disappointed that you didn't lose more weight right away. You realize that the "civilian" clothes you brought to wear home from the hospital won't fit. You still look about 4 months pregnant. Some women (very few) manage to look great in 2 weeks; others are still waiting for everything to shift back 6 to 12 months later. Start walking, pumping iron, doing the exercises in Appendix 1 and keep your fingers crossed.

Physiologically, your body is beginning the 6-week journey back to its prepregnant state. In addition to the immediate weight loss after birth, you've lost about 5 more pounds of water weight. Afterbirth pains tell you that your uterus is getting smaller already. Your vaginal flow at first looks like a normal period and then turns into a clear discharge by the tenth day. However, you may notice an increase in bright red bleeding for a time as you increase your activity and after nursing. Don't worry as long as you're not soaking a pad an hour. You might pass a blood clot or two when you get up from lying down. The blood sits in your vagina and coagulates; when you stand up, it falls out.

During the first 2 days or so, you'll be undergoing psychological as well as physical recovery. You find yourself with an intense desire to put the pieces of your birth experience together. You recount the tale of your labor and delivery with anyone who'll listen. It's common for the first few weeks postpartum to dream you're still pregnant and going through labor and delivery again. The dreams mirror your leftover fears. Your baby appears and disappears in the dream. This important process helps you bridge the old to the new.

In the hospital, you spend time checking your baby over to make sure everything is perfect. You fret over a bruise, scratch, or a head that still seems a little banana shaped. By the time you go home, everything will have returned to normal. Not to worry.

You want to identify your baby as yours by looking for family similarities. He looks just like his father, or he has Aunt Gertrude's eyes. You've begun the "bonding-binding" process that occurs intermittently and continues for the next 6 months. Right now, you just *know* everything is going to be great as you roll up your sleeves and get ready to plunge headlong into motherhood. Your little doll won't have any feeding problems or colic and won't keep you up many nights. Well, hold on to those thoughts—they may come in handy later.

WHERE'S THAT LOVIN' FEELIN'?

We're taught to believe that mothering is an instinct. The moment our baby is born, we expect motherly love to ooze from the primal depths of our being for this little stranger who now belongs to us. It doesn't actually happen that way.

Many women feel secretly guilty because they don't have that immediate loving feeling. To be honest, few women do. It takes time to build a relationship and to love anyone, including your baby. This goes for any one of your babies.

214

For the second-time or plus mom, her greatest fear is that she won't have enough room in her heart to share with her new baby. She loves the child she already has so much, it's hard for her to conceive that she could love another baby that much too. But the feelings come eventually, gradually, naturally, as if by instinct.

THE SIBLING SITUATION

Every mother agonizes over the potential reaction of the other children in the family to the new arrival. What can you do to smooth the way?

Kids have their own particular attachment behaviors with new babies. Initially, they tend to be very subdued, at least until they're reunited with you. Keep in mind, you're still the most important person in their world. They need assurance from you that you still love them and you're OK. At first, they'll pay more attention to you than the new baby brother or sister. Give them your undivided attention.

The most common acquaintance behavior of children is to look at the baby and then smile. Some may touch the baby briefly with their fingertips. The child younger than 7 usually wants to touch the head first. The over-7-year-old prefers to touch the arms and legs first. The kids are more interested in touching than talking at first. Other attachment behaviors are kissing the baby, verbalizing that they love the baby, and referring to the baby as their brother or sister. Stroking is also a common behavior.

Taking pictures of the baby, talking about a painful birth, and forcing the child to touch the newborn **delay** attachment to the baby. Siblings also become anxious if caretaking duties or procedures make the newborn cry.

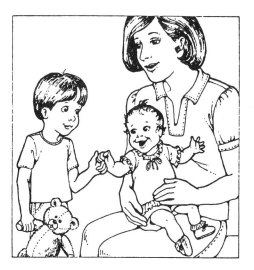

Children who've experienced a previous loss of some kind, such as death of a grandparent or parent or through divorce, take longer to attach. They may not respond as readily to the new baby, and the typical attachment behaviors may be delayed. These children need extra love, time, and reassurance.

Give your child permission to touch the new baby, but don't insist she do it. Kids need to interact with the new baby at their own pace, with the support of nurturing parents. You can't rush things.

THOSE "BABY BLUES"

By now you've probably heard of the infamous "baby blues." It's not a popular song or the color of Paul Newman's eyes. It describes the great letdown after the euphoria—depression amid joy. Every woman encounters these feelings to some degree in the first 10 days or so after birth. Let's look at what throws a damper on the natural high of your honeymoon phase of motherhood. Physiologically, you must cope with afterbirth pains, perineal soreness and/or stitches, vaginal flow, breast engorgement, hormone fluctuations, reestablishment of normal bowel and bladder function, and muscular discomforts. Your once adequate motor function seems to have taken a holiday. You feel like the world's biggest klutz, clumsy and off balance. This doesn't do much for your self-image.

Emotional upsets are very common the first 10 days after birth. You can feel unloved and unlovable. Apathy sets in, and you become disinterested in food. You're too tired to think about how tired you are. Along about the second week at home, a sense of isolation sets in. You find you aren't as thrilled about holding your baby as you were the first few days. You keep him nearby, but he spends more time in his bassinet. This pattern may continue until he becomes charming enough to entice you to spend more time cuddling him again. Reconciling your optimistic expectations of parenthood with the realities you face is no easy task. There's hope! Luckily, this "down" phase doesn't last long for most women.

A small percentage of women (8 to 12 percent) will experience a full-blown postpartum depression, which is different than those baby blues. With postpartum depression, your usual symptoms of irritability, loss of interest in your baby, sleep disturbance, loss of appetite, fatigue, and feelings of worthlessness are like a black hole. You can't seem to see your way out. If you experience a "blue" day every day for at least 2 weeks with no end in sight, call your doctor.

HELP!

Your desire to be Supermom, Wife Wonderful, and Mrs. Clean probably outweighs your available energy. Don't get caught in the trap of trying to be all things to all people at your own expense. In the early weeks, your body is trying to recover. You need lots of rest at a time when you least have the opportunity to get it. Get a head start on avoiding fatigue, your biggest enemy postpartum. Remember, fatigue magnifies any other problems you have during your postbirth adjustment. Pretend you're a five-star general planning for the D day invasion. You want to win this campaign—not end up like a burned out bomb on the shores of exhaustion.

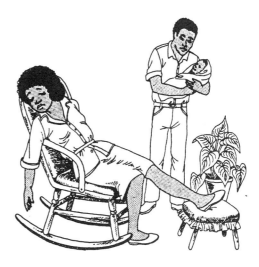

Before you deliver, cook as many meals in advance as you can and freeze them. Tell grandma(s) that if she really loves you, she'll add some goodies to your stash in the freezer. Investigate the best take-out places for future use. Make a list of all those errands you need done those first few weeks at home and assign them to willing friends or relatives. Tell your friends you don't want any more teething rings and rattles; you want gift certificates for free baby-sitting—use the certificates when you get them.

If you can afford it, hire a cleaning lady. Assign some household tasks to your husband. Tell him you're giving him a chance to relive his military days; assign him latrine duty or KP. Find a desperate teenager; teenagers are used to working for minimum wages. Let nonessential chores slide. If you continue to iron your husband's underwear, you need professional help!

Don't make any major life changes like moving, changing jobs, or letting cousin Billy come to stay for a month or two until he gets back on his feet. Plan in advance to curtail visitors. Share your D day plan with anyone you suspect will be camped on your doorstep. You don't want to have to hide in the closet while dad tries to run interference. Extend invitations, in advance, with specific dates so friends know when they can see you. Let them know your bedtime and stick to it. Posting the rules saves time and hard feelings later.

You need the emotional support of friends and other mothers in your same boat. Inquire about new parent-support groups in your community, such as *Parents Are People, Too*. Establish a relationship with the nurse in your doctor's office so you can call for advice when you need it.

217

Sleep deprivation is a real killer, devastating your mood and ability to cope with the increased demands on your time and energy. Nap when the baby sleeps. Household tasks can wait.

At some point you may find yourself thinking you'd gladly kill for some uninterrupted sleep. Dark shadows intrude on your dream scenario if daddy doesn't seem interested in 2 A.M. feedings. Your anger at his detachment can become fertile ground for resentment and future disharmony. To quote my genteel Southern friend, Miss Judy, "Why, honey, I don't get mad—I get even!" You really have to watch that stuff. Talk to each other and . . .

Get dad involved from the start. Some companies give new fathers paternity leave. Check this out, or have him take vacation time. Don't hog the baby; let dad help. The more he participates in caring for your new baby, the more confident he'll be in his new role. He needs on-the-job training. He can do anything you can do, except breast-feed, and there may be a way to work that out. For those middle of the night feedings, he can go get the baby, change his diaper, and bring him to you in bed. He can cuddle up to you both and keep an eye on junior while he's nursing. If you're really tired, you can sleep through anything. You're in this together.

Set aside time for yourself every day. Get out of the house, even if to just take a quick walk while someone watches the baby. Continue your relaxation and meditation exercises. Have your husband massage your feet and revisit those acupressure points; the massages are beneficial anytime. Turn the tables and give him a treatment—he needs pampering too.

BREAKING AWAY

After the first month, the dark cloud over your head disappears as you cast off apathy and depression. You want to see what the world is doing. You want conversation. You feel the urge to dress up: dinner, dancing, movies, the works! You can't wait to get out.

So how come while you're out, you spend all your time thinking about and missing your baby? You and your husband have an attack of the guilts for being so self-indulgent. You dash home early to seek forgiveness from your baby. It's another milestone in parenting. You're both hooked.

YOUR LIMPING LIBIDO

It won't be long before your husband is anxious to fan the flame in your sexual furnace to get that old fire going again. Romance is in the air, and he has that gleam in his eye. When can you let the games begin?

Doctors vary as to how long you should wait before resuming intercourse. Few stick to the old 6-week limit. Some advise waiting until the episiotomy is healed, and others merely suggest that a gentleman waits until the episiotomy is repaired. It doesn't really matter because most couples wait about 3 weeks before giving into temptation. Jumping the gun makes you feel a little guilty and wicked, but excited. One word of caution: If getting pregnant again right away isn't high on your list, use some kind of birth control. Condoms plus foam is a good temporary method. Don't count on breast-feeding to keep you safe; it won't. Consult Appendix 2, "Contraceptive Guidelines."

In spite of your husband's enthusiasm and your doctor's go ahead, you may find your libido hiding out. It's quite normal to be a little hesitant about resuming intercourse. For a couple of weeks, or up to 3 months postpartum, you may not respond to sexual stimulation as quickly or intensely as before. Even when your full response returns, you may be bone-weary, weak, and still a little gun-shy. Maximize your chance for a successful rendezvous by making a date with your husband. Pick the time of day when you're least tired. Farm out the little one to understanding friends, neighbors, or relatives for a few hours so you and your husband can get reacquainted.

Occasionally, some men find their sex drive derailed after watching the birth of their baby. They can't get the picture out of their mind, and it interferes with their ability to perform sexually. If this disturbing occurrence happens to your husband, encourage him to talk to a qualified professional who can help him constructively deal with and resolve his feelings.

If you still aren't sure whether your perineum is healed enough, here are a few helpful hints to try before you take the plunge. Have your husband insert one finger gently into your vagina and rotate it to find possible tender areas before you proceed with the real thing. If he can fit two fingers comfortably, intercourse shouldn't be painful. Before penetration, bear down to relax those muscles in your perineum. If you're breast-feeding, use some lubricant to counteract any dryness. Try the side-by-side or woman on top positions to control the depth of penetration. If you find it's just a little too soon to resume intercourse, get out the bag of tricks you devised while still pregnant. Be wild and crazy! Pretend you're back in high school and "make out." Or as the sex manuals say, "practice mutual manual or oral stimulation of genitalia." You can still recapture the romance and intimacy you both need right now.

The good news is that once your response and your bottom are back to normal, you may have more intense orgasms than ever due to the "pregnancy effect." The increased blood flow still circulating to your pelvis can heighten erotic sensations. Your husband may think he has a tiger on his hands.

MACHO MAN OR MR. MOM?

During "your" pregnancy, you proba- bly gave a lot of thought to your relationship with your own father, either grieving or rejoicing. In any case, you wonder if you can measure up to your idea of what an ideal father should be. Fathering isn't a spectator sport. Up until now, in the parenting game, you've been warming the bench. Now is your chance to make first string.

The concept of fathering has un- dergone a real metamorphosis. Values and expectations are changing. So what do you do? If real men don't eat quiche, do they change diapers and feed babies? Absolutely!!! Many men who think nothing of risking life and limb on a football field find a small baby very intimidating. How do you hold a baby? Like a football. You cuddle babies the same way, and it's a lot less dangerous.

You can overcome your fear of handling your baby before he's born. Community organizations offer baby care classes. You can easily learn bathing, diapering, and infant massage if you need help. Practice on your friends' babies. You can't breast-feed, but you can have lots of other meaningful contact with your baby. Buy a baby carrier of some kind to wear and take him for a walk. Make a weekend routine of giving him a massage. Borrow the rocking chair and snuggle up and talk to him. Start living that mental image you have of what a dad should be. The more you become involved in caring for your baby, the more confident you become . . . and the more you enjoy it.

FACING FATHERHOOD

The first few weeks at home are stressful for you too. The focus may be on baby and mom, but you need a few kind words and some support.

That wonderful woman who captured your heart and spoiled you rotten has temporarily weirded out on you. You thought things were going to be back to normal after the delivery. You yearn for those romantic days of yesteryear. You feel like the "Lone Stranger." You might wonder what you've gotten yourself into.

The mother of your child cries easily and is, probably, inconsolable about her figure for now. She needs reassurance that you still think she's attractive. She's depressed, tired, and preoccupied with the baby. You feel as if sexual deprivation has become a way of life. The crisis is temporary. You can make things a lot easier on all of you by anticipating how you can best help.

Decide, in advance, which caretaking duties you're willing and able to manage. It's very important to reach an agreement before the birth, when she's calm, coherent, and rational. If you don't clearly communicate your mutual expectations, you can stir up a real hornet's nest. Your willingness, patience, and stable influence will reap benefits later. The more you help with housework and your baby, the less of those baby blues she'll experience. She won't forget that you were there for her when she really needed you.

BABY TALK

You're home and ready to start your job as the ultimate parent. When you realize all the job entails, your mind whirls and you become weak in the knees.

You also discover that your great attachment to your obstetrician has switched to your baby doctor. You aren't fickle, just pragmatic. To add to the confusion, all that well-meaning advice your friends and family gave you while you were pregnant doubles now that you're parents. Hang onto your sanity by listening to your pediatrician and to your own instincts. As you and your baby get to know each other, you'll work out your own routine and way of doing things. Remember that it takes a little time and experience to cross over that bridge from novice to confident parent. It's a whole new world and you have a lot to learn. Give yourself time.

Here are some basic ground rules and updated information. They'll help you avoid enough of the "agony" so you can enjoy more of the "ecstasy" of parenting in the first 6 weeks at home. The following tidbits will keep you going until you find a comprehensive baby book as your primary reference (see Recommended Resources section).

DIAPERS

Unless you're into animal hides stuffed with peat moss, your choices are still between cloth diapers and the DDs. In diaper lingo, DDs stand for disposable diapers, not the measurements of your husband's favorite movie star. There are a few pros and cons to consider for each method.

The DDs hook you on convenience, which we all dearly love, but they have a few drawbacks you might want to consider. DDs are made of a plastic, waterproof backsheet and a fluffed wood pulp liner, both nonbiodegradable. DDs then aren't as disposable as we're led to believe. They're far from being recyclable. DDs add 84 million pounds of raw fecal matter to our land-fill sites every year; 30 percent of our nonbiodegradable garbage comes from DDs. It's enough to make the ecologists crazy.

On a more personal level, DDs cause three times more diaper rash than cloth diapers because of their super absorbency and highly effective plastic liners: The plastic retains heat and promotes bacterial growth. You stay dry, but baby stays very wet. If you decide to use DDs try to find a brand that doesn't have elastic in the waist band, to allow as much air circulation as possible.

Also, DDs are very expensive compared to diaper service. Do some comparison shopping before you're seduced by the convenience factor.

There are two ways to go with cloth diapers: do it yourself or diaper service. The cheapest way is to do them yourself. You need at least three dozen to start unless you want to spend all your time at the washer and dryer. Here's how to do it yourself:

- Buy a long-handled clip or "Diaper Duck" for rinsing dirty diapers in the toilet bowl and a padded clothespin for your nose.

- Put the used diapers into a plastic diaper pail with a solution of water and Dreft or Borateem, which cuts down the smell and helps kill bacteria.

- On wash day, drain the diaper pail into the toilet. An average load should not exceed 24 diapers. Use the spin cycle first to whirl away the undrained dirty water. Use a mild soap or detergent with a minimum of additives, such as Dreft. Use the *hot* wash and *warm* rinse cycle with a high water level.

- Dry the diapers in sunlight or on high heat in the dryer for 45 minutes to help kill bacteria. Realize that you can't sterilize diapers the way the diaper service can because the noncommercial water and drying temperatures aren't hot enough.

Diaper service is a nice civilized alternative to DDs and do it yourself. All you do is put the dirty diapers into the bag provided—you don't even have to swish the diapers in the toilet anymore. The service will wash, dry, and deliver clean, sterilized diapers to your doorstep every week. Diaper service makes a nice baby gift for mom and is more economical than using disposables. Mother Nature and the ecologists will love you.

THE CLEAN TEAM

No matter what method of diapering you choose, remember grandma and her edict that "Cleanliness is next to Godliness." When you change your baby's diaper, use warm water and a soft cloth to wipe the creases and folds. Clean little girls from front to back (top of vagina to rectum) to avoid infections from contamination. Reinforce this method of wiping when you start to potty train her. Don't use commercial wipes routinely because they contain alcohol or other drying agents that can cause skin irritation. Once a day, wash with a mild soap such as Dove. Rinse well with warm water and dry baby completely before rediapering.

The best advice on creams, powders, and ointments is not to bother. Healthy skin doesn't need synthetic additives, and they just interfere with air circulation. Especially avoid skin products made from a petroleum base or parabens, which are common allergens. One of the best things you can do for your new baby's bottom is to not use rubber pants. They aren't necessary at this young age. Also let baby "go bare" for part of the day because fresh air is a good preventive and cure for diaper rash (see the later "Common Concerns" section).

BOTTLES AND BURPING

The bottle-feeding equipment is very basic. You have a choice of glass, plastic bottles, or disposable bags. Glass bottles are easier to clean than plastic, but glass breaks and plastic doesn't. Disposable bags have the advantage of no cleanup, and the baby swallows less air during feeding.

Formula preparation involves nothing more than following the directions on the can and using tap water to mix. You no longer need the heart of a compulsive, paranoid chemist. You've been set free!

THE KISS (KEEP IT SIMPLE SUPERMOM) FORMULA

- Sterilizing water by boiling is unnecessary. Water from the tap, unless it's well water, is essentially bacteria-free.

- If you have well water, have it professionally tested to determine if it's safe for your baby's use without having to be boiled.

- Sterilizing bottles is unnecessary. A good scrubbing with hot soapy water and/or a tour through the dishwasher is sufficient. Clean nipples by forcing hot, soapy water through the hole and rinsing well.

- Forget warming baby's bottle. He doesn't care, and a room-temperature bottle won't cause any problems with his digestion.

- If you feel the need to warm bottles, beware of the microwave because it can create hot spots and burn your baby's mouth. Shake the bottle well after warming.

- Use prepared bottles within 30 minutes or refrigerate them. Don't use leftovers for later; start fresh with each feeding.

- Don't insist baby finish his bottle if he falls asleep during the feeding or doesn't seem interested in continuing his meal. If he's able to go 2-1/2 hours between feedings and taking the amount your doctor suggested, he's not starving. Overfeeding can be a big problem with bottle-feeding if you force it.

- Check the nipple opening—it's correct if the milk flows in drops when you invert the bottle. A larger hole could result in choking.

Burp your baby in the upright position over your shoulder, on his stomach over your lap, or with him leaning forward in a sitting position. Massage or stroke his back. Try burping him in the middle of the feeding and at the end.

Feedings are a perfect time to hold and cuddle your baby. Entertain him by talking softly and smiling at him. This is supposed to be a relaxing time for you too, so don't be tempted to prop his bottle to save time. Feeding him in a flat position can result in ear infections or choking.

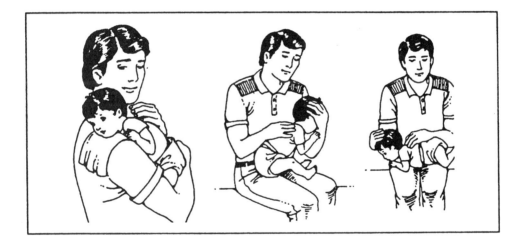

SIPPING AND SLEEPING SCHEDULES

For the first 4 weeks, your baby will want to be fed every 3 to 4 hours. By 5 to 6 weeks, 50 percent of bottle-fed babies sleep in 8-hour stretches and by 4 months, almost all of them can. From the beginning, breast-fed babies eat a little more often than bottle-fed babies and take an extra month before sleeping 8 hours without being fed. By 3 to 4 months, night feedings have usually dwindled down to one. You'll find yourself living for that time.

Just when you think you have this feeding stuff down to a predictable routine, your little angel seems to be hungry all the time and fussy. If you don't know what's happening, you can be frantic. At about 2, 6, and 12 weeks of age, both bottle- and breast-fed babies have growth spurts. Solve the problem by feeding the breast-fed baby more often to increase milk production. In addition to feeding the bottle baby more often, add 1 to 2 ounces more of formula to her feeding. As her stomach is able to hold more, she'll decrease her time between feedings again.

Establishing good sleeping habits in your baby is important to her well-being and your sanity. If you want to avoid a raging sleep deficit, here are some guidelines.

Don't use your breast as a pacifier or your baby will become a "snacker" accustomed to small frequent feedings that will continue during the night hours when you need your sleep. Help her realize that eating and sleeping don't always go together. Babies normally wake up several times during the night, so try to determine the source of the crying. Is she dreaming, simply fussing, or is she really hungry? If it has been 2 hours or less since her last feeding, don't nurse her or give her a bottle simply as a means of putting her to sleep; you don't want to nurture the belief that she can't sleep without eating first. As a routine, put her in her crib at bedtime when she's still awake so she realizes that she can fall asleep without the aid of breast or bottle. If she isn't hungry but wants to suck, give her a pacifier. A pacifier is very comforting to some babies and won't cause dental abnormalities before the ages of 3 or 4. She'll swallow less air with a pacifier compared to using her thumb or fist. A pacifier is useful for the first 3 months before she discovers her hands, fingers, and rattles. The need for supplemental sucking decreases by 3 months, and you can start weaning her from the pacifier.

Somewhere between 3 and 6 weeks is a good time to consider moving her out of your bedroom if she's still rooming with you. Babies are regular noise factories; they snort, snuffle, snore, grunt, sigh, groan, and moan. All those fussy little noises she makes keep you awake and may encourage you needlessly to disturb her because you think she needs something. Don't make each other nervous. You both need your sleep.

SOLID FOODS

One of the long perpetuated myths says "Feed a baby solid food before bedtime and he'll sleep through the night." It doesn't work. Don't be tempted to try it, even if you're experiencing a sleep deficit. You can cause problems by introducing solid foods too soon. The first 4 to 6 months baby isn't ready to handle the mechanics of swallowing or digesting solid food. It just passes through undigested and may wreak havoc on the way through. Turn a deaf ear to aunt Betty, who swears she had all her babies eating T-bone steak before they had teeth. Listen to your pediatrician!

BATHS AND BELLY BUTTONS

For the first week at home, limit baths to a simple sponging until the cord heals and falls off. Use a clean, warm washcloth, first to wipe her eyes, then her head, behind her ears, face, neck, and chest. South of the border regions need more frequent cleaning to avoid irritation and diaper rash from contact with dirty or wet diapers.

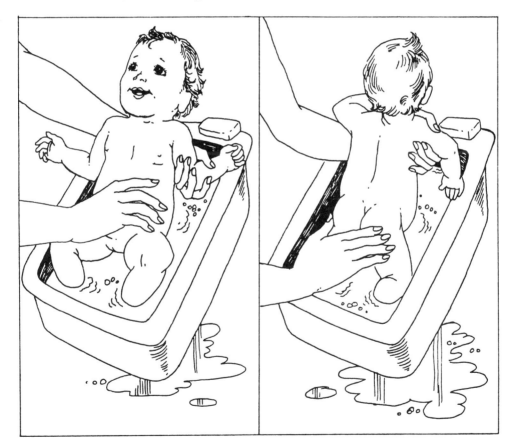

After the cord has fallen off, you can start regular baths in a baby tub, clean dishpan, or clean sink. Put a small towel or washcloth on the bottom to keep him from slipping and sliding around. The tub needs only 1 or

227

2 inches of water, and the room should be warm. Use the same washing sequence as the sponge bath. About once a week wash his hair with a nontears' baby shampoo. If he has a scaly, waxy rash (cradle cap), use an adult dandruff shampoo and scrub with a soft brush. Don't worry about the "soft spot." It's not so soft that you should avoid washing it. Lather his body from the neck down with a mild soap. Wash the penis or vaginal folds (labia) gently, just as you do the rest of the body. Don't use cotton-tipped sticks to wash anything! Your grandma was right: If you can't get to it with the corner of the wash cloth, forget it. Rinse thoroughly from the neck down, and wrap your baby in a clean towel to dry.

Some babies love their baths from the start, but others take a little time to adjust. Some babies simply don't like having all their clothes and blankets off; it makes them nervous and they put up a real fuss. Don't worry that he will grow up to be "Pig Pen." Eventually he'll get used to it and stop protesting. You can help him relax by talking softly, keeping your hand securely under his neck, and avoiding hurried, jerky movements.

You don't need to be too compulsive with baths. For the first few months, two or three times a week is often enough for a full bath. How dirty can a baby get in a day? Wash her hands, wipe off drools and spills, keep her bottom clean, and save your energy for other things.

Belly buttons appear by the fifth to ninth day after birth when the umbilical cord heals and falls off. When the cord dries, it feels like those thick rubber bands that supermarkets use to hold vegetables together. The oozing or bleeding that commonly occurs after the cord falls off can be cleaned three or four times a day with alcohol. If the oozing or bleeding lasts more than 2 or 3 days, call your baby's doctor.

HYGIENE FOR THE HAVES AND HAVE-NOTS

Care of the Uncircumcised Penis

The uncircumcised penis requires very little care. The foreskin protects the glans of the penis from irritation. Don't attempt to retract the foreskin; retraction isn't possible until around 3 years of age or older. Think of the foreskin as Mother Nature's special protective coat and leave it alone.

Occasionally, you may notice white spots on the tip of the penis. Don't panic; the family "jewels" are still safe. It's just the normal shedding of skin cells. With the uncircumcised penis, just wash what you see and forget the rest.

228

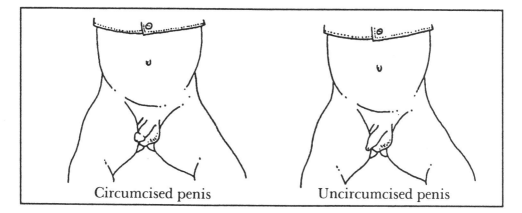

| Circumcised penis | Uncircumcised penis |

Care of the Circumcised Penis

A baby circumcised with the Plastibell device has a plastic ring that's left on the penis for 5 to 8 days, at which time it falls off by itself. Forget it's there. No care is required. If the Gomco clamp method has been used, a gauze strip with petroleum jelly is usually wrapped around the penis and stays on for 24 hours. The jelly protects the glans from irritation and prevents it from sticking to the diaper. Stop using the jelly after 2 or 3 days to let air circulate and aid healing. You can help out by keeping his diapers and any outer clothing loose and not laying him on his stomach for a few days until the area isn't so tender. In the normal process of healing, a yellowish discharge will adhere to the penis. This isn't an infection, so don't try to remove it. Use only clear water for cleaning until healing is completed. After that, wash the penis like all other parts.

Problems to watch for include any bleeding, infection, foul odor, or any apparent trouble urinating. If you have any questions, call his doctor.

FUN AND GAMES

Your baby is ready from birth to start interacting with you. She isn't the little lump she appears to be. She can focus on objects 8 to 10 inches away, and within a short period of time she can recognize her mom and dad from the other faces in her life. Babies prefer to look at faces rather than objects. Notice that she can mimic your expressions when you're smiling, frowning, and even sticking out your tongue. Babies love faces that are expressive and prefer voices with a high pitch. Few people can resist a baby. Even big hulks will turn themselves into a soprano to get a baby's attention—they can't help it. Communication from the first day is very important, so take advantage of every opportunity. During her awake times, put her in her baby carrier or infant seat where she can see you as you work around the house. Talk to her while you work and while you change her diaper and bathe her. You can enhance her language development by using the correct word spoken in the correct way. In other words, don't use baby talk. Besides, you might embarrass yourself at your next dinner party when you hear yourself asking "Is dinner yum, yum on your tum tum, tweetie?"

CRY ME A RIVER

Each baby comes into the world equipped with a unique temperament ready for expression from the first breath. Ask any delivery room nurse. Some babies are as serene as a monk in meditation. "Go with the flow" is their motto. Others arrive as high-strung and nervous as a preacher without a pulpit on Sunday. This baby needs a lot of comforting and reassurance to alleviate his anxiety. All babies cry, and it can be very confusing at first trying to decode what he wants and needs.

Let's put crying babies into perspective. Babies cry when they want to eat, but sometimes babies cry as a way to relieve tension. They can't jog, meditate or work out, so they cry. Babies cry when they're tired or overstimulated. Many babies have a certain time of the day when they're fussy. A fourth of newborns have crying periods three times a week that last 3 or more hours. Some babies are able to console themselves quite well. One might cry for a few minutes, stick a fist in his mouth, and drop off to sleep. Other babies can be inconsolable no matter what you do. Try to be objective and not take it personally if your baby falls in the inconsolable category. It's more of a challenge to find what soothes her soul, and eventually you'll figure it out. Here are a few tips to remember for those fussy times:

- **Swaddling** your little papoose is an old Indian trick of wrapping the baby tightly in a blanket with her arms inside. Restricting movement seems to be calming.

230

- **The plug** can be a thumb, fist, or pacifier. Some babies have a greater need to suck than others. If a pacifier makes him happy, do it. If he's still attached to it by the time he gets married, let his wife worry about it.

- **Temperature changes** can sometimes disturb your baby. Check to see if you have too many or too few clothes on her. Judge by how you're dressed: If you have two layers of clothes on and she has six, she's probably too warm.

- **Sounds** can be soothing. Devices that mimic the sound of the placenta, ocean waves, or a heartbeat can be very comforting. For the really hard to console baby, try the SleepTight device (see "The Colicky Kid" section). Taping your baby's own crying, mom's voice, or any soothing music, and playing it back to him may have a quieting effect also.

- **Rocking chairs and swings** work well. Get a long windup time for the swing. They are great for dinner times when you're tired of eating with one hand or having your husband cut your meat all the time.

- **Baby carriers** work well for babies who like constant contact. The ones that strap to your front also have the advantage of the baby being able to hear your heartbeat.

If you've tried the entire repertoire and nothing works, keep calm. Put Baby Cakes in her crib on her stomach and get out your earplugs. You've given it your best shot. Use your relaxation techniques on yourself and think positive. This too shall pass.

INFORMATION PLEASE

Most hospitals are very conscientious about helping you learn about and become comfortable with your new baby before you go home. In this early stage of parenthood, you can be bombarded by a lot of information that somehow doesn't stay with you. Once you're home, you may have a lot of questions but you can't remember the answers. You aren't alone. Here are some helpful hints to tide you over until you can buy that baby book.

COMMON CONCERNS

Diaper Rash

The most common cause of diaper rash is wet diapers left on for long periods of time, especially disposable diapers. After you introduce solids at 4 to 6 months, new foods can cause an allergic rash or irritation because of the food protein in the stool. Teething goes along with diaper rash when the urine becomes more alkaline at that time. If you're washing your own diapers, keep in mind that detergent residue or fabric softener can cause irritation. What to do?

- Go bare. Let the sunshine in—behind a closed window. Fresh air is the best medicine for diaper rash.

- Avoid plastic pants or disposable diapers. Wool diaper covers, sold at baby specialty stores, are perfect substitutes for plastic pants. You may find you prefer them over plastic pants.

- Change diapers more frequently. Also, when washing diapers, give an extra rinse with 1/2 cup vinegar added to the final rinse water.

- Use only natural creams that include vitamin E on the affected areas. Desitin with zinc oxide is a particularly effective barrier to moisture and bacteria; healing often occurs overnight. Aloe vera gel is another option, but it stings when applied.

If the diaper rash problem becomes chronic, your best bet is diaper service and wool diaper covers. Some babies just can't tolerate disposable diapers.

Constipation

Constipation isn't usually a problem in the first few weeks of a baby's life. We're a very bowel-oriented society and become anxious if we think the plumbing is clogged. The definition of constipation in a newborn is straining to have a bowel movement and no results. The number of bowel movements per day isn't a factor in determining constipation. Babies vary according to how often the plumbing gets purged. Formula-fed babies are more prone to constipation, especially during hot weather. Adequate fluid intake by mom helps avoid constipation in the breast-fed baby. The important factor is the result, not the regularity. If you think your baby is constipated, call your pediatrician for advice.

Skin Condition

It's very common for a newborn to have little whitish bumps on his nose. These plugged skin pores, known as milia, disappear in a few weeks. Nothing needs to be done except washing his face with warm water. Save the Noxzema and Sea Breeze for his teen years.

Fifty percent of babies have light red areas on the neck or eyelids, sweetly referred to as "stork bites" by grandma. Your pediatrician may use a more earthy description and call them salmon patches. Most of these spots fade and disappear over months or a year.

Half of all full-term babies have physiologic jaundice—a yellow coloring of the skin that appears on the second or third day after birth. You first notice the yellow on the face and trunk, later on the arms and legs. With dark-skinned babies, you notice the coloring in the gum and in the whites of the eyes. What you're seeing is the effects of the body destroying the system's extra red blood cells that the baby doesn't need. The liver may not be able to keep up with the cleanup job for the first few days. By the seventh day, the liver matures enough to handle the job more efficiently. Within 2 weeks the yellow disappears. Mild cases of jaundice aren't harmful and require no treatment.

If you think your baby is yellow, call your pediatrician. Don't wait until he looks like the Yellow Rose of Texas all over.

Breast Engorgement and Vaginal Discharge

Both newborn boys and girls can have some degree of breast engorgement. You can see and feel a little nodule under the nipple area. This temporary condition is caused by the transfer of maternal hormones across the placenta. After birth, when the supply is cut off, the engorgement disappears. Not to worry.

For the first few days, the genital area of both sexes is a little swollen. Little girls commonly have a whitish, blood-tinged vaginal discharge for a few days after birth.

Choking

Choking is uncommon in babies under 6 months of age. The newborn may choke if the milk flows too fast, but he'll quickly recover. If you get worried, hold him with his head lower than his body and let gravity do the work. It's not necessary to pound his back, which may scare him.

The Colicky Kid

The colicky kid isn't a western hero from your mother's era. It's that child of yours who screams so hard her face is red from the effort. She draws her legs up, and her abdomen is hard and distended. Her feet and hands are cold as ice, and you're on the verge of losing your mind. You need all your emotional and physical strength to pass this grueling test of motherhood.

The cause of colic is still a mystery, and the only sure cure is tincture of time. Colic usually disappears by the third month of age or sooner. Meanwhile, in addition to the remedies for the fussy baby, your survival techniques could include the colic hold position to alleviate pressure in the baby's abdomen. Put him in his carrier or stroller and go for a walk. Put him in his infant seat on the clothes dryer while it's running, but don't leave him alone. Take him for a ride in the car. Ask a neighbor to try all the above, for an hour or so, while you escape to restore the thin threads of sanity you have remaining.

A new device that looks very promising in the treatment of colic is SleepTight,* a sound and vibration unit that attaches to the baby's crib and simulates riding in the car. In a 3-year study funded by the National Institute of Child Health and Human Development, the SleepTight device lessened colic symptoms in 96 percent of the babies tested; 85 percent of the babies stopped crying within 4 minutes. You might want to check it out.

Until the colic problem resolves, sleep when your baby does; get help with the housework and pay attention to your diet. You don't need the mood swings that go with your fluctuating blood sugar. During your darkest hours, keep this thought: Your present inconsolable wretch of a baby will soon be an infinitely charming toddler who will be the delight of all your

---

* SleepTight, 3613 Mueller Rd., St. Charles, MO 63301, or 1-800-325-3550.

days. It's worth the wait. Meanwhile, throw yourself on the mercy of your friends and ask for some baby-sitting relief. Now's when you discover who your real friends are. Ask your pediatrician for additional tips and remedies.

WHEN TO CALL THE DOCTOR

The prospect of a sick baby can be very scary for any parent, especially a new one. How can you tell if a baby is sick? One of the first signs of illness is loss of appetite. If she cries, whines, and refuses one or two feedings in a row while seeming listless and apathetic, that's a good clue. Call the doctor.

Fevers

Fever is another sign. If your baby has a rectal temperature of 101.8°F (Fahrenheit), or an axillary temperature of 99.8°F, call your pediatrician. If you don't have any experience with thermometers, don't despair. Here's a quick lesson on what to do.

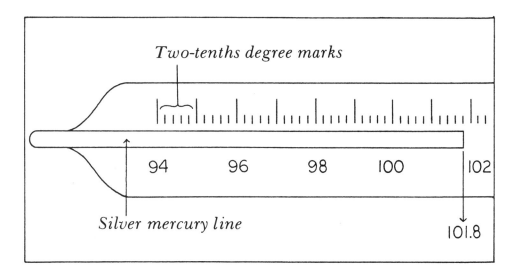

It isn't necessary to take a baby's temperature rectally. Putting the tip of the thermometer under her armpit (axillary area) and placing her arm down to keep the thermometer in place works equally well. Check that the tip of the thermometer isn't peeking out the other side of the arm. The digital thermometers are really great because they beep when the reading is done and display the number on the viewer.

If you prefer the old-fashioned kind of thermometer, shake it down until the silver line (see illustration) is below 98.6°F. After placing the thermometer, hold it there for 5 minutes. The normal axillary temperature is 98°F.

Read a thermometer by holding the blunt end in your right hand with the silver tip pointing toward your left. Rotate the thermometer very slightly until you can see the silver mercury line. Read the temperature where the line ends. Even numbers appear under the heavier, dark lines as shown. The uneven numbers aren't written but are represented by the dark lines between the written numbers. The smaller, finer lines between the dark lines represent two-tenths of a degree. For example, the mercury line on the illustration stops at 101.8°F.

If you'd rather do a rectal temperature, lubricate the silver tip with petroleum jelly. Place baby on his stomach, with a clear view of his rectal area, and insert the thermometer very carefully to a depth of only 3/4 inch. Hold the thermometer and wait 3 to 4 minutes. Remove and read. The normal rectal temperature is 99.5°F.

If you think your baby has a fever, take his temperature before you call the doctor; it's important information. If you're still unclear as to how to take a temperature, have a nurse show you before you leave the hospital.

Diarrhea

True diarrhea, if untreated, can become a serious problem for a newborn. Your baby has diarrhea if he passes a large amount of fluid from the rectum with a small amount of stool or has an increase in the frequency of stools with a liquid consistency. The appearance becomes yellowish-brown or green stained with flecks of mucus. Intestinal cramps may precede the sudden explosive bowel movement. To avoid serious dehydration, maintain a balance between what goes in and what comes out. If your baby has diarrhea, call his doctor.

HEALTH AND WELFARE

Car Seats

Car accidents and falls are the biggest threat to your baby's safety during the first 2 months of life. Every month, nearly 400 children under the age of 4 die from accidents that could've been prevented.

236

Your baby's first ride home from the hospital should be in a rear-facing, properly secured, FAA-approved infant seat—not in your arms. Your pediatrician can give you the pamphlet titled, "A Family Shopping Guide To: Infant/Child Automobile Restraint" provided by the American Academy of Pediatrics.

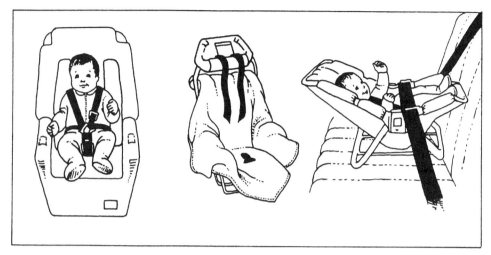

When shopping for a car seat, look at the labels and make sure it meets federal standards (FAA approved). Ask the clerk if you can try it before you buy to make sure it fits your car and you know how to secure it properly. These things aren't easy to figure out, so ask for help if you need it.

Falls

Accidents and injury from falls are easy to prevent. Don't put your baby on countertops, sofas, or changing tables and leave him unattended and unsecured. Even very small babies can manage to fall. If you have to leave him even for a minute, put him on the floor.

Drowning

One-fourth of all childhood drownings occur at home in the bathtub. Never leave your baby alone while in the bathtub for any reason. Don't develop bad habits that can be disastrous.

Siblings

It's best to not leave small children (1 to 4 years) alone with a new baby because the well-meaning toddler may be tempted to pick him up and could lose control and drop him. He can be hugged too hard or fed something he's not ready to eat. The time small children spend with the baby should be enjoyable but supervised until they're old enough to understand what isn't harmful.

Pets

It's a good practice to not allow your pets in the baby's room. Cats especially can be a problem because they love to sleep next to warm bodies, and what's more snuggly than a baby? They can easily get into the baby's crib. There have been cases where a cat slept with a new baby and inadvertently smothered him. Well-mannered family dogs have bitten infants and small children without warning.

In general, the guidelines for protecting your baby from small children apply to pets as well. They aren't responsible for what they don't understand.

Cribs

A safe crib is another must. Whether the crib is old or new, check to see that the side rails or slats are no further apart than 2-3/8 inches. The mattress height should be adjustable so you can lower it as your baby grows and learns to sit and stand up. There should be no spaces between the mattress and the sides and ends of the crib. A bumper pad works well to fill in the gaps. Be certain that crib decorations aren't a potential hazard to a curious teething baby at a later time.

Immunizations

Having your baby immunized against the numerous childhood diseases is a very important factor in safeguarding her health. Diseases such as diptheria, whooping cough (pertussis), measles, and polio haven't been eradicated—they're still there just waiting for an unprotected child. If children aren't vaccinated, epidemics can occur and take their toll.

The immunizations begin around 2 months of age. Your pediatrician has pamphlets that explain the various vaccines and what they do. Ask any questions and concerns you have so they can be cleared up in advance. Do your part for your baby and your community.

SO LONG FOR NOW

Your 6-week postpartum exam officially ushers you back into the regular nonpregnant world. You've spent the last 6 weeks saying hello to your baby. Now it's time to say goodbye to your doctor, at least for a while. Most women over the months have established a nice comfortable rapport with their doctors and often with the doctor's office staff. They are those friendly faces who made you feel special and delighted in your pregnancy. It's natural to miss all that attention that was once all yours but now belongs to your baby.

It probably never occurred to you, but your doctor and staff will probably miss you too. Be sure to let them know how you feel, and give them the opportunity to reciprocate. Kind words are always appreciated.

It's an exciting trip you've been through, and a new one is just beginning. So gather all your resources together—yourself, your husband, and your new baby—be patient and loving with each other. Remember for the journey to come, keep your sense of humor; it comes in handy.

ΔΔΔ

Breast-feeding

Use this chapter as your support and starter kit for breast-feeding your baby. It can be a jungle out there. Your ticket to successful breast-feeding is knowledge and confidence. Hang in there. Breast-feeding in humans isn't instinctual; it's learned behavior.

MYTHS AND MISCONCEPTIONS

The old wives' tales concerning breast-feeding die hard, but here goes.

You don't need 44 double Ds to breast-feed your baby. Whether full- or flat-chested, everyone has an equal chance to be successful.

Breast-feeding doesn't cause your breasts to sag or lose their shape. Wearing a good support bra is all the protection you need. Breast-feeding actually hastens the return of your prepregnancy figure because your uterus is quicker to get back into shape, and you tend to lose weight more rapidly when you nurse.

Almost all women have enough milk. Use it or lose it. If you nurse often enough, the milk will be there.

Babies don't become allergic to breast milk. It's good protection against infections for your baby. Just practice good handwashing techniques.

Even with a passle of other kids at home, you can still breast-feed. It takes two hands to bottle-feed, but only one to breast-feed. You have a free hand for another child who may need a hug at the same time.

Your baby isn't affected by what you eat. You don't have to give up chocolate, eggs, onions, or other spicy foods.

Drinking alcohol (beer, wine) won't increase your milk supply or improve your letdown reflex. Drinking lots of fluids will.

Nix on nipple preparation—spending hours preparing your nipples for breast-feeding doesn't prevent nipple soreness. Don't waste your time. Rolling and tugging on your nipples causes uterine contractions. Doing it for several minutes at a time can hyperstimulate your uterus. (This definitely isn't a good idea if you have a complicated pregnancy.) The result of hyperstimulation is a temporary decrease in your baby's heart rate. Stimulation of your nipples during lovemaking is not usually a problem since the stimulation tends to be intermittent, not prolonged.

Limiting the amount of nursing time on each breast doesn't prevent nipple soreness; it only delays it. You reduce the amount of stimulation you need to produce more milk. By nursing only a few minutes, the baby only gets the "foremilk." The real calories and hunger appeasement come from the "hind milk." Let your baby nurse at her own frequency and for her own duration. Unlimited sucking also prevents engorgement.

DETERRENTS TO BREAST-FEEDING

Misinformation

Misinformation creates confusion and raises havoc with the new mother. You tire of trying to hurdle the endless obstacles on your path to success. Nursing personnel vary widely in their knowledge of effective and current breast-feeding techniques. If each new nurse tells you something different, it's easy to get confused and discouraged. Take matters into your own hands. Bone up on breast-feeding before you deliver. Read this chapter, and check the Recommended Resources section for more books. Find a breast-feeding class. Call the La Leche League. Lots of resources are out there.

Hospital Schedules and Routine

The hospital routine doesn't easily coordinate with the "feeding-on-demand" policy that makes for successful breast-feeding. Many hospitals routinely put a supplemental bottle of formula or water into the bassinet of a breast-fed baby. There's a message there. Supplemental feeding of formula sabotages your efforts to establish a good milk supply. Babies also become confused by trying to switch back and forth from one type of nipple to another (sucking on a bottle is very different than sucking on a breast).

When you shop for a hospital, be sure and ask about nursery routines and just how accessible your baby will be to you.

Exhaustion and Tension

These are real killers. You have to take extra pains to get enough rest. You save a lot of time by not heating bottles, but it takes longer to feed a baby by breast. No one else has the proper equipment in working order, and you won't find wet nurses in the yellow pages. You're stuck with those round-the-clock feedings. In the early days you can keep your baby by your bed at night for easy access. You can also coax your husband to bring the baby to you. He can supervise nursing while you go back to sleep.

Tension interferes with the milk letdown reflex. Use your relaxation techniques to keep you calm, not alcohol. Extra sleep helps keep you off the edge too.

Lack of Support

Lack of support and encouragement from those around you makes a difference. Some pediatricians, at the first sign of problems, will suggest bottle-feeding or encourage supplementing with formula. Be sure the people you turn to for advice have the right answers to keep you going.

How about your husband? If he views your breasts as his personal property, how willing is he to share them? Check it out. Discuss his pros and cons and educate him at the same time you're gathering your information. The more he knows, the more supportive he can be.

A well-meaning friend or relative often delivers the coup de grace at home when the baby cries and she tells you that the poor dear must be

244

starving to death. The kiss of death comments are "Are you sure your milk is rich enough?" "The poor thing looks like he's losing weight." Amid exhaustion and remorse, you collapse into a vat of despair and reach for the free formula the hospital sent home with you—just in case.

Get off to a good start by knowing correct procedures and anticipating those circumstances that may sabotage your efforts.

ITEMS OF INTEREST

Your baby's first food is colostrum; the yellowish, sticky, sweet substance you can squeeze from your nipples; it's high in calories and protein. Colostrum contains high levels of agents that protect the baby from infection, and also has a laxativelike effect. The stools of the breast-fed baby are loose and watery—constipation isn't a problem. She may have a stool every time she eats or only one every 5 to 6 days.

Transitional milk makes its appearance about 1 to 2 weeks postpartum. Your mature milk looks pale and bluish white. This is the only food your baby needs for the first 4 to 6 months of life.

Uterine cramping can be a minor problem while breast-feeding but it usually disappears in 7 to 10 days. Two over-the-counter drugs, Advil and Nuprin, provide excellent relief from cramps. Take one tablet 1/2 hour before you nurse. If you're totally breast-feeding your baby, you probably won't menstruate. Intercourse may be painful from decreased vaginal lubrication; Astroglide and Replens, available in drugstores, are designed specifically for this problem.

Many women find nursing an erotic experience that can be disconcerting, depending on how comfortable they are with their sexuality. Occasionally, women even report experiencing orgasm. Now we know what kept the species going until the formula manufacturers got into the act and ruined the fun.

GOOD BEGINNINGS

For the first 2 or 3 hours after birth, your baby's sucking reflex is going to be its strongest; after that, it'll dwindle for several days. Don't become discouraged if he just doesn't seem that interested at first. Even though few babies are hungry enough to nurse well right away, it's a good idea to let him become familiar with your breast at delivery, if possible. If not, you can catch up later.

The goal in breast-feeding is to avoid sore nipples. The best way to accomplish that is to learn to put your baby to breast in the proper fashion, to minimize trauma to your nipples.

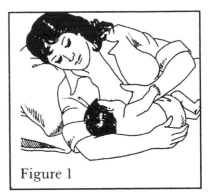

Figure 1

Sit upright in a chair or bed and put the baby across your abdomen with her head in the crook of your arm (Figure 1). Turn her entire body toward you. Her face, chest, abdomen, and knees should be facing your body. This position places the nipple directly in front of her mouth. You can bend your knees to bring her closer. If you've had a cesarean, place a pillow between your knees and the baby to lift her off your abdomen or lie on your side.

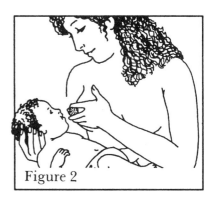

Figure 2

Don't use the incorrect position in Figure 2, which is a common mistake. Grasp your breast with your thumb on top and your fingers underneath (Figure 3). The correct position will allow stimulation and emptying of the nipple ducts to help prevent clogged ducts and engorgement.

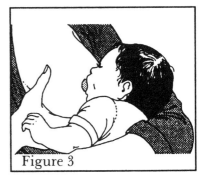

Figure 3

Express some colostrum, if possible, to get her interested. Tickle her upper lip with your nipple very gently (Figure 4), to elicit the rooting reflex. When she opens her mouth wide, pull her close with her stomach toward you. She'll be able to breathe if her body is straight against yours. If you think she needs more of an airway, lift up on your breast slightly rather than depress it with your thumb. Be careful not to disengage the good contact you have.

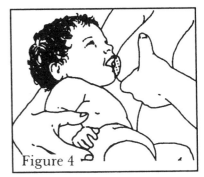

Figure 4

To suck properly, and to save your nipple, her jaw should fit behind the nipple and your breast to position the nipple deep in her mouth. Most of your areola (dark part of your nipple) should be in her mouth.

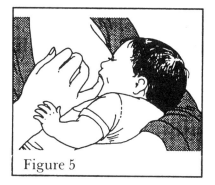

Figure 5

If you feel the need to time the feeding, 10 minutes on each breast is average; 90 percent of the milk supply can be obtained in 7 minutes. To end the feeding, insert your little finger into the corner of her mouth to break the suction (Figure 5). At the next feeding, begin with the breast you used last. For example, if you finished with the left breast, begin the next feeding with the left breast, to ensure that the breast is fully emptied.

Nipple care is simple. Let your nipples air-dry for 15 to 20 minutes. Cleanse your nipples only with water when you bathe. If you have dry skin, natural lubricants such as pure lanolin, pure cocoa butter, vitamin E oil, and vegetable oil help avoid cracked nipples. Avoid products such as Masse and Mammol creams, which you have to wash off before each feeding.

Leaking breasts are a temporary inconvenience. The baby cries and you think the dam has burst. To stop the flow, press the heels of your hands firmly against the breast. Use white washable cotton handkerchiefs for pads. Leaking usually subsides when breast-feeding is well established.

Some babies need burping after each breast, but others may not need to burp after both. If your baby doesn't burp, put her on her stomach in bed, which may help.

Nursing babies should be fed at least every 3 hours with only one 5- to 6-hour period between feedings in any 24 hours. This assures that your baby is getting enough fluid intake and increases your milk production. Your baby is getting enough milk if you're changing six wet diapers a day. You can expect her to gain about 1 pound per month.

WEAN TO WORK?

If you plan to return to work after having your baby and you really want to breast-feed, you can do it. There are ways, but you have to be highly organized and committed to seeing it through.

Arranging for a baby-sitter near where you work is a thought. You can feed you baby before you go to work. At noontime you can dash to the sitter's to provide lunch. Store up supplements by pumping your breasts and saving the milk for later. Breast milk can be stored in the refrigerator for 24 hours in a clean unsterilized container. With freezing, it lasts 2 weeks in a one-door freezer and several months in a two-door freezer. You can defrost the milk in the refrigerator for 2 hours and then under warm running water. A consideration: heating, freezing, and thawing decreases breast milk's anti-infective properties. Don't thaw or warm the milk in the microwave because doing so destroys vitamins. Also, hot spots are a problem and might burn the baby's mouth.

An opportune time to pump your breasts is when you're nursing your baby because letdown is in full force. One breast is for him and the other for the breast pump. Hand expression is an alternative, but those who've had experience say it takes too long if you're in a hurry. Breast pumps come in many forms and prices. Consult your childbirth educator for recommendations.

DOUBLE YOUR FUN

Since milk supply is determined by demand, one mom can feed two babies successfully. Nursing twins takes time, practice, and coordination. The old double football hold comes in handy. Or you can mix and match positions—one in football, the other in cradle position; both in front cradle hold, cross-crossing. Try different combinations to see which works best for you. Rest for you is crucial since you're doing double duty. See the Recommended Resources section for more comprehensive instructions.

FEEDING FOLLIES AND REMEDIES

You may run into a few snags along the way in your new breast-feeding career. Here are the potential problems and their solutions.

Baby Won't Latch On

The problem may be a sleepy baby or one who needs to burp. Try not to feel as if she's rejecting you. It's just going to take longer to generate a little interest.

■ **HELPFUL HINTS**

1. Try unwrapping the blankets.

2. Express some colostrum to stimulate sucking.

Flat, Inverted, or Retractile Nipples

■ **HELPFUL HINTS**

1. Pinch your nipple between thumb and index finger. Stroke the side of the nipple, not the tip (Figure 6).

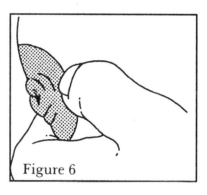

Figure 6

2. Grasp the outer edge of the areola and gently compress it to help introduce it into her mouth (Figure 7). If she still isn't sucking, give her a sip from a bottle and quickly shift to your nipple.

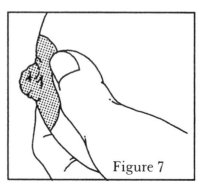

Figure 7

3. Breast shields help correct inversion and retraction of nipples by applying an even, continuous and painless pressure that gradually forces the nipple farther through the central opening of the shield. You wear the shield between feedings; remove it before nursing. Don't save the milk that leaks into the shield to feed your baby. Wash shields frequently with hot soapy water; rinse them thoroughly and dry

carefully. Air-dry nipples for 15 to 30 minutes after feeding. Use lanolin ointment to help prevent sore nipples from the moisture retained in the shield.

Sore, Cracked, or Bleeding Nipples

Sore nipples are common, especially in fair-skinned women. A number of factors contribute to the problem, such as the baby chomping or biting the nipple. Overly full breasts make it difficult for the baby to attach properly. Occasionally, blood blisters form around the nipple. If they break, even though blood may seep into her mouth—it's not a problem. Keep going.

■ **HELPFUL HINTS**

1. With biting or chomping of the nipple, break the baby's suction and start over.

2. Hand express a little milk to start the flow so the baby doesn't have to suck vigorously before letdown.

3. More frequent, shorter feedings may help.

4. Nursing in different positions puts pressure on different parts of the nipple.

5. Take the handles off two tea strainers and wear them inside your bra to allow circulation and aid healing. You can apply lanolin (it doesn't need to be washed off).

6. Offer the less sore nipple first.

7. You might try taking some pain medication 1/2 hour before nursing.

8. For cracked nipples, air dry or use an electric lamp (60 to 90 watt), placed 18 inches away, two or three times a day. Don't use soap, petroleum jelly, alcohol, or any other irritating substance on your nipples. Use a mild emollient such as lanolin.

9. If pain is severe, stop nursing for 2 to 3 days until healing can occur. Meanwhile, manually pump your breast(s) to maintain your milk supply.

Engorgement

Engorgement usually happens the second to fifth day after delivery. Your breasts become so full that they feel like two boulders painfully perched on your chest. You might have a slight fever of less than 100.6°F. Overly full breasts make it hard for the baby to properly grasp the nipple. Only the nipple is sucked, and it becomes very painful. The collecting ductules aren't milked, and the baby is frustrated by the lack of milk. Neither of you is having a good time! You can avoid engorgement by sticking to the on-demand feeding schedule.

■ HELPFUL HINTS

1. Stand in a hot shower.

2. Use gentle, manual expression to soften the areola and reduce congestion.

Fever

Fever may occur when your milk comes in. Your temperature should be less than 100.4°F. If your temperature is higher, other causes such as infection should be investigated. **Call your doctor.**

Breast Infection (Mastitis)

Infections don't usually develop until 2 to 3 weeks postpartum. Your breast(s) become hot, red, and tender. You have a fever and chills and feel achey. You might be nauseated and feel generally rotten. Call your doctor; you need an antibiotic if you have mastitis.

■ HELPFUL HINTS

1. Even with an infection, you don't need to stop nursing because milk remains sterile unless there's an abscess. Start feeding on the affected side to empty the breast.

2. Get lots of rest and drink plenty of fluids. Take Tylenol to lower your fever.

Clogged Milk Ducts

Sometimes, one or more milk ducts become plugged. A small lump that may be reddened and painful can be felt.

■ **HELPFUL HINTS**

1. Massage the lump in a circular motion while nursing. Make sure your bra isn't too tight; it could be pressing on the milk gland.

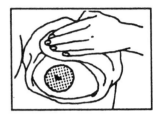

2. Apply heat 15 to 20 minutes before feeding.

3. Offer the sore breast first so it can be completely emptied. Rotate positions with every feeding to exert pressure on different ducts.

4. Hand express or pump milk from the affected breast after each feeding to completely empty it.

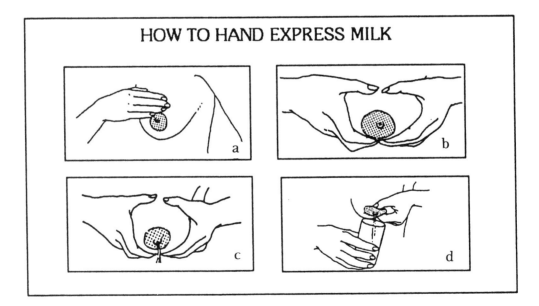

HOW TO HAND EXPRESS MILK

Breast Milk Jaundice

This type of jaundice occurs in less than 1 in 200 babies. Breast milk jaundice appears later than physiologic jaundice and peaks in 7 to 10 days. Your baby isn't allergic to your milk, and you aren't poisoning him. The cure is simple.

■ **HELPFUL HINTS**

1. Stop breast-feeding for 12 to 24 hours and then carry on as usual.

2. Pump your breasts to keep up your milk production.

SOME PARTING SUPPORT

If you find you need some outside support for your endeavors, there are people out there who'll be happy to help you. It could be a friend or acquaintance who's breast-feeding or has breast-fed her baby successfully. The La Leche League, the International Childbirth Education Association (ICEA), and the Nursing Mothers Council undoubtedly have chapters in your area. Ask your childbirth educator for the name of a certified lactation consultant. Give her a call if you need some help.

Remember, not all babies know instinctively what to do. Not all mothers do either. But if you both persevere, you'll eventually get the hang of it.

DRUGS AND BREAST-FEEDING

Most drugs that you take find their way into your breast milk, but the question is how much? It's a matter of degree. It's a relief to know that there are only a few drugs you can't take while breast-feeding. Beginning on page 254 is a list of the more common drugs and their effects on breast-feeding and your baby.

Drugs Contraindicated During Breast-feeding

Drug	Effect on Baby or Lactation
Indocin	Manufacturer recommends drug not be used.
Parlodel	Suppresses lactation.
Tagamet	Potential effects on baby's gastric acidity and central nervous system stimulation.
Cafergot	Vomiting, diarrhea.
Tapazole	Potentially interferes with thyroid function.
Thiouracil	Decreases thyroid function. Doesn't apply to propylthiouracil.
Valium	Levels accumulate in baby.
Benadryl	Newborn has increased sensitivity to antihistamines.

Drugs That Require Temporary Cessation of Breast-feeding

Drug	Effect on Baby or Lactation
Flagyl	Stop breast-feeding while on drug. Wait 12 to 24 hours after last dose before resuming.
Active radiopharmaceuticals	Prior to study, pump breasts and store milk in freezer. After study, consult radiologist as to length of excretion time for drug and continue to pump breasts—discard milk until drug is excreted.

Maternal Medication Usually Compatible with Breast-feeding

Drug	Effect on Baby or Lactation
Central Nervous System Depressants	
Alcohol	May decrease milk letdown.
Phenobarbital, Secobarbital	Watch for sedation effects on baby.
Magnesium sulfate	None.
Anticoagulant	
Dicumarol, Coumadin	None.
Antiepileptic Drugs	
Dilantin	No adverse effects.
Decongestants, Bronchodilators	
Theo-Dur	None.
Antihypertensive, Cardiovascular Drugs	
Digoxin	None.
Aldomet	Excreted in small amounts.
Inderal	No adverse effects reported.
Antibacterial Drugs	
Ancef, Kefzol	Excreted in low doses.
Claforan	Excreted in low doses.
Furadantin,* Macrodantin	Negligible in amounts in milk.
Tetracycline	Excreted in low doses.
Septra	No risks for full-term, healthy infant.
Ampicillin	None.
Antithyroid	
Propylthiouracil	Periodically evaluate infant's thyroid function.

* Infants with glucose-6-phosphate dehydrogenase deficiency may develop hemolytic anemia.

Drug	Effect on Baby or Lactation
Diuretics	
Diuril, Hydrodiuril	May suppress lactation. Do not use first month of breast-feeding.
Hormones	
Birth control pills with estrogen/progesterone	Decrease in milk production and protein content.
Narcotics, Nonnarcotic Analgesics, Anti-inflammatory Agents	
Datril, Liquiprin, Tempra, Tylenol	Excreted in low doses.
Codeine	Excreted in small amounts.
Motrin, Advil, Nuprin	None.
Demerol	No adverse effects.
Morphine	Only trace amounts in milk.
Prednisone	None.
Darvon	None.
Aspirin	Potentially may affect blood clotting.
Antidepressants	
Elavil	No clinical effects noted.
Norpramin	No adverse effects noted.
Tofranil	None noted.
Antianxiety drugs	
Equanil	No clinical signs in baby noted.
Thorazine	None noted, but observe for sedation.
Stimulants	
Caffeine	No adverse effects reported.

ΛΛΛ

APPENDIX 1

Exercises

These exercises can be used prenatally and postpartum. The following illustrated exercises help you to:

- Tone the pelvic floor muscles
- Reduce lower back stress from the added weight of pregnancy
- Reduce sciatic pressure
- Strengthen upper back
- Reduce the tendency to rounded shoulders
- Strengthen arms for carrying your baby
- Increase your endurance and muscle control for labor and birth

1. Inner thigh lifts. Lay on your side. Bend your top leg and place it on the floor in front of your straight leg. Lift your straight leg and lower it slowly.

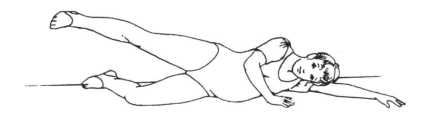

2. Outer thigh lifts. Lay on your side with both knees bent. Straighten your top leg and lift. Raise your thigh only to hip level as you lift. Press your top leg down as you lower it into the other leg. You should feel only the outer thigh muscles working.

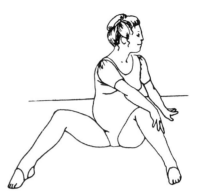

3. Pregnancy curls. Sit with your legs apart, knees bent, and feet flat on the floor. Place your hands behind your thighs. Without rounding your lower back (keep it flat), lean back just far enough to feel your abdominal muscles tighten; hold for 5 seconds.

4. Pregnancy pretzel. Sit on the floor with your feet and knees apart. Sit firmly on your tailbone. Keep spine straight; lift and extend your torso. Pretend you have a hoist attached to your breastbone that is pulling you up. Place one hand on your opposite thigh. Twist your body (not just your neck) to look over your shoulder. Hold the stretch for 5 seconds. Return to starting position and switch sides to repeat.

5a. Cat back. Assume a hands and knees position. Relax your stomach and lower back but keep your spine straight.

5b. Contract your stomach and buttock muscles. Pull your pelvis forward and round your back. Relax and repeat.

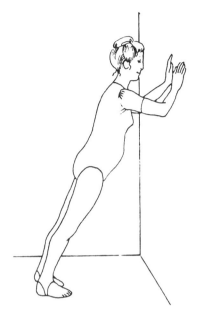

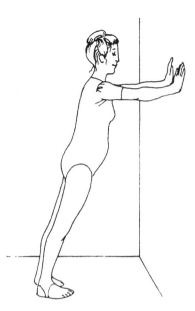

6a. Wall push ups. With your feet hip width apart, place both hands on the wall about shoulder height. Lean toward the wall with your elbows bent. Pause 1 to 2 seconds.

6b. Push away slowly. Do not fully straighten your elbows.

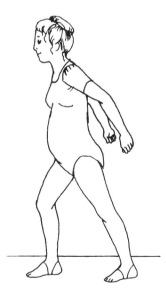

7a. Tricep extension. With one leg in front of the other, bend your knees slightly. With your hands touching your ribs, relax your shoulders.

7b. With palms facing in, extend your arms behind your body. Extend your elbows like a chicken. Contract the triceps as you extend. Return to starting position.

 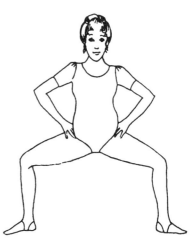

8a. Pregnancy squat. With your feet wider than shoulder width apart, toes pointing out and knees bent slightly , contract your buttock muscles.

8b. Press down slowly into a comfortable deeper squat. Keep balance forward and distribute your weight evenly. Repeat 2–3 times. If this exercise strains your knees and back, eliminate it.

9a. Bicep curl. Begin in the pregnancy squat position. Stabilize your elbows into your rib cage. Face palms up with hands next to your thighs.

9b. Contract your upper arms as you move your palms to your shoulders. Continue to tighten the muscles as you return your hands to your thighs. Use 3-pound weights if you wish.

260

10a. Postnatal squats with baby lifts. With your legs apart, feet pointing out, and knees slightly bent, hold your baby under the armpits. Lower your baby as you press down into the squat position.

10b. Lift your baby up as you extend your legs out of the squat position. Move slowly through the positions. This is a great exercise for you and fun for the baby!

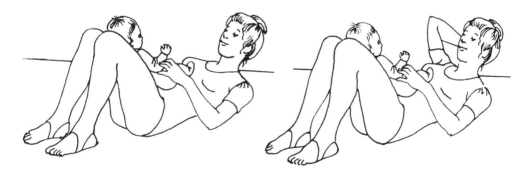

11a. Postnatal curl-ups. Lay on your back with your knees bent. Place your baby on your thighs, facing you. Lift your shoulders off the floor as you curl your torso toward your baby.

11b. If your neck is weak, support your head with one hand while holding your baby with the other hand. Lift from your chest, not your head, when you do the curl.

APPENDIX 2

CONTRACEPTIVE GUIDELINES*

Method	Advantages	Disadvantages/Precaution	Risk for Pregnancy**
No method	None.	Unplanned pregnancy.	60–80%
Withdrawal	No drugs or devices.	Unplanned pregnancy.	23%
Diaphragm with spermicides	Available over-the-counter (OTC). Protection against sexually transmitted disease (STD).	Need prescription. Must use every time. Potential allergy to rubber or spermicides.	19%
Condom	No drugs, protects against STD.	Must use every time. Some people allergic to rubber.	10%
Spermicides (jellies, cream, foam, suppositories)	Available OTC. East to use. Provides protection against STD.	Must follow instructions exactly and use every time. Some people allergic to spermicides.	18%
Sponge	Same as for spermicides. May be left in place. Is effective up to 24 hours.	Same as spermicides. Do not leave in place longer than 24 hours.	9–15%
Natural family planning	No drugs or devices. Doesn't interfere with religious beliefs.	Needs careful monitoring of menstrual cycle. Change in regular cycle due to infection, fever, etc. can be confusing. Requires abstinence. Unplanned pregnancy can result.	24%
Intrauterine device	Effective, reversible. One-time decision.	May have increased menstrual flow and cramping. Risk for perforation, expulsion, and tubal infection. Not recommended for women with multiple partners because of risk of infection and infertility risks, or women who have never been pregnant.	5%

262

Method	Benefits	Risks	Pregnancy risk**
Combination birth control pill	Reduces risk of certain malignant tumors and iron deficiency anemia, and may reduce incidence of premenstrual syndrome. Most effective means of reversible contraception. Decreases menstrual irregularity, flow, and menstrual cramps. Reduces incidence of pelvic inflammatory disease, benign breast disease, and benign ovarian tumors.	Minor side effects: nausea, vomiting, break-through bleeding, breast tenderness and enlargement, facial pigmentation, weight gain. Requires taking pill daily. Cardiovascular complications, mostly in women older than 35 who smoke, such as: blood clots, stroke, heart disease, high blood pressure, and in rare cases, benign liver tumors.	2–4%
Vasectomy	Permanent. One-time decision. No known long-term health effects.	Minor operation. Another operation needed to reverse procedure. Success of reversal depends on surgical technique and time elapsed since vasectomy.	Less than 1%
Tubal sterilization	Permanent. One-time decision. No known long-term health effects.	Major surgery requiring anesthesia. Additional surgery needed to reverse. Success depends on type of sterilization procedure done.	Less than 1%

* Adapted from "Benefits, Risks, & Effectiveness of Contraception" by the American College of Obstetricians and Gynecologists. The information contained in this table isn't meant to be a complete summary of risks, benefits, and effectiveness of every contraceptive method. No decision about the use of a contraceptive method should be based solely on the information contained in this table. Consult your physician to help determine the best contraceptive method for you.

** Pregnancy risk based on 100 couples using this method for 1 year.

Recommended Resources

Pregnancy and childbirth books are like the Marines . . . you only need a few "good" ones. Audiotapes and videotapes are a welcome addition to your pregnancy library. The Emmett Miller, M.D., tapes are highly recommended. You can order them from Source Cassette Learning Systems, P.O. Box W, Stanford, CA 94309, 1-800-52-TAPES (1-415-328-7171 inside California).

PREGNANCY AND BIRTH PREPARATION

Books

ASSERTIVE CHILDBIRTH, THE FUTURE PARENTS' GUIDE TO A POSITIVE PREGNANCY. McKay, 1983. Discusses birth alternatives and how to plan for choices.

A CHILD IS BORN. Nilsson, 1977. Outstanding photographs of human reproduction from conception to birth.

MAKING LOVE DURING PREGNANCY. Bing and Coleman, 1982. Illustrated guide. Discusses sex during pregnancy, myths, emotional aspects, and related topics.

THE MASSAGE BOOK. Downing, 1972. A beginner's guide to giving and receiving massage with an introduction to reflexology.

THE THERAPEUTIC TOUCH: HOW TO USE YOUR HANDS TO HELP OR HEAL. Krieger, 1979. An introductory guide to hands-on healing by a professor of nursing, an expert in the field.

BIRTH—THROUGH CHILDREN'S EYES. Anderson and Simkin, 1977. Guide to preparing siblings for labor and birth. Well illustrated.

INFANT MASSAGE. Schneider, 1982. A well-done guide that includes basic techniques and application for problems such as colic.

Audio Tapes

Eastern Peace, Steven Halpern. Provides background music to augment relaxation/visualization exercises.

ACOG Childbirth Preparation Program. A good supplement to childbirth classes or for those who need a brush up. Includes techniques for relaxation, massage, breathing, and visual imagery. The video version contains brief highlights from fourteen actual labors and births.

Emmett Miller, M.D.:

Great Expectations. A wonderful guide to augment prepared childbirth classes. Visual imagery and relaxation techniques geared for pregnancy.

Healing Journey. Helps to attain a calm, relaxed state. Provides imagery for dealing with minor ailments. Good for common complaints of pregnancy.

Rainbow Butterfly. Designed to produce feelings of peace, security, and trust in oneself. Helps improve ability to visualize and develop a positive self-image.

Easing into Sleep. For those nights of insomnia.

Letting Go of Stress. May be especially helpful for those with blood pressure problems or threatened preterm labor. Trains you to recognize tension and stress and use effective ways to relax.

Writing Your Own Script. Guides you in clearing your mind of unwanted data and replacing it with positive input.

Relaxercise, David Zemach-Bersin and Mark Reese. Easy-to-do micromovement exercises you can do in a chair. Exercises to ease tensions in back, shoulders, and neck and to relieve eye strain from computer work. Order from Source Cassette Systems.

Videotapes

ACOG Childbirth Preparation Program. See audiotapes.

The ACOG Pregnancy Exercise Program. Provides safe exercises for the pregnant woman.

Baby Basics. What you need to know to care for your new baby. Video Health Communications. 1-800-526-4773 to order.

Kathy Smith Pregnancy Workout. SyberVision #6012. 90-minute video on how to relieve minor discomforts of pregnancy and get back into shape after your baby is born. Especially recommended. 1-800-777-5885.

Yoga for Beginners. SyberVision #6029. 75-minute video with step-by-step instruction on how to develop stamina, flexibility, strength, and a healthy back. Comes with 48-page handbook. 1-800-777-5885.

DRUGS IN PREGNANCY

PEACE OF MIND DURING PREGNANCY: AN A-Z GUIDE TO THE SUBSTANCES THAT COULD AFFECT YOUR UNBORN BABY. C. Kelly-Buchanon. The author, an experienced teratogen counselor, presents an overview of birth defects and prenatal diagnosis techniques. Summarizes possible risk from individual substance exposures in pregnancy such as commonly prescribed drugs and specific teratogenic infections, chemical exposures, pesticides, and vaccinations. Environmental influences such as x-rays, microwaves, high altitude, pregnancy exercise, and tanning booths.

LIFESTYLE, EXERCISE, AND NUTRITION

STRETCH AND RELAX. Tobias and Stewart, 1985. A beautifully illustrated and helpful book on stretching, toning, and strengthening the body. A special chapter on pregnancy. Exercises based on yoga poses.

ESSENTIAL EXERCISES FOR THE CHILDBEARING YEAR. Noble, 1982. Exercises for pregnancy and postpartum.

GETTING STRONGER. Pearl, 1986. Good all-around weight training and fitness book.

PICKLES AND ICE CREAM. Hess and Hunt, 1984. An enjoyable book on nutrition in pregnancy.

FOOD VALUES OF COMMONLY USED PORTIONS. Pennington, 1989. A very valuable resource for evaluating the foods you eat for calories, proteins, fats, carbohydrates, and calcium.

MATERNITY STYLE: HOW TO LOOK YOUR BEST WHEN YOU'RE AT YOUR BIGGEST. Bucknum-Brinely, 1985. Fun book to read with lots of great illustrations. Shopping, sewing, and style advice are provided.

BREAST-FEEDING

THE COMPLETE BOOK OF BREAST-FEEDING. Eiger and Olds, 1987. The best sourcebook on breastfeeding. Includes tips for the working mom, diet and nutrition, and sexuality during the nursing period.

YOU CAN BREASTFEED YOUR BABY . . . EVEN IN SPECIAL SITUATIONS. Brewster, 1979. Comprehensive guide to breast-feeding twins, preterm babies, and handicapped babies while working and traveling.

COMPLICATED PREGNANCIES

HAVING A CESAREAN BABY. Hausknecht and Rattner-Heilman, 1983. Informative guide to cesarean birth.

PREVENTING PRETERM BIRTH: A PARENTS' GUIDE. Katz, Gill, & Turiel, 1988. The best book on preterm labor from prevention to delivery. Written by experts in the field.

THE PREMATURE BABY BOOK. Harrison, 1984. Well-illustrated guide to coping with the birth of a preterm baby.

THE PAIN OF PREMATURE PARENTS: A PSYCHOLOGICAL GUIDE FOR COPING. Michael T. Hynan, 1987.

POSTPARTUM

CARING FOR YOUR BABY AND YOUNG CHILD—BIRTH TO AGE 5. The American Academy of Pediatrics. Absolutely the best book on baby care and child development. It has everything you need to know from emotional, cognitive, physical development to what kinds of toys are appropriate for what age. If you buy only one book, this should be it.

THE WORKING PARENTS' SURVIVAL GUIDE. Sally Wendkos Olds, 1989. A comprehensive guide to the perils, pitfalls, and pearls for working parents written in a warm style.

THE VERY BEST CHILDCARE AND HOW TO FIND IT. Danalee Buhler, 1989. The ins and outs of day care, live-in help, basic health and safety from newborns to children 3 years of age.

PARENTS' GUIDE TO RAISING TWINS. Friedrich and Rowland, 1984. Survival handbook for parents of twins from prebirth to early school days.

PERINATAL LOSS AND GRIEF

ENDED BEGINNINGS: HEALING CHILDBEARING LOSSES. Panthos and Romeo, 1984. Covers spectrum of perinatal loss: birthing disappointments, death of a baby, stillbirth, miscarriage, birth defects, unplanned cesarean, and many more.

Prenatal Genetic Screening History Questionnaire*

NAME _____ DATE _____

QUESTIONS 1-5 pertain to both you and the baby's father.

Use space provided at the end of the questionnaire to explain "YES" answers.

		1. Have either of you, or anyone in your families, had any of the following disorders?
Y	N	a. Down's syndrome (mongolism)
Y	N	b. Chromosomal abnormality
Y	N	c. Neural tube defect (abnormality of spinal column such as spina bifida, open spine, or anencephaly)
Y	N	d. Hemophilia (blood clotting disorder)
Y	N	e. Muscular dystrophy
Y	N	f. Cystic fibrosis
Y	N	g. Mental retardation
Y	N	h. Any other birth defects or family disorders not listed above
Y	N	2. Have either of you had any children, dead or alive, from previous marriages or relationships with a birth defect not listed above?
Y	N	3. As a couple, or with previous partners, have you had a stillborn child or three or more miscarriages in the first three months of pregnancy?
Y	N	4. Have either of you had a chromosomal study?
		5. If either of you are of the following ancestry, have you been screened for any of these diseases?
Y	N	a. Jewish: Tay-Sachs
Y	N	b. Black: Sickle Cell
Y	N	c. Mediterranean background Italian, Greek, etc.: Thalassemia
Y	N	d. Southeast Asian, Chinese, Philippine: Thalassemia
Y	N	6. When your baby is born, will you be 35 years or older?

Use space provided below to answer "YES" questions.

_____

_____

_____

_____

_____

*Adapted from the American College of Obstetricians and Gynecologists Technical bulletin #105–September 1987.

Bibliography

GENERAL REFERENCE

Cunningham, G. F., MacDonald, P. C., & Gant, N. F. *Williams obstetrics.* 18th ed. Norwalk, CT: Appleton & Lange, 1989.

EMOTIONS OF PREGNANCY AND SEXUALITY

Bing, E., & Colman, L. *Making love during pregnancy.* New York: Bantam Books, 1977.

Bray, P., Myers, R. A., & Cowley, R. A. Orogenital sex as a cause of nonfatal air embolism in pregnancy. *Obstetrics and Gynecology* 61: 653 (1983).

Colman, A. D., & Colman, L. L. *Pregnancy: The psychological experience.* New York: Herder and Herder, 1971.

Dameron, G. W., Jr. Helping couples cope with sexual changes pregnancy brings. *Contemporary OB/Gyn* 21: 23 (1983).

Longobucco, D. C., & Freston, M. S. Relation of somatic symptoms to degree of paternal-role preparation of first-time expectant fathers. *JOGNN* 18(6): 482–488 (1989).

Mueller, L. S. Pregnancy and sexuality. *JOGNN* 14(4): 289–294 (1985).

YOUR BODY AND BABY'S GROWTH

Ingelmen-Sundbert, A. *A child is born: The drama of life before birth.* New York: Dell, 1969.

Moore, K. *The developing human.* Philadelphia: W.B. Saunders, 1977.

COMMON COMPLAINTS

Cunningham, G. F., MacDonald, P. C., & Gant, N. F. *Williams obstetrics.* 18th ed. Norwalk, CT: Appleton & Lange, 1989.

PREGNANCY FITNESS

Chez, R. A., & Pitkin, R. M. Nutritional supplements during pregnancy. *Contemporary OB/Gyn* 19: 199 (1982).

Fishbein, E. G., & Phillips, M. How safe is exercise during pregnancy? *JOGNN* 19(1): 45–49 (1990).

Johnstone, F. P. Nutrition intervention and pregnancy: What are clinicians' choices? *Contemporary OB/Gyn* 21: 211 (1984).

Juice: Comparing apples and oranges. University of California, Berkeley *Wellness Letter* 4(10): 3 (1988).

News Commentary: Dealing with weight-gain goals. *OBG Management,* July 1990, p. 6.

O'Grady, J. P. More on maternal exertion and fetal heart rate. *OB/Gyn Alert* 5(3): 9–10 (1988).

WORK AND PLAY

Birnhardt, J. H. Potential workplace hazards to reproductive health. *JOGNN* 19(1): 53–62 (1990).

Sherer, D. M., & Schenker, J. G. Accidental injury during pregnancy. *OB Gyn Survey* 44(5): 330–338 (1989).

Zuber, C., Librizzi, R. J., & Bolognese, R. J. Do aspartame and video display terminals pose pregnancy risks? *Postgraduate Obstetrics & Gynecology* 9(26): 1–6 (1989).

DRUGS IN PREGNANCY

Aaronson, L. S., & Macnee, C. L. Tobacco, alcohol, and caffeine use during pregnancy. *JOGNN* 18(4): 279–287 (1989).

Briggs, G., Freeman, R., & Yaffe, S. *Drugs in pregnancy and lactation.* 2nd ed. Baltimore: Williams & Wilkins, 1986.

Matteson, D. R., Kozlowski, K., Quirk, J. G., & Jelovsek, F. R. Effects of drugs and chemicals on the fetus. *Contemp OB Gyn* 33(5): 131–145 (1989).

PREPARED CHILDBIRTH

Beck, N. C., & Hall, D. Natural childbirth: A review and analysis. *Obstetrics and Gynecology* 56: 371 (1978).

Lindell, S. G. Education for childbirth: A time for change. *JOGNN* 17(2): 108–112 (1988).

Willmuth, L. R. Prepared childbirth and the concept of control. *JOGN* 4 (5): 38 (1975).

BIRTH OPTIONS

Emrey, M. A., & Mundell Kowalski, K. Alternatives to traditional birth settings and practices. In Sonstegard, Kowalski, & Jennings (eds.) *Women's health: Crisis and illness in childbearing*, volume II. New York: Grune & Stratton, 1983.

Feldman, E. Comparing low-risk births in hospital and birth center settings. *Birth* 14(1): 18 (1987).

Pearse, W. H. The "four myths" about out of hospital births. *American College of Obstetricians and Gynecologists Newsletter*, March 1984.

PRENATAL CARE

The American College of Obstetricians and Gynecologists: *Standards for obstetric-gynecologic services.* 6th edition. Washington, D.C.: ACOG Pub., 1983.

Cohen, Llan. Chlamydia trachomatis in the perinatal period. *Contemp OB/Gyn* 33(6): 22–134 (1989).

Ritter, S. E., & Vermund, S.H. Congenital toxoplasmosis. *JOGNN* 14(6): 435–439 (1985).

COMPLICATED PREGNANCY

Coustan, D. R., et al. Screening for gestational diabetes mellitus. *Obstet. Gynecol.* 73: 557–560 (1989).

Creasy, R. K. Ways of preventing preterm birth. *Contemp OB/Gyn* 32(4): 64–77 (1988).

Gabbe, S. G. Routine use of fetal movement counting. *OB/Gyn Alert* 6(7): 25 (1989).

Gershon, A. Chickenpox: How dangerous is it? *Contemp OB/Gyn* 31(3): 41–56 (1988).

Gill, P. J., & Katz, M. Early detection of preterm labor: Ambulatory home monitoring of uterine activity. *JOGNN* 15(6): 439–442 (1986).

Katz, M., Gill, P., & Turiel, J. *Preventing preterm birth: A parent's guide.* San Francisco: Health Publishing, 1988.

Kemp, V. H., & Page, C. K. The psychosocial impact of a high risk pregnancy on the family. *JOGNN* 15(3): 232–236 (1986).

Long, J., & Lieberman, E. Prolonged pregnancy: The management debate. *Br. Med. J.* 297: 715 (1988).

Maslow, A. S., & Bobitt, J. R. Herpes in pregnancy: Exploring clinical options. *Contemp OB/Gyn* 32(4): 44–61 (1988).

O'Grady, J. P. More on prevention of prematurity. *OB/Gyn Alert* 6(3): 10–11 (1989).

Sibai, B. M., & Moretti, M. M. PIH: Still common and still dangerous. *Contemp OB/Gyn* 31(2): 57–70 (1988).

FETAL WELL-BEING TESTS

Manning, F. A., et al. Fetal assessment using the biophysical profile. *Am. J. Obstet. Gynecol.* 162: 703–709 (1990).

Marshall, C., & Schneider, J. Assessments of fetal well-being and maturity. In Sonstegard, Kowalski, & Jennings, (eds.), *Women's health: Crisis and illness in childbearing,* volume III. San Diego, CA: Grune & Stratton, 1987.

Matteson, D. R., Angtuaco, T., & Long, C. Magnetic resonance imaging in obstetrics and gynecology. *Contemp OB Gyn* 29(1): 48–81 (1987).

O'Grady, J. P. First trimester chorionic villus sampling. *OB/Gyn Alert* 6(1): 3 (1989).

Paul, R., & Chez, R. F. Fetal acoustic stimulation. *Contemp OB/Gyn* 32(1): 123–125 (1988).

Schifrin, B. S., & Clement, D. Why fetal monitoring remains a good idea. *Contemp OB Gyn* 35(2): 70–86 (1990).

Wallach, E. E. When a child is brain-damaged. *Contemp OB/Gyn* 35(9): 11–16 (1990).

SPECIAL DELIVERY

Berkowitz, G. S., et al. Pregnancy outcome in the mature gravida. *N. Engl. J. Med.* 322: 659–664 (1990).

Cunningham, F. G., & Leveno, K. J. Pregnancy after 35. *Williams obstetrics supplement.* 18th ed. Norwalk, CT: Appleton & Lange, 1989. Pp. 1–12.

Galvan, B. J., & Broekhuizen, F. F. Obstetric vacuum extraction. *JOGNN* 16(4): 242–248 (1987).

Marshall, C. C. The art of induction/augmentation of labor. *JOGNN* 14(1): 22 (1985).

Phelan, J. P., Clark, S. L, Porreco, R. P., & Van Dorsten, J. P. Finding alternatives to cesarean section. *Contemp OB/Gyn* 31(1): 191–210 (1988).

LABOR AND DELIVERY

Apuzzio, J. J. Clinical dialogue: Anesthesia for newborn circumcision. *Contemp OB/Gyn* 35(1): 108–112 (1990).

Berry, L. M. Realistic expectations of the labor coach. *JOGNN* 17(5): 354–355 (1988).

Fortier, J. C. The relationship of vaginal and cesarean births to father-infant attachment. *JOGNN* 17(2): 128–134 (1988).

Grant, A., et al. Intrapartum asphyxia: Uncommon cause of cerebral palsy. *Lancet* 2: 1233–1236 (1989).

Rossi, M. A., & Lindell, S. G. Maternal positions and pushing techniques in a non-prescriptive environment. *JOGNN* 15(3): 203–208 (1986).

Scanlon, J. W. Foreskin foibles. *Perinatal Press* 12(5): 71 (1989).

Slavazza, K. L., Mercer, R. T., Marut, J. S., & Shinder, S. Anesthesia, analgesia for vaginal childbirth: Differences in maternal perceptions. *JOGNN* 14(4): 321–329 (1985).

Wallace, D., & Cunningham, F. G. Obstetrical anesthesia. *Williams obstetrics supplement.* 17th ed. Norwalk, CT: Appleton & Lange, 1988. Pp. 1–12.

POSTPARTUM

Anderberg, G. J. Initial acquaintance and attachment behavior of siblings with the newborn. *JOGNN* 17(1): 49–54 (1988).

Hampson, S. J. Nursing interventions for the first three postpartum months. *JOGNN* 18(2): 116–122 (1989).

Inturrisi, M., Camenga, C. F., & Rosen, M. Epidural morphine for relief of postpartum, postsurgical pain. *JOGNN* 17(4): 238–243 (1988).

Keefe, M. R. The impact of infant rooming-in on maternal sleep at night. *JOGNN* 17(2): 122–126 (1988).

LaFoy, J., & Geden, E. A. Postepisiotomy pain: Warm vs. cold sitz bath. *JOGNN* 18(15): 399–403 (1988).

Machol, L. Single room maternity care gains converts. *Contemp OB/Gyn* 34(5): 62–70 (1989).

Marecki, M., Wooldridge, A., Dow, P., Thompson, J., & Lechner-Hyman. Early sibling attachment. *JOGNN* 14(16): 418–423 (1985).

O'Hara, M. W., & Engeldinger, J. Postpartum depression. *Postgraduate Obstetrics & Gynecology* 10(4): 1–6 (1990).

Watters, N. E. Combined mother-infant nursing care. *JOGNN* 14(6): 478–483 (1985).

Wong, S., & Stepp-Gilbert, E. Lactation suppression: Nonpharmaceutical versus pharmaceutical method. *JOGNN* 14(4): 302–309 (1985).

BREAST-FEEDING

Eiger, M. S., & Olds, S. *The complete book of breastfeeding*. New York: Workman Publishing, 1987.

LeEsperance, C., & Frantz, K. Time limitation for early breastfeeding. *JOGNN* 14(2): 114 (1985).

Index

measles, 94
medications
    during pregnancy, 57
    during labor and delivery, 186,
        187
membranes, rupture of, 142,
    168, 180
midwife, 80, 83
milia, in newborn, 233
milk
    breast, 68, 245
    cows, 67
    formula, 68
    intake during pregnancy, 28
    suppression after delivery, 200
    transitional, 245
monitoring, fetal
    external, 176
    internal, 178
morning sickness, 45
morphine, 186
mucus plug, 168
multiparas
    concerns, 215
    length of labor, 170
muscular dystrophy, genetic
        study, 128
myths, labor, 164

N

nausea in pregnancy
    remedies for, 45
    during labor, 163, 191
navel, baby
    care of, 228
nembutal, 187
neonatologist, 124
neural tube defects, 129, 130
newborn (*see* baby)
nicotine
    use in pregnancy, 63
nightmares, 46

nipple
    care for breast-feeding, 247
    preparation for breast-feeding,
        243
    problems in breast-feeding, 248
    stimulation
        for CST, 126
        to augment labor, 190
nipple stimulation
    with breast-feeding, 245
    with intercourse, 12, 243
nonstress test (NST), 126
nosebleeds, 47
nubain, 186
numbness
    arms or legs, 47
nutrition
    during pregnancy, 21
nutritional hints, 23

O

obstetrician, 124
oxytocin
    for induction of labor, 140
    release with nipple stimulation,
        12, 125, 190
    use after delivery, 198
oxytocin challenge test (OCT),
        125
orgasm, 10, 13, 220, 243
overdue pregnancy, 122

P

pacifiers, 226, 231
pain
    abdominal, 100
    headache, 42, 100, 113
    heartburn, 41, 113
    hemorrhoids, 43
    in labor, 151
    in vagina, 49
    pubic symphysis, 48
    round ligament, 48

287

T

tace, 201
talwin, 186
Tay-Sachs disease, 269
tea
   use in pregnancy, 64
temperature
   maternal, 101
   newborn
      axillary, 235
      rectal, 236
tempra
   use in pregnancy, 59
TENS (transcutaneous electrical
      nerve stimulation)
   for nausea, 45
   for pain, 48
tests
   alpha fetoprotein (AFP), 130
   amniocentesis, 128
   antibody screen, 93
   Apgar score, 197
   biophysical profile, 127
   blood count, 93
   blood sugar, 94
   blood type and Rh factor, 93
   chicken pox, 95
   chlamydia, 95
   chorionic villus sampling
      (CVS), 130
   contractions stress, 125
   CMV (cytomegalovirus), 96
   fetal acoustic stimulation (FAS)
      test, 127
   genetic, 128
   hepatitis B, 96
   HIV (human immunodefi-
      ciency virus), 96
   Kleihauer-Betke, 101
   magnetic resonance imaging
      (MRI), 133
   nonstress, 125, 126
   parvovirus, 96

   rubella (measles), 94
   serology, 94
   serum alpha fetoprotein (AFP),
      130
   sickle cell disease, 128
   Tay-Sachs syndrome, 269
   thalassemia, 128
   toxoplasmosis, 97
   ultrasound, 130
   urinalysis, 93
   VDRL (serology), 94
therapeutic touch, 157–160
temperature
   maternal, 101
   baby, 235
third stage of labor, 198
thumb-sucking, 226
toxoplasmosis, 97
transition stage of labor, 191, 193
transitional breast milk, 245
travel
   air, 56
   car, 55, 56
twins, 177
Tylenol
   use in pregnancy, 59

U

ultrasound
   safety of, 131
   test, 130
   uses for, 132
umbilical cord
   newborn, 228
urinary tract infection
   maternal, 50, 101
   in uncircumcised infant, 199
uterine
   cramping
      after amniocentesis, 128
      after intercourse, 11
      postpartum, 198
      with breast-feeding, 245

incisions
    classical, 148
    low cervical, 148
uterus
    size, 94
    weight of, 20

V

vacuum extractor
    for delivery, 144
Vagette device, 174
vagina
    shooting pains in, 49
vaginal birth after cesarean
        (VBAC), 147
vaginal bleeding
    maternal, 99, 167
    newborn, 233
vaginal discharge
    maternal, 50
    baby, 233
valium, 187
varicose veins, 50
vibrator
    use in pregnancy, 13
video display terminals (VDTs),
        52
vistaril, 186

vitamins
    supplements, 27, 59
vomiting, persistent, 100

W

walking
    exercise during pregnancy, 31
water breaking, 168
water pills, 59
weight gain
    and low birthweight baby, 20
    prenatally, 19, 20, 21, 94
weight loss
    postpartum, 213
weight training
    during pregnancy, 33
wool diaper covers, 232
working
    during pregnancy, 51

X

x-rays, 61

Y

yoga
    exercise during pregnancy, 34

Z

zoster immune globulin (ZIG), 96

OTHER SUCCESSFUL PRENATAL BOOKS
FROM CONNIE MARSHALL

De Aquí a La Maternidad
A user friendly pregnancy guide especially for the Hispanic family. Written with warmth and sensitivity, it combines up-to-date information with cherished pregnancy and birth practices from the Hispanic culture.
....U.S. $9.95

The Expectant Father
A one-of-a-kind pregnancy guide written specifically for the expectant father. In a witty and reassuring manner, the pregnancy process is demystified, and commonsense guidelines put the expectant father on the path to positive parenting. Written not only by an expert in the field, but filled with actual quotes from men as they share their nine-month journey to fatherhood. The expectant mother will also be reading this book to see what her husband is experiencing during this important time in his life.
....U.S. $10.95

Helping Moms Have Healthy Babies
A prenatal booklet offering very basic, easy-to-understand, but important information and guidelines for having a healthy pregnancy. This guide has a wide appeal. Public health agencies to busy working women love this handy purse-sized guide. **Available in Spanish.**
....U.S $2.95

FOR ORDERING INFORMATION CONTACT:

CONMAR PUBLISHING, INC.
P.O. BOX 641
CITRUS HEIGHTS, CA 95611
1-800-428-8321
(916) 332-9872